FOOTPRINTS OF HOPI HISTORY

Edited by
LEIGH J. KUWANWISIWMA,
T. J. FERGUSON, and
CHIP COLWELL

FOOTPRINTS OF
HOPI HISTORY

Hopihiniwtiput Kukveni'at

THE UNIVERSITY OF
ARIZONA PRESS

TUCSON

The University of Arizona Press
www.uapress.arizona.edu

ISBN-13: 978-0-8165-3698-6 (cloth)
ISBN-13: 978-0-8165-4097-6 (paper)

Cover design by Leigh McDonald
Cover illustration: *Talavie #4* by Dan Namingha, photograph by Nicole Namingha, courtesy of Niman Fine Art

Library of Congress Cataloging-in-Publication Data
Names: Kuwanwisiwma, Leigh J., editor. | Ferguson, T. J. (Thomas John), 1950– editor. | Colwell, Chip (John
    Stephen), 1975– editor.
Title: Footprints of Hopi history : Hopihiniwtiput kukveni'at / edited by Leigh J. Kuwanwisiwma, T. J. Fergu-
    son, and Chip Colwell.
Other titles: Hopihiniwtiput kukveni'at
Description: Tucson : The University of Arizona Press, 2018. | Includes bibliographical references.
Identifiers: LCCN 2017047628 | ISBN 9780816536986 (cloth : alk. paper)
Subjects: LCSH: Hopi Indians—History. | Community archaeology. | Ethnoarchaeology.
Classification: LCC E99.H7 F59 2018 | DDC 979.1004/97458—dc23 LC record available at
    https://lccn.loc.gov/2017047628

Printed in the United States of America
♾ This paper meets the requirements of ANSI/NISO Z39.48-1992 (Permanence of Paper).

Leigh J. Kuwanwisiwma dedicates this book to Dalton Taylor and the other advisors whom he first worked with at the Hopi Cultural Preservation Office, including ValJean Joshevama Sr., Frank Mofsi, LaVern Siweupmptewa, Owen Numkena, and Bert Puhuyestewa. The cultural knowledge and wisdom shared by these advisors helped establish research protocols at the Hopi Cultural Preservation Office that protect and benefit the Hopi people. The work of the first generation of cultural advisors is now ably carried forward by new members of the Hopi Cultural Resources Advisory Task Team. The Hopi Tribe is fortunate to have their advice on cultural and historical matters.

CONTENTS

PREFACE

T. J. FERGUSON AND CHIP COLWELL

*K*UKVENI—FOOTPRINTS—ARE A POWERFUL historical metaphor that the Hopi people use to comprehend their tangible heritage. Hopis say that the deity Máasaw instructed their ancestors to leave footprints during their migrations from their origin place to their home today as evidence that they had fulfilled a spiritual pact to serve as stewards of his land. Today, Hopis understand these footprints to be the archaeological remains of former settlements, pottery sherds, stone tools, petroglyphs, and other physical evidence of past use and occupation of the land. The fourteen chapters in this book focus on Hopi footprints as understood through a variety of research techniques, including archaeology, ethnography, documentary history, plant genetics, and educational outreach. In summarizing this body of research, Leigh J. Kuwanwisiwma conceived this book's title, *Footprints of Hopi History: Hopihiniwtiput Kukveni'at*.

The chapters in the book are organized to provide an arc from the Hopi Tribe's philosophy of collaborative research, through the methodology employed in Hopi community-based participatory research, to the substantive results of research projects, and finally to a reflexive consideration of how collaboration with the Hopi Tribe shapes anthropological inquiry. The book features managerial uses of research, cultural landscape theory, use of geographical information systems in research, archaeological interpretations of social identity and immigration, analysis of corn genetics, heritage education of youth, and research of oral traditions and documentary history. The volume offers a fresh and innovative perspective on Hopi archaeology and history, and demonstrates how one tribe has significantly advanced knowledge about its past through collaboration with archaeologists and cultural anthropologists.

All of the work presented in this book was conducted in collaboration with the Hopi Tribe under the auspices of the Hopi Cultural Preservation Office directed by Leigh J. Kuwanwisiwma. Since 1985, the Hopi Cultural Preservation Office has worked with archaeologists and cultural anthropologists on a wide range of research projects, including academic research, archaeological field schools, historic preservation compliance projects, implementation of the Native American Graves Protection and Repatriation Act (NAGPRA), and research related to land and water rights. This collaborative research has produced more than 150 scholarly publications, technical reports, dissertations and theses, and websites (see appendix). While the Hopi Tribe's program is not unique—more than a dozen tribes in the American Southwest have established similar offices (Anyon et al. 2000)—the Hopi Tribe has been a leader in the breadth, depth, and sustained effort necessary to create bridges between tribal goals and anthropology.

As Leigh Kuwanwisiwma explains in chapter 1, "the initial impetus for creating the Hopi Cultural Preservation Office was the Hopi Tribe's interest in participating in the environmental review process associated with the National Historic Preservation Act of 1966 (NHPA) and the National Environmental Policy Act of 1969 (NEPA). These two laws provide the foundation for cultural resources management (CRM) by requiring federal agencies to consider the effects of their undertakings on the environment, including the historical and cultural environment. To do this, federal agencies must identify historic sites and cultural resources that are important to the Hopi Tribe and evaluate them during project planning. Many federal agencies accomplish this by funding the Hopi Cultural Preservation Office to identify and evaluate Hopi cultural resources using tribal research participants who can explain how historic properties are associated with community values and history.

In conducting the research needed to identify Hopi cultural sites and historic properties, the Hopi Cultural Preservation Office developed a uniquely Hopi protocol for cultural preservation, as Chip Colwell and Stewart B. Koyiyumptewa discuss in chapter 2. As this chapter demonstrates, a core element of the Hopi research protocol is the involvement of many tribal members in fieldwork and research. Beyond technical reports and publications, these research participants share their personal experiences about fieldwork and their thoughts about Hopi ancestral sites with their families and friends, and the Hopi Cultural Preservation Office considers this traditional form of oral transmission to be an important means of disseminating project information.

One long-term endeavor of the Hopi Cultural Preservation Office has been a series of research projects associated with the adaptive management of the Grand Canyon, as Michael Yeatts explains in chapter 3. The research conducted in the Grand Canyon by the Hopi Cultural Preservation Office has greatly increased our understanding of Hopi history and cultural resources along the canyons of the Colorado River.

Under Leigh Kuwanwisiwma's direction, the Hopi Cultural Preservation Office realized that the many small discrete CRM projects in which they were participating could be organized into a larger overarching research program directed at documenting Hopi migrations and cultural history. While the results of any one project are geographically circumscribed, the Hopi Cultural Preservation Office significantly advances knowledge about Hopi clan migration in the Southwest. The Hopi Cultural Preservation Office has extended its research program by working with university- and museum-based scholars on academic research projects that fill in the geographical and topical gaps left by CRM research. These projects make external funding and resources available to the Hopi Tribe, and help synthesize information from CRM projects. In chapter 4, Saul Hedquist, Maren Hopkins, Stewart Koyiyumptewa, Lee Wayne Lomayestewa, and T. J. Ferguson use Hopi place-names and oral traditions to investigate Hopitutskwa (Hopi land) as a cultural landscape. A landscape perspective is further developed in chapter 5, where Wesley Bernardini uses Hopi insights to analyze the visual prominence of mountains, commenting on the role of these landforms in past and present social landscapes.

On several projects, the Hopi Cultural Preservation Office has made it possible for Hopi tribal members interested in the footprints of ancestral villages to work with archaeologists exavating or intepreting the sites. In chapter 6, E. Charles Adams explains how his long-term collaboration with the Hopi Tribe has benefitted the Homol'ovi archaeological research program. In chapter 7, Patrick D. Lyons draws upon his interaction with Hopi cultural advisors in his archaeological interpretaton of a fourteenth-century village in the San Pedro Valley of southern Arizona that was occupied by Pueblo migrants from the Kayenta area.

The Hopi Cultural Preservation Office values long-term collaboration with scholars. For example, Kelley Hays-Gilpin and Dennis Gilpin have worked with Leigh Kuwanwisiwma and Hopi cultural experts for more than twenty years on a variety of research projects that include CRM investigations, preparation of museum exhibits, and repatriation. In chapter 8, Hays-Gilpin and Gilpin reflect on how Hopi oral traditons inform archaeological interpretations and how archaeological research helps place clan migration in a chronological framework.

One of the research priorities of the Hopi Cultural Preservation Office has been studies needed to implement NAGPRA. This law was passed in 1990 to protect Native American graves on federal and Indian land and to create a process for tribes to claim ancestral human remains and certain cultural items in museum collections. In order to have a claim under this law, the Hopi Tribe must demonstrate cultural affiliation—a historically traceable shared identity—with past groups, and this often requires scholarly study. In chapter 9, Laurie D. Webster uses information collected during two cultural affiliation studies sponsored by the Hopi Cultural Preservation

Office to demonstrate how analysis of textiles provides important information about Hopi clan migration.

Because corn and farming are important Hopi cultural and subsistence activities, the Hopi Cultural Preservation Office has worked with Crow Canyon Archaeological Center in southeastern Colorado to study ancestral Pueblo agriculture. Chapter 10, by Mark D. Varien, Shirley Powell, and Leigh Kuwanwisiwma, describes the use of DNA analysis to investigate varities of corn and considers how corn varieties relate to clan migrations.

Hopi cultural preservation entails the transmission of traditional knowledge and practices from one generation to the next. As the twenty-first century unfolds, the Hopi Cultural Preservation Office is developing new ways to connect Hopi youth with their heritage and language. One successful educational outreach program entails a long-term parnership with Northern Arizona University, as discussed in chapter 11 by Joëlle Clark and George Gumerman IV. This innovative program connects Hopi youth and elders during trips to ancestral sites, allowing cultural knowledge about Hopi footprints to be shared between generations.

Interaction between outside scholars and the Hopi Cultural Preservation Office has shaped the research methods, ethics, and goals of several generations of anthropologists. In chapter 12, Thomas E. Sheridan lays out a methodology developed in partnership with the Hopi Cultural Preservation Office for using oral traditions to improve the interpretation of the documentary record. Gregson Schachner, in chapter 13, reflects on how work with the Hopi Cultural Preservation Office has positively changed the practice of archaeology in the Southwest and the training of new scholars entering the field. Finally, in chapter 14, Peter M. Whiteley draws upon his ethnographic fieldwork at Hopi to consider how Native thought influences the development of anthropological explanation. Whiteley concludes that Hopi analytical and historical perspectives improve anthropological theory.

In sum, this book highlights research collaboration between the Hopi Tribe and scholars who have significantly advanced anthropological understanding of Hopi archaeology, history, and heritage. This body of research directly benefits the Hopi Tribe by providing it with the information it needs to participate in government-to-government consultation pursuant to the NHPA, NEPA, NAGPRA, and other federal laws. More broadly, Hopi tribal members and the scholarly community both benefit by documenting and illuminating Hopi history and its relationship to the landscape.

This book grew out of a symposium held at the 78th Annual Meeting of the Society for American Archaeology (SAA) in Honolulu, Hawaii, in 2013 to honor Leigh Kuwanwisiwma's contributions to the field of anthropology. After the symposium, many of the participants said that, while they had known about their own projects with the Hopi Cultural Preservation Office and the projects of one or two other scholars, they had not realized the breadth and depth of the overall research program directed by Kuwanwisiwma and the Hopi Cultural Preservation Office. The participants in the SAA session all contributed to this book in order to help the Hopi Tribe share the insights and successes of the Hopi Cultural Preservation Office's research program. The research presented in this volume all lies on the spectrum of what have been variously called collaborative (Colwell 2016), community-based (Atalay 2012), and Indigenous archaeologies (Colwell-Chanthaphonh et al. 2010). The book aspires to be a case study to illustrate how this movement toward inclusiveness and empowerment provides important new methodological and theoretical frameworks for anthropology while serving a Native community's needs and reflecting its values.

In a short volume like this, it is not possible to include all the anthropological and historical research conducted by and for the Hopi Tribe. This volume focuses on research conducted by a network of scholars who participate in meetings of the SAA. In conjunction with the Hopi Cultural Preservation Office and its staff, other scholars are pursuing important research not featured in this book. Among other research efforts, Justin Richland (2008) has researched Hopi courts and has worked with Susan Secakuku on an Intellectual Properties in Cultural Heritage (IPinCH) project. Wendy Holliday has conducted historical research to document the Hopi political prisoners incarcerated at Alcatraz in the nineteenth century (https://www.nps.gov/alca/learn /historyculture/hopi-prisoners-on-the-rock.htm). *Hopi People*, a book by Stewart B. Koyiyumptewa, Carolyn O'Bagy Davis, and the Hopi Cultural Preservation Office (2009), features commentary about historic photographs. These works should be considered alongside the projects discussed in this book to fully appreciate how the Hopi Tribe has played a leading role in scholarship since 1989, when Leigh Kuwanwisiwma became the director of the Hopi Cultural Preservation Office.

The Hopi Cultural Preservation Office continues to dedicate its efforts to protecting Hopi culture and history. Embracing science and incorporating Hopi traditional knowledge, the Hopi Cultural Preservation Office is a model of critical thinking combined with action that respects the Hopi people and shares the results of research with them. The long-term research partnerships that the Hopi Cultural Preservation Office has formed with scholars have proven to be mutually beneficial to the Hopi Tribe and the field of anthropology.

REFERENCES CITED

Anyon, Roger, T. J. Ferguson, and John R. Welch. 2000. Heritage Management by American Indian Tribes in the Southwestern United States. In *Cultural Resource Management in*

Contemporary Society: Perspectives on Managing and Presenting the Past, edited by Francis P. McManamon and Alf Hatton, pp. 120–141. Routledge, London.

Atalay, Sonya. 2012. *Community-Based Archaeology: Research with, by, and for Indigenous and Local Communities*. University of California Press, Berkeley.

Colwell, Chip. 2016. Collaborative Archaeologies and Descendant Communities. *Annual Review of Anthropology* 45:113–127.

Colwell-Chanthaphonh, Chip, T. J. Ferguson, Dorothy Lippert, Randall H. McGuire, George P. Nicholas, Joe E. Watkins, and Larry J. Zimmerman. 2010. The Premise and Promise of Indigenous Archaeology. *American Antiquity* 75(2):228–238.

Koyiyumptewa, Stewart B., Carolyn O'Bagy Davis, and the Hopi Cultural Preservation Office. 2009. *The Hopi People*. Arcadia, Charleston, South Carolina.

Richland, Justin B. 2008. *Arguing with Tradition: The Language of Law in Hopi Tribal Court*. University of Chicago Press, Chicago.

FOOTPRINTS OF HOPI HISTORY

1

THE COLLABORATIVE ROAD

A Personal History of the Hopi Cultural Preservation Office

LEIGH J. KUWANWISIWMA

I N 1985, FEDERAL AND STATE agencies sent requests to the Hopi Tribe to consult on a range of cultural issues. Recognizing the need for a special tribal office to handle such requests, then Vice Chairman Stanley Honanie pursued funding through Public Law 93-638, which provides tribal grants for self-determination and self-government through the Bureau of Indian Affairs. The Hopi Tribal Council passed a resolution to secure the money and establish a staff position to be supervised by Vice Chairman Honanie. Patrick Lomawaima accepted the position of cultural preservationist and the Hopi Cultural Preservation Office began.

Then the funding for the Cultural Preservation Office ran out. A subsequent vice chairman, Vernon Masayesva, shared the vision of establishing an office to deal with all of the tribe's cultural issues. He took the initiative to fund this office from his own budget and to appoint a director rather than filling the position through a competitive hiring process. When Vice Chairman Masayesva asked me to come work for him, I was unsure why I was summoned. At that time, I was the assistant director for the Tribal Health Department, primarily responsible for contracts and budgets, but also working with the elderly. I'd also served several terms on the board for the Hotvela-Paaqavi School when Masayesva was the principal. Additionally, we are first cousins.

I hesitated to accept the position because it was a political appointment, and I was a regular tenured employee. I worked with Vice Chairman Masayesva to develop a position description and had it classified as a competitive position. Vice Chairman

This chapter is based on interviews with Leigh J. Kuwanwisiwma conducted by T. J. Ferguson on January 7–8, 2014, and edited by Chip Colwell.

Masayesva called me and said that the job was going to be publicly advertised and that he expected me to apply. I was hesitant because I didn't know the extent of the job; I didn't even know enough about heritage preservation to wonder about all the federal laws and state laws that affect decisions. Those concerns would all be new to me once I started the job.

Growing up in the village of Paaqavi on Third Mesa, I learned bits and pieces of Hopi philosophy. In the 1980s, I began to learn more about formal historical research. This early experience established in my mind the possibility of community-based participatory research, which directly involves tribal members and allows the tribe to review the production of documentation and reports. My village governing board called on me to assist anthropologist Peter Whiteley. For whatever reason, the board told Whiteley, "Go see Leigh. He will be the best person to help you." At that time, I didn't know how essential it was to document Hopi history. When I grew up, the oral tradition and teachings were still strong and "commoners" like me—a member of the Greasewood Clan without any religious title—didn't have to worry about documenting culture in writing. When Whiteley came along, I became fascinated with documenting Hopi history.

Previously, my life had been focused on my village of Paaqavi, but through Whiteley's research I was exposed to the whole history of Third Mesa—including the history of Orayvi, its famous split in 1906, and the subsequent establishment of the villages of Kiqötsmovi, Paaqavi, and Hotvela. My eyes were suddenly opened by the many interviews of older Hopi people, which I helped conduct and interpret. Together, Whiteley and I captured a lot of information. Whiteley proposed to publish a book on Paaqavi history and the Board of Governors agreed. This work—published in 1988 as *Bacavi: Journey to Reed Springs*—further motivated me to pursue the position with the tribe (Whiteley 1988).

After two weeks, no one had applied for the Hopi Cultural Preservation Office directorship, including me. Vice Chairman Masayesva called me again and encouraged me to apply. He advertised the position for two more weeks and I finally applied. I was the only applicant so we began to work out my transition from the Health Department to this position. Nevertheless, I was still hesitant and told the vice chairman that he needed more candidates and that there were more qualified people. He was unhappy with my response, but I was the only applicant. I told him that, if he advertised one more time and I was the only applicant, I'd accept the position. It's a Hopi custom for a leader to ask someone multiple times to take on a responsibility. The job was posted again, and again I was the only applicant. This time Vice Chairman Masayesva was serious; he called me into his office and said, "Leigh, you have the job. You know that." By this time, Ivan Sidney had become chairman of the Hopi Tribe, and he supported my hire. My first day on the job was March 18, 1989. I was thirty-nine years old.

We have been fortunate that the Cultural Preservation Office has not been politi-
cized by changing administrations. All of the seven administrations I've worked under
have provided good support. What motivates all of us is that we are Hopi people.
Because it has always been clear that the Hopi would face a tough future, cultural preservation and the integrity of the tribe's culture have been important. In my years on
the job, I have come to learn the wisdom of the tribe's older leadership. Chief Loloma,
who lived a century ago, declared that the Hopi people have a mission to maintain
and sustain their culture for as long as possible amidst dramatic change. I admired
the traditional leadership of my grandfather's and my father's generation. I sought to
learn from them the philosophy of the Hopi—to be who they are in their Southwest
home and to maintain the integrity of their culture in ceremonies, farming, social and
kinship systems, and every other part of their lives. It was their philosophy to maintain
their culture as much as possible so that the future generations of Hopi would benefit
from it, learn from it, and hopefully carry it on. I understood my mission to be simple:
to uphold the Hopi philosophy of unity, reciprocity, cooperation, industriousness,
respectfulness, and most importantly humility.

DEVELOPMENT OF THE HOPI CULTURAL PRESERVATION OFFICE

The Hopi Cultural Preservation Office quickly undertook an array of projects and
programs including creating Hopilavayi, a language preservation program; conducting extensive research to support lawsuits, such as those pertaining to water and land
rights; and protecting sacred places. The tribe also became more involved in evaluating
the potential impacts of development projects on the environment.

One of the first and largest environmental protection efforts began when I attended
a public meeting in Flagstaff, Arizona, about Glen Canyon, a region north of the
reservation with deep spiritual and cultural connections to the Hopi. There I learned
that the Bureau of Indian Affairs was representing all of the Arizona tribes as part of
its trust responsibility to assist tribes with the protection of treaty rights, lands, assets,
and resources related to the mandates of federal law. I returned home and convinced
the tribal council and Vernon Masayesva, who by then was tribal chairman, that the
Hopi Tribe needed to represent Hopi interests. With the assistance of Kurt Dongoske,
a non-Hopi archaeologist, I developed a proposal, and the Hopi Tribe became the first
tribe to engage in research for the Glen Canyon environmental impact statement as
part of the National Environmental Policy Act (NEPA) process. The tribe focused on
this work until 1997, but even today it remains a member of the Glen Canyon Adaptive
Management Working Group. These were huge responsibilities for the office.

Another major area of work revolves around assisting the tribe in consultations with federal and state agencies, museums, and private institutions. This involves reviewing and commenting on federal compliance activities related to historic preservation and environmental protection legislation. I developed a rule of thumb that the Hopi Cultural Preservation Office would respond to everything that comes to the Hopi Tribe. This, too, represents a big investment of time and energy. Assisted by a non-Hopi employee, Terry Morgart, I typically edit, review, and sign about ten letters a day.

I did not always have as much help or as many resources. On my first day, I walked into Vice Chairman Masayesva's office and said, "I'm reporting to work." He looked at me and said, "I don't even have a place for you to work yet." He told me to wait for a couple of days while he figured it out. I talked to my former boss, Leon Nuvayestewa, at the Health Department, and he allowed me to stay in my former office and gave me the supplies I needed because I didn't have a budget for supplies. My first budget included only salaries. Today, the Hopi Tribe invests about $380,000 each year into the office. We once had more than $500,000, but in 2005 with the shutdown of the Black Mesa Mine, which supplied coal to the now defunct Mohave Generating Station, tribal royalties dwindled and the Hopi Cultural Preservation Office budget was reduced. The Hopi Tribe funds the core staff and the office receives additional funding from a variety of sources for specific projects. Project-specific funding comes from the Bureau of Reclamation to monitor Glen Canyon Dam and for river trips in the Grand Canyon. There are other grants for the Hopi language program and numerous research contracts for historic preservation projects, many of them focusing on traditional cultural properties. The Hopi Cultural Preservation Office is the only program within the Department of Natural Resources that deals with issues outside the political boundaries of the Hopi Reservation. It's a huge responsibility to conduct the consultation that informs the tribe's decisions on various projects—whether to support a project or to reject it and whether adverse impacts can be mitigated. We're currently working on several major initiatives, including the Four Corners Power Plant environmental impact statement, the Navajo-Gallup Water Supply Project, and the Navajo Generating Plant environmental impact statement (including the power grid, rail spur, and two coal mines). All of these projects require funding from external sources.

In 1989, my staff consisted of three people: Merwin (Lefty) Kooyahoema (who was technically still with the Health Department); Rhonda Kyasyousie, a volunteer secretary; and me. Over the years, the staff size has varied from a handful to more than a dozen people, depending on the projects being conducted and their budgets. Currently the staff consists of seven people: Mike Yeatts, senior archaeologist; Sue Kuyvaya, administrative manager; Lee Wayne Lomayestewa, research assistant; Terry

Morgart, legal researcher; Joel Nicholas, archaeologist; Stewart B. Koyiyumptewa, archivist and project manager; and me.

Although this staff has been central to the success of the Hopi Cultural Preservation Office, I also depend on help from Hopi religious leaders and community elders. During the office's first year, I was charged with the reburial of an infant whose remains had been excavated from an archaeological site. This was a traumatic moment for me because I had never anticipated having to oversee reburials of ancestral remains and I had no idea how to deal with it. I quickly understood that repatriation and reburial are not a one-man job; I would have to draw upon the resources of the tribe itself. That's when I brought in Dalton Taylor, a Sun Clan member from Songòopavi, Second Mesa, as one of our first advisors.

Early on I realized I needed help—I'm a commoner, not initiated into any major Hopi religious societies. Therefore, I formed a core of central advisors, the Cultural Resources Advisory Task Team (CRATT), which consists of eighteen men representing the Hopi clans and villages on the three mesas. Meeting monthly, CRATT includes many of the tribal members whom we engage in historic preservation research. For field and museum research projects, a team of CRATT members joins us to share their knowledge of our history. During fieldwork, ideas are passed around among cultural advisors, and there are many diverse opinions. Hopis belong to different clans—so that clan identity helps to shape CRATT contributions to a project—but no matter which clan they belong to, all Hopis share a common way of thinking. I rely on CRATT as the first sounding board for issues that I need help with. The team's cultural advice is valuable, even though I ultimately have to make executive decisions.

People have come and gone from CRATT. Some have passed away and some new people have joined, but the group has been stable over the years. The influx of newer, younger cultural advisors is consistent with the culture; it's a natural thing to bring in younger people and new thinking. As older advisors retire or pass on, we must prepare for a transition to the next generation. New, younger advisors can be listeners and learners as they start to work on projects.

There is a transition on the horizon for my position as well. I've been engaged in developing a new cadre of young academics. Lyle Balenquah worked for the Hopi Cultural Preservation Office for a time and received a master's degree in anthropology from Northern Arizona University (NAU) in 2002. Lloyd Masayumptewa received his MA from NAU in 2001 and has since worked for the National Park Service. He is currently superintendent at Hubble Trading Post. Stewart Koyiyumptewa has a BA in anthropology from the University of Arizona and is completing a master's in anthropology at NAU. Joel Nicholas received his BA in anthropology from the University of Arizona. From an academic and technical standpoint, we must prepare. Although I had no formal background, I had a lot of help from outside professionals. But one of these days, we must take the reins ourselves. I'm engaging other Hopi staff members to apply their real world experience to tribal and legal responsibilities. There is a political part of the job for which you have to tough it out and develop a strong skin to survive. That is part of the challenge—to find someone who is willing to do that.

COMPLIANCE ISSUES

In terms of compliance, especially with regard to eligibility issues concerning the National Register of Historic Places, there is still much work to do. Early on, we worked with Kurt Dongoske, who began to understand how the Hopi think and to explain that to non-Indians. Part of the technical debate in the compliance process of determining eligibility for the National Register concerns whether or not an archaeological site is a traditional cultural property. The site is fifty years old, but regulators have argued that archaeological sites are not a living part of our culture today because they are ruins. Why are we calling ancestral archaeological sites traditional cultural properties? Under the National Register criteria, they are a part of our history, part of our "footprints." We use ancestral sites to teach young Hopis about their history and culture. Therefore, to me, they qualify as traditional cultural properties. Nonetheless, that issue is still under debate. Often when we read reports we realize that unfortunately not all archaeologists agree that archaeological sites are traditional cultural properties. Therefore, this needs to be further argued in the compliance process.

Similarly, archaeologists considered a cairn documented on a recent Arizona Public Service (APS) survey (Ferguson et al. 2015; Hopkins et al. 2014) to be an isolated feature; therefore, it's not eligible for the National Register. If you collaborate with the Hopi Tribe, you understand that those cairns are in fact part of a greater landscape, part of a living culture, probably associated with ruins nearby. The Hopi have cultural knowledge about some of the clans that came from the Grand Canyon and areas to the north as part of the final footprints. Things like this, as well as the designation of the law as a "national" historic preservation act are still bothersome. It's ironic that this act caters to development. I have a hard time dealing with how the law encourages compliance through mitigation, which for archaeological sites means testing or full data recovery. Cultural and spiritual values are intangible and the law cannot accommodate that; it deals with the tangible. For example, within a coal mine there may be thousands of archaeological sites, and many of those are bulldozed while the mining company and federal agencies tell us that they have complied with the law. We've taken this question to administrative law hearings and had the judge decide that the federal agencies have complied and that they are required to notify the Hopi only when burial remains need to be recovered—if anyone reports them.

I still wrestle with compliance issues such as these because the process is simply not good for tribes. That's the irony of the National Historic Preservation Act. It's bothersome because we lose sites, and once we lose them, either through data recovery, which is an adverse impact, or through outright destruction, Hopi culture is diminished. We just don't agree that burial sites should be disturbed but legally we can't do much about it.

The problem with NEPA is that it's a remandable law; therefore, someone who doesn't agree with the act can sue for noncompliance. If the suit goes to court, the judge may decide that the proponents must bring their work into compliance with the law and regulations. It's remandable but that doesn't mean much for the tribes. The case is remanded to the proponents or the federal agencies, and then it goes back to court and the decision is up to one judge. Changing the law is not feasible because of the political process, so unfortunately nothing is going to change for a long time.

REPATRIATION

The motivation for some of the research that the Hopi Cultural Preservation Office has endorsed is the Native American Graves Protection and Repatriation Act (NAG-PRA). Under NAGPRA, anything that we can produce to fight for ancestral history is important—anything that will support NAGPRA's ten lines of evidence, ranging from biology to kinship to oral tradition, that are used to establish cultural affiliation between the tribe and claimed cultural items or human remains. For example, the baseline data on corn DNA being documented by Mark Varien and his colleagues at Crow Canyon is important. Crow Canyon funded that research for us, and the Hopi Tribe agreed on the research protocols and intellectual property rights issues. As a result, Varien and colleagues produced the first DNA study on eight Hopi varieties of corn compared to the current database of Hopi corn (see chapter 10, this volume). That study will be useful in NAGPRA research because it points to continuities of cultural practices and social identities between Hopis and our ancestors over the millennia. Frances E. Smiley at NAU is ready to do similar work.

With the help of John McClelland at the Arizona State Museum in Tucson, we've looked at dental morphology in terms of physical anthropology lines of evidence. Christy Turner, a physical anthropologist at Arizona State University, held a collection of 200 Hopi dental casts. No one knew what to do with the casts after he passed away. When the university offered to return the dental casts, I recommended to the tribal chairman that the Hopi Tribe should get custody of the dental casts. We'll have to work through the ethical issues if the casts are from living people or if they are from deceased people who have descendants. In any case, the dental casts are important for

NAGPRA research. There's a lot more work to be done. People who are majoring in physical anthropology can talk to the Hopi people about what we want in terms of research.

More generally, diet is of interest to the Hopi. We sometimes romanticize about the old times of our people, but they struggled to survive. They dealt with drought and environmental changes, and they didn't live very long. When they were sixty, they were old. Our ancestors foraged for food before they became farmers. They were gatherers. They knew about edible food such as the wild grains and what the Hopis call starvation food, such as the new leaves on greasewood. The salt from salty clay supplemented their diet. They knew the environment. We've lost some of that knowledge.

The diet of our ancestors can be determined from their remains. Anomalies in bones are important. Once there was an oil leak at Springerville, Arizona, that affected an ancestral cemetery. In the cemetery were stacked burials of people of all ages, interspersed with brush, like a mass burial. Dalton Taylor and I agreed that these remains should be recovered. We told the archaeologists that we needed to know why there were stacked burials; we needed to know if there was disease because there are special prayer feathers for different kinds of events. We found out that the lack of calcium caused a huge epidemic of rickets and these people couldn't survive. Once we knew what had happened, Dalton made the right prayer feather to ask that these health problems never come back again.

The technical and scientific sides of research can benefit the Hopi people. Over time, we've become more open in our thinking about research and capacity building. Working with outside researchers helps train tribal members in research techniques, and that benefits us. The Hopi Tribe continues to need more NAGPRA research.

Implementing NAGPRA is difficult, and since the 1990s we've been handling reburials all over the Southwest. We didn't have a tradition of reburial, but Dalton Taylor said, "Let's help our ancestors out." Later, Wilton Kooyahoema, a Kookopng-yam (Fire Clan) leader from Hotvela, took over the reburials. When Wilton retires, who will come forward? If no one wants to, I'll do it even if I'm retired. It's been a rollercoaster of decisions. There are so many ancestral remains: 600 at Bureau of Land Management in Dolores, 800 at Chaco Canyon, 3,000 at Coconino, and 1,500 at White River.

At Mesa Verde, a region in southwestern Colorado filled with Pueblo sites, there are remains of 1,500 ancestors. The cultural advisors and I had seen the spreadsheet of data, but when we opened the boxes and the remains were handed to us, we saw the cradle boarding—the flat backs of the skulls that had been shaped by continuously placing the children's soft heads against the hard wood of a cradle board. We had to ask who they were. I don't dwell on it, but when I talk about it now, it comes back and I visualize it again. So we cleansed ourselves. There were twenty mummies. I handled those. There were four mummified remains of mothers and infants in swaddling. Mummified remains are the most challenging visually and emotionally. There is a personal reaction, an anger that comes with the reburial process. We felt this anger and we tried to balance it with what the Hopi Tribe and the Hopi Cultural Preservation Office have decided to do, which is to rebury these people, hopefully for the last time. There is a sort of ledger where you ask why these people were exhumed and then you try to balance that emotion by personally accepting that the tribe's decision was the best thing that could be done. After every reburial, there are strong emotional responses that are balanced by knowing that reburying these people is the right thing to do. Even so, it's tough to do, especially because of the spiritual aspects.

Now we're turning our attention to Hopi sacred objects. There are so many in museum collections. In the late nineteenth century, Frank H. Cushing raided our shrines to get prayer sticks and J. Walter Fewkes raided our cemeteries to get funerary objects. Nancy Parezo at the University of Arizona finally decoded their notes so that we can figure out how much they got from cemeteries and shrines. These are stolen material that shouldn't be subject to NAGPRA. We never released those items to anybody, but when NAGPRA was passed, Congress gave property rights to museums and federal agencies—"possession and control" as the law calls it—and the Hopi Tribe has to beg for them and prove that they belong to the Hopi.

Hopi ceremonial and sacred objects in museums outnumber those of other tribes. Repatriating these objects is a long-term project. Consultation and including the right people from the Hopi villages to help takes time, not to mention the whole process of making a claim. Both the Hopi Cultural Preservation Office and the Flute Clan from First Mesa were needed to prove that the Flute Ceremony artifacts in Cambridge, Massachusetts, had to be returned (McManamon 1997). They opened the medicine bundle and altar to prove that the paraphernalia found at Tseigi Canon is the same as that found at First Mesa today. These struggles are draining.

The Paris auctions of Hopi sacred artifacts taught me a lot (Hopi Tribe 2015; Mashberg 2013). Time was not on our side. When we finally received legal help from Jim Scarborough (legal services are expensive), we learned that French law is different from U.S. law in that it requires a certificate of rightful possession. The auction house deals with that issue. If stolen items are bought and sold several times, rightful possession is established. A sacred object that is commodified under French law loses its sacredness. That was a problem for us. However, under NAGPRA, sacred objects can't be sold so we wanted a delay to determine if the sale to French citizens occurred after 1990, when NAGPRA was passed. Also there were eagle feathers and we wanted to know if there was any French law that applied to endangered species. France and the

United States are signatories to the UNESCO treaty that was stimulated by Nazi theft of art; because Hopi artifacts were looted, we argued that the treaty should apply to the Hopi. We lost the case. Whether there is room for appeal is uncertain. We need a new law; it's frustrating.

Without our knowledge, the Annenberg Foundation (2013) bid on twenty-four items at the Paris auction, and those are now being returned to the Hopi Tribe. Unfortunately, someone profited from the sale. Culturally the return of these items is probably satisfying, but the market for such items remains.

There are changes every year. Repatriation is frustrating, but it stimulates your thinking; it triggers you to be proactive and to anticipate issues and how you want to deal with them. It's rewarding to learn so much.

COLLABORATION

The Paaqavi project with Peter Whiteley set the precedent for successful collaboration. Although this project required working with an outside researcher, it produced a significant resource for the village and for the entire Third Mesa. I'm seeing the same results today. We control the research and we hire the contractors or we have a key role in determining who is hired. Over time we've engaged with different consultants and now Stewart Koyiyumptewa is getting into fieldwork and acting as lead on some of the smaller projects to gain the experience he needs.

It's the legacy that is important. The tribe is under a lot of stress, and like the prophets of old, the old leadership teaches you to be a visionary. You must look not only at the next twenty years, but at a hundred years from now. You look at your grandchildren and you ask yourself what is their future going to be like in these rapidly changing times. Language loss is a huge problem. The ceremonial way of life is slowly being eroded. It bothers me to say that one day we may need to rely on written documentation for our culture. I hope not, but research preserves Hopi knowledge and will be a resource for future generations.

As I reflect back over the last twenty-five years and all the people whom we've engaged with over the years—from Hopi Cultural Preservation Office employees to the tribal constituency to the highest political levels of the tribe—what stands out most in my mind is trust. Trust is what matters with us. In particular, scholars from outside the tribe need to understand where the tribe is coming from and where the tribe is heading in terms of, in some cases, the legacy of researchers who exploited the Hopi people. Today we are in the driver's seat in controlling research. It's trust that a lot of our villagers, advisory team, and others need to feel about people coming in to work with the Cultural Preservation Office.

Over time, I've tried to guide the Hopi Cultural Preservation Office to embrace research. I'm impressed with the type of research—ethnographic and applied collaborations—that we've accomplished (see appendix). Consider, for example, the curriculum development for several schools that has been accomplished by NAU with Hopi teachers and elders (see Clark and Gumerman, this volume). That's a direct benefit to the Hopi constituency. Another example is Wesley Bernardini's work to map a lot of our archaeological sites with state-of-the-art equipment and to train our staff to learn that technology (see Bernardini, this volume; Hedquist et al. 2015). We've engaged with the APS to build a fence around one of our major petroglyph sites, Tutuveni, which was being heavily vandalized (Bernardini 2007). In addition, with APS and World Heritage Fund support, we now have cameras to monitor the site. Over the last four years, although the site is publicly accessible, we haven't seen any more vandalism. Yet another benefit is the 1997 language fluency survey completed with the University of Arizona and a Hopi linguist (Hopi Cultural Preservation Office 1998, Hopi Language Assessment Project 1997). We still use these data to help guide the Hopi language program.

There are bridges that have developed over time. For example, during the initial stage of his master's degree, Wes Bernardini chose to come to the Hopi Reservation. When he became a doctoral student he continued to interact with the Hopi Cultural Preservation Office, and now as a professor he still works with us. There is also a bridge between the generations of older archaeologists and younger students. Patrick Lyons, now the director of the Arizona State Museum, also approached us as a student. He had been tutored and mentored by people like Chuck Adams, who has long worked with us. Chip Colwell is also someone who has worked with us for a long time, as is Wolf Gumerman. The transition has happened; the bridge has been created.

This story is about both how the tribe has dealt with research and academia and how it has been able to attract a high level of technical support from scholars who mean what they say when they say they want to work with the Hopi Tribe. The current generation of students is the beneficiary of that.

Many students contact the Hopi Cultural Preservation Office through their professors who have worked with the Hopi Tribe. Those students have a way of getting in touch with us. Other students come in cold without a referral from their professors. Over time we have developed a standard research protocol. If students are interested in research, we ask them to look at the research protocol on our website (Hopi Cultural Preservation Office 2016). If they have something in mind that they want to do, we ask them to answer those questions first and then see what happens. Eventually we meet students one-on-one. Through reciprocity, we learn from the students.

Students and scholars who want to work with the Hopi are always welcome to come to the regular CRATT meetings. We like to hear what they are doing. There is always a way to build a relationship with them so that they can help meet tribal needs. Some undergraduate students like Tai Johnson, who eventually wrote a master's thesis on diet and nutrition (2007), develop a working relationship with the Hopi Cultural Preservation Office that carries them forward into their graduate work. We deal with all types of interests, and we try to accommodate students. We'll sit down and talk about any research that is of interest to the Hopi.

THE FUTURE OF RESEARCH AT HOPI

I hope that this book summarizes the research that the Hopi Cultural Preservation Office has conducted and sponsored so that it can be used in school curricula and public education programs. It must be available in different venues, including schools and villages. This book can be a road map to all the research so that people can read the synopses and then seek more detailed information.

What does the future hold for collaborative research between the Hopi Tribe and anthropologists (archaeologists and ethnographers)? I can speak only for the Hopi. The tribe, through the Hopi Cultural Preservation Office, has embraced both the traditions of the Hopi ancestors and the need to have our culture documented in different ways. We now have a large collection of oral history interviews for language preservation. From some of the older folks we interviewed, we captured the old style of Hopi talking and the dialects. We hope that people can benefit from that.

I see the tribe's effort to maintain the collaborative road, whereby in many cases traditional Hopi history is being corroborated. Science has come in and taken a look at some of our traditions and, lo and behold, they do support each other. We are discovering new bridges between science and tradition. I think we can do more with Wesley Bernardini's and Kelly Hays-Gilpin's work in ceramic typing. That is a research area that hasn't been fully explored to trace the literal footprints of the Hopi people.

There is room for even more exciting collaboration between people who want to work together. My vision is to also look at capacity building and to encourage our Hopis to go through the academic world and come back, as Joel Nicholas and Stewart Koyiyumptewa have done. It's about challenging them to go farther, to develop the capacity for the tribe to eventually take full control and leadership in research about the Hopi.

This book can be an outreach to both the Hopi Tribe and the academic world. I think the book is also a legacy of all the people who have gone through the last twenty-five years with the Hopi Cultural Preservation Office, including the early cultural advisors. This book, with all its contributions, is something I leave for my family.

REFERENCES CITED

Annenberg Foundation. 2013. Annenberg Foundation and Hopi Nation Announce Return of Sacred Artifacts to Native American Tribe. Electronic document, http://www.annenberg foundation.org/node/51351, accessed January 30, 2016.

Bernardini, Wesley. 2007. *Hopi History in Stone: The Tutuveni Petroglyph Site*. Arizona State Museum Archaeological Series 200. Arizona State Museum, University of Arizona, Tucson.

Ferguson, T. J., Stewart B. Koyiyumptewa, and Maren P. Hopkins. 2015. Co-creation of Knowledge by the Hopi Tribe and Archaeologists. *Advances in Archaeological Practice* 3(3):249–262.

Hedquist, Saul L., Stewart B. Koyiyumptewa, Wesley Bernardini, T. J. Ferguson, Peter M. Whiteley, and Leigh J. Kuwanwisiwma. 2015. Mapping the Hopi Landscape for Cultural Preservation. *International Journal of Applied Geospatial Research* 6(1):40–59.

Hopi Cultural Preservation Office. 1998. Hopi Language Preservation and Education Plan. Hopi Tribe, Kiqötsmovi, Arizona.

———. 2016. Protocol for Research, Publication, and Recordings: Motion, Visual, Sound, Multimedia and Other Mechanical Devices. Electronic document, http://www8.nau.edu/hcpo -p/ResProto.pdf, accessed January 30, 2016.

Hopi Language Assessment Project. 1997. *Presentation of Hopi Language Survey Results*. Hopi Cultural Preservation Office and Bureau of Applied Research in Anthropology, University of Arizona, Tucson.

Hopi Tribe. 2015. Hopi Tribe Demands Return of Sacred Objects Being Sold Illegally in Paris Auction. Press Release, May 20, 2015. Hopi Tribe, Kiqötsmovi, Arizona.

Hopkins, Maren P., Saul L. Hedquist, T. J. Ferguson, and Stewart B. Koyiyumptewa. 2014. *Talwi'pikit Tuuwuhiyat Ang Hopit Navoti'at*: Hopi Traditional Knowledge on the Arizona Public Service 500kV El Dorado Transmission Line Corridor on the Hopi Reservation. Prepared for Arizona Public Service Company. Hopi Cultural Preservation Office, Kiqötsmovi, Arizona.

Johnson, Tai. 2007. *Surviving the Transformation, Hopi Farming, Food, and Labor*. Master's thesis, Department of History, Northern Arizona University, Flagstaff.

Mashberg, Tom. 2013. Hopis Try to Stop Paris Sale of Artifacts. *New York Times* 3 April:C1.

McManamon, Francis P. 1997. Notice of Intent to Repatriate Cultural Items from Arizona in the Possession of the Peabody Museum of Archaeology and Ethnology, Harvard University, Cambridge, Massachusetts. *Federal Register* 62(48):11462.

Whiteley, Peter M. 1988. *Bacavi: Journey to Reed Springs*. Northland Press, Flagstaff, Arizona.

2

TRADITIONAL CULTURAL PROPERTIES AND THE HOPI MODEL OF CULTURAL PRESERVATION

CHIP COLWELL AND STEWART B. KOYIYUMPTEWA

SINCE 1989, THE HOPI CULTURAL PRESERVATION OFFICE (HCPO) has effectively used the social sciences as an instrument to serve the Hopi people. Through a broad range of projects, the HCPO provides an important example of how a Native American community is eager to use rigorous research to understand its own history and culture—as long as the scientific process is relevant, respectful, and beneficial to the people it studies. By putting science in the service of its community, the Hopi approach to cultural preservation provides a key model of mutual benefit to both scholars and Native peoples.

In its twenty-five years, the HCPO has covered an impressive array of topics, such as ancient history, social identity, migration, cultural landscapes, plant genetics, ethnobotany, heritage management, repatriation, cultural education, and language preservation. Equally impressive is the number of academic fields the HCPO has used to address these themes: anthropology, archaeology, archival and library sciences, biology, botany, ethnohistory, geography, and museology.

Unifying and underlying all of these projects is a method that in recent years has been labeled variously as collaborative, community-based, and Indigenous (Colwell 2016). In a sense, the HCPO bridges these different approaches and practices. Many of the projects are collaborative in that they involve non-Hopis and Hopis working together toward shared goals, freely sharing information, offering stakeholders full involvement, giving full voice to descendants, and seeking to meet the needs of all parties (Brighton 2011; Colwell-Chanthaphonh and Ferguson 2008; Kerber 2006; Kuwanwisiwma 2002; McAnany and Rowe 2015). Community-based projects are similar but fundamentally arise from the community itself and can involve methods that are deeply participatory and action oriented (Atalay 2012; Gumerman et al. 2012; Supernant and Warrick 2014; Welch et al. 2011). Indigenous archaeologies are those pursued by both Indigenous researchers and their allies who work toward incorporating local values, perspectives, and traditions into scientific practice (Colwell-Chanthaphonh et al. 2010; Silliman 2008; Smith and Wobst 2005). Even legally mandated consultation has given rise to new and positive forms of interaction and collaboration (Ferguson 2009; Fuller 1997; Versaggi 2006). But, for the HCPO, these would just be fancy labels to describe a rather straightforward proposition: that research on the Hopi people should include Hopi voices, perspectives, needs, and values.

This chapter will demonstrate how this idea has been put into practice in one key area of work for the HCPO: facilitating compliance with historic and environmental preservation laws. The example we will present concerns the effort to document Hopi traditional places in the path of a new transmission line. Although the research conducted for this project identified numerous cultural and natural resources—ranging from water sources to eagle nests to medicinal plants—we focus on three particular traditional cultural properties. Our goal is to show how Hopi interests are served at the same time as new knowledge is being generated and documented through a collaborative process. We will conclude by discussing the ways in which this kind of research has created a unique approach to cultural preservation.

CULTURAL PRESERVATION
ACROSS 744 KILOMETERS

The Navajo Transmission Project (NTP) involved the proposed construction of a 744-kilometer-long 500-kV (500,000-V) alternating current transmission line from the Shiprock Substation in northwestern New Mexico to the Marketplace Substation in southeastern Nevada (figure 2.1). The project was proposed by the Diné Power Authority, a business enterprise of the Navajo Nation that wanted to link new power-generating stations to expanding markets. The new transmission line included numerous construction components: approximately 2,310 towers (26 to 49 meters high), four substations, a right-of-way and access roads, and ancillary facilities such as equipment storage areas.

The HCPO sought to be consulted on the NTP because the proposed transmission line would go through much of the Hopi ancestral homelands and potentially affect numerous cultural and natural resources that are important to the Hopi people. Hopis are deeply tied to the land, which in turn feeds their identities, cultural practices, and spiritual beliefs (Balenquah 2012; Koyiyumptewa and Colwell-Chanthaphonh 2011; Whiteley 2011).

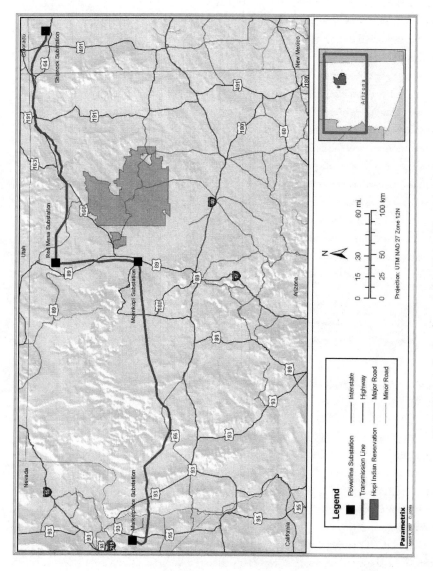

FIGURE 2.1 Proposed route of the Navajo Transmission Project.

The first federal law that guided this project was the National Environmental Policy Act (NEPA) of 1969, which established a national policy for the environment to "encourage productive and enjoyable harmony between man and his environment; to promote efforts which will prevent or eliminate damage to the environment and biosphere and stimulate the health and welfare of man; to enrich the understanding of the ecological systems and natural resources important to the Nation" (42 U.S.C. §4321). This act defines the environment broadly to include natural, cultural, and historic resources so that the United States may "preserve important historic, cultural, and natural aspects of our national heritage, and maintain, wherever possible, an environment which supports diversity, and variety of individual choice" [42 U.S.C. §4331(b)(4)]. Unless a federal undertaking is categorically excluded from review, a report must be made examining how federal actions will significantly affect the quality of the human environment.

The second federal law used in this work was the National Historic Preservation Act (NHPA) of 1966, which recognized that the spirit and direction of the United States are founded upon our historic heritage. The law thus declared that "the preservation of this irreplaceable heritage is in the public interest so that its vital legacy of cultural, educational, aesthetic, inspirational, economic, and energy benefits will be maintained and enriched for future generations of Americans" [16 U.S.C. §470(b) (2)(4)]. Section 106 of the NHPA required the lead federal agency for the NTP to consider the effects of proposed projects "on any district, site, building, structure, or object that is included in or eligible for inclusion in the National Register" (16 U.S.C. §470f). Of special importance to Native American tribes is the traditional cultural property that is "eligible for inclusion in the National Register because of its association with cultural practices or beliefs of a living community that (a) are rooted in that community's history, and (b) are important in maintaining the continuing cultural identity of the community" (Parker and King 1998:1).

Because the NTP requires federal permits and crosses federal lands it is a federal undertaking. Under NEPA and the NHPA, the lead federal agency and project proponents must consult with Native American tribes [40 C.F.R. §1501.2(d)(2) and 36 C.F.R. §800.2(c)(2)(ii), respectively]. Participation of the Hopi Tribe in the consultation process was in no way intended to imply implicit or explicit support for the proposed project.

The HCPO secured funding from the project proponents to determine which cultural and natural resources the NTP might affect. The HCPO then subcontracted with Anthropological Research, LLC, to assist in the documentation of cultural resources and with Parametrix to assist in the documentation of natural resources. Significantly, this research and the report produced from it (Albert and Colwell-Chanthaphonh 2007) did not constitute consultation under federal law. Rather, this

FIGURE 2.2 One group of CRATT members, with the authors, in the project area (photo by T. J. Ferguson, October 11, 2006).

work provided the scientific basis for the Hopi Tribe to articulate its concerns during its government-to-government consultations with the lead federal agency.

In 2006, the HCPO research team was assembled. A vital part of this team was the Hopi Cultural Resources Advisory Task Team (CRATT). This team consists of men versed in Hopi religion and culture who are designated representatives of the tribe's twelve autonomous villages (see chapter 1). For this project the HCPO research team focused on documenting both general environmental resources and specific historic properties in the path of the proposed transmission line. Once any resource or property was identified, the team evaluated the potential short-term, long-term, and cumulative effects of the transmission line—and whether any of these effects could be mitigated. For three weeks in 2006, a group drawn from CRATT conducted vehicular surveys of the proposed project area (figure 2.2). This involved driving along the proposed route and stopping at various points to document and discuss resources as they were identified. This effort was followed by a week of interviews and one large group meeting to review the report's findings. As cultural experts giving their time, each CRATT member (like each contracted scientist) was paid a modest stipend. By the end of the project, the team had worked with twenty-eight Hopi researchers and CRATT members (see table 2.1).

TABLE 2.1 Hopi cultural advisors who participated
in the Navajo Transmission Project in 2006.

NAME	AGE	CLAN	VILLAGE
Norman Albert	42	Sun	Hotvela, Third Mesa
Kevin Crooke	30	Sun	Hotvela, Third Mesa
Donald Dawahongnewa	49	Water/Corn	Songòopavi, Second Mesa
Harold Dawavendewa	66	Sun	Upper Munqapi
Jerry Honawa	70	Tobacco/Rabbit	Hotvela, Third Mesa
Wilton Kooyahoema	69	Fire	Hotvela, Third Mesa
Stewart B. Koyiyumptewa	34	Badger	Hotvela, Third Mesa
Leigh J. Kuwanwisiwma	56	Greasewood	Paaqavi, Third Mesa
Marvin Lalo	50	Tobacco/Rabbit	Wàlpi, First Mesa
Floyd Lomakuyvaya	57	Bearstrap	Songòopavi, Second Mesa
Lee Lomayestewa	47	Bear	Songòopavi, Second Mesa
Victor Masayesva Jr.	55	Water Coyote	Hotvela, Third Mesa
Harlyn Monongye	62	Greasewood	Hotvela, Third Mesa
Harlan Nakala	61	Flute	Wàlpi, First Mesa
Augustine Mowa Jr.	48	Sun	Songòopavi, Second Mesa
Theodore Namingha Sr.	76	Corn	Hotvela, Third Mesa
Gilbert Naseyowma	72	Sun	Lower Munqapi
Owen Numkena Jr.	70	Corn/Water	Musangnuvi, Second Mesa
Harold Polingyumptewa	71	Sand/Snake	Hotvela, Third Mesa
Raleigh Puhuyaoma Sr.	72	Sun Forehead	Supawlavi, Second Mesa
Morgan Saufkie	71	Bear	Songòopavi, Second Mesa
Ferrell Secakuku	68	Snake	Supawlavi, Second Mesa
Michael Sockyma	64	Corn	Hotvela, Third Mesa
Sharon Sockyma	47	Corn	Hotvela, Third Mesa
Theodora Sockyma	63	Bear	Musangnuvi, Second Mesa
Herschel Talashoma Jr.	43	Greasewood	Hotvela, Third Mesa
Jim Tawyesva Sr.	66	Roadrunner	Polacca, First Mesa
Max Taylor	49	Sun	Songòopavi, Second Mesa

KIIKIQÖ (RUINS)

Among the most prominent parts of the cultural landscape in the NTP project area
are scores of archaeological sites. In their own language Hopis call ancient villages
kiikiqö (singular *kiiqö*; lit. ruins) and emphasize that these sites give testimony to
their ancestors' ancient migrations and their living pledge of land stewardship. Many
ancestral sites are named, and stories of ancient days recalled. Other sites are actively
visited and sacred offerings are left. At other times, prayers for entire ancestral areas

are offered from the Hopi Mesas. Although each clan once lived in a particular village, these "footprints" are important to all Hopis today because each clan is historically, ritually, and spiritually interconnected to every other clan, and they collectively contribute to the whole of Hopi society. *Kiikiqö* are thus an essential part of Hopi history and culture. They are monuments to the Hopi past and integral features of religious practices and beliefs in the present.

Many Hopi traditionalists emphasize the origin histories that go back to the emergence of their ancestors onto the earth, the Fourth World, where they met the spirit-being Màasaw, with whom they entered into a covenant whereby they would become stewards of the Earth in exchange for its use. "We [Hopis] first emerged all one people—one language, one culture," Hopi advisor Ferrell Secakuku told us in an interview, "but at the beginning they got into a fight, and so Màasaw changed the language. He spread out the corn and each was a different language, a different destiny. The Hopi picked up the short corn, which represents endurance, wisdom, and a spiritual inclination to survive. Then they migrated."

The people set out to find their destiny at the center of the universe, the Hopi Mesas. In this search, they formed into clans, settling in one village after another, moving in every direction. The migrations were not easy; the people were confronted by many obstacles. Some clans moved to the far south, suffering the heat, while others moved to the far north, suffering the bitter cold. Generations passed. At last, the clans began to coalesce at the Hopi Mesas, each bringing its own unique rituals, stories, histories, and knowledge. Hopis believe that Màasaw instructed the Hisatsinom, these ancient ancestors, to leave their footprints on the land as proof that they had fulfilled the covenant. These footprints, in the form of springs, shrines, villages, and petroglyphs, give evidence of the Hopi historic pathways (Colwell-Chanthaphonh and Ferguson 2006; Dongoske et al. 1993; Kuwanwisiwma and Ferguson 2004). These oral traditions of Hopi movement tie into numerous archaeological cultures across northern New Mexico and Arizona (figure 2.3) (Welch and Ferguson 2016). From Chaco Canyon to the Kayenta region to the Grand Canyon, scholars have found myriad lines of evidence that link at least several thousand years of history to the Hopi people (Brew 1979:514; Lyons 2003; Reed 2004; Schwartz 1989:67).

Because of limited time and funding, the Hopi research team could visit only a sample of the archaeological sites in the NTP right of way. No matter the site's type or period, whether an isolated artifact or a pueblo, Paleoindian or historic, the Hopi cultural advisors consistently identified the sites as culturally important. In part this is because many Hopis reference ancestral places in their prayers and will visit them on religious pilgrimages. As Floyd Lomakuvaya explained, "Every time I make prayer feathers, I make them for all the ruins that my ancestors lived in. And I go out to Montezuma Well, Walnut Canyon, and those places. That's what my uncles told me,

FIGURE 2.3 Stewart B. Koyiyumptewa holds a complete arrowhead, with extant power lines in background, found in northern Arizona (photo by Chip Colwell, October 25, 2006).

the stories. They said, 'Keep coming because your ancestors are still down there.' That's why I make the pilgrimages."

When visiting archaeological sites, advisors frequently made more specific connections to things left behind. For example, at various sites, they identified such artifacts as a *paavalwi* (a type of stone tool ground down to fit the hand and used to apply plaster and whitewash to walls), a *mata* (metate, or a stone used as the base when grinding corn and other botanicals) fragment, a *qalap'owa* (chipping rock), a *yoysiva* (flint arrowhead), and a *tsqapta* (pottery bowl). At one petroglyph site (AZ J:29:47 [ASM]) Donald Dawahongnewa identified a white chalky rock called *toko'owa* that is used medicinally (figure 2.4). Asked the significance of finding this kind of rock at an ancient site, Dawahongnewa responded, "This rock tells me a long time ago, they were sick and collected these. My medicine is here. They did this long ago." He then set the rock back down and left an offering of cornmeal.

At another petroglyph site (AZ J:30:35 [ASM]) there is a distinctive panel with a procession of human figures, possibly as many as twenty-four, all in a line. Hopi advisors agreed that these dancers very likely represented the Wuwtsim ceremony, and more specifically, because of the depiction of the hair, the Natnga, a special initiation

FIGURE 2.4 Donald Dawahongnewa holds a white chalky rock called *toko'owa* that is used medicinally at an ancestral petroglyph site, AZ J:29:47 (ASM) (photo by Chip Colwell, October 10, 2006).

held about every seven years. One particular figure was thought to depict the Yayat ritual, which is conducted at the Second Mesa village of Musangnuvi and includes elaborate headdresses decorated with wings and long feathers. Farther up the canyon wall at this site, at the end of a staircase etched into the bedrock, advisors located a *tuwvota* (shield symbol) protected by a nook in the bedrock. The *tuwvota*, a highly significant and distinctive Hopi symbol had been pecked into the rock and later carefully retraced with white paint (figure 2.5). "This is the shield, earth symbol, associated with ceremonial leaders because they do ceremonies for all people, all the world," Leigh J. Kuwanwisiwma explained. "It's land, life, all directions. From the time of creation, each dot represents each of the four worlds until humanity destroys it. The symbol honors ceremonial leaders. It's a purposeful, thoughtful location, facing Hopi, and it has the carved stairs leading to it."

Based on the sample of sites visited and Hopi traditional knowledge of clan migrations, as well as Hopi cultural and religious meanings imbued in ancestral sites as footprints, all the recorded archaeological sites in the NTP corridor that were associated with the Pueblo and antecedent periods —at least 303 sites—were considered

FIGURE 2.5 Leigh J. Kuwanwisiwma sits next to a pecked and painted *tuwvota*, a highly significant and distinctive Hopi symbol, at AZ J:30:35 (ASM). Note also the *tuwvota* on Kuwanwisiwma's jacket (photo by Chip Colwell, October 17, 2006).

traditional cultural properties. These sites were deemed eligible for the National Register under criterion A (for their association with events that have made a significant contribution to the broad patterns of our history) and criterion D (for their potential to yield or be likely to yield information important in prehistory and history).

Hopi advisors are concerned that construction activities associated with the NTP will physically harm or destroy documented and undocumented *kiikiqö*. For scientists and non-Hopis, the adverse impacts on historical and scientific values of the archaeological sites can be mitigated through archaeological research. But the Hopi's values are based on the existence of the *kiikiqö* standing on the landscape as living monuments; for Hopis, scientific study does not constitute mitigation. Advisors emphasize that scientific study and documentation are preferable to careless destruction, but archaeological research cannot lessen the impact of the NTP on these traditional cultural properties. As Ferguson and Koyiyumptewa (2007:83) have emphasized, the destruction of each ancestral site and footprint constitutes an incremental and irrecoverable loss for the Hopi people, resulting in "acute feelings of sadness, depression, anxiety, shame, powerlessness, and sleeplessness."

KAWESTIMA (SNOWY PLACE)

Thirty-two Hopi place-names listed in table 2.2 were sites identified within the view-shed of the project corridor (see Hedquist et al. 2014). Of these, five would be seriously affected by the transmission line: Yotse'vayu, Kawestima, Nayavuwaltsa, Tokotsmo, and Palavayu.

Of these places, Kawestima provides an especially rich example of how Hopis imbue named places with historical meanings that they connect to their living traditions (figure 2.6). To the Hopi people, Tsegi Canyon in northern Arizona is a layered landscape, suffused with different histories, stories, and names. Many Hopis, particularly those on Third Mesa, know the area as Kawestima, a word borrowed from the Keresan language. However, the exact "geographical referent for Kawestima depends on context and dialect" (Ferguson et al. 2007:41). Some speakers refer to the ruin of Betatakin and others to the ruin of Keet Seel in the Navajo National Monument as Kawestima. Others refer to Betatakin as Talastima. Similarly, First Mesa speakers know Betatakin as Talatismayo and Tsegi Canyon as Lenaytupqa (Flute Canyon).

In fieldwork and interviews, most Hopi cultural advisors said that Kawestima includes all of Tsegi Canyon and Marsh Pass. Victor Masayesva Jr. emphasized the large area encompassed by Kawestima: "Kawestima is more like an ecosystem, it's a system, not so much villages." Masayesva described the canyon's waterway not as a *muuna* (a stream), but as a *muumuna* (literally meaning a continuously flowing liquid), a steady stream that is the place's defining characteristic. He added that the entire landscape is a traditional cultural property because archaeologists have so clearly identified Hopi ancestral sites in the area dating back more than 1,000 years. The canyon is not just in the past; it connects to the living traditions of the Fire Clan, Water Coyote Clan, Snake Clan, Spider Clan, and Flute Clan. "This is who they are," Masayesva said, "this area."

Ritual paraphernalia, taken by archaeologists in 1915 from Sunflower Cave in Marsh Pass, were repatriated to the Flute Clan of First Mesa (McManamon 1997). These items date to the Pueblo I period (AD 750–975) and are still used today by clan members. Flute Clan leader Harlan Nakala spoke of the repatriated objects: "Those sunflowers and birds, those are ours. So I believe we did migrate through there. When we first got those back we used them in a ceremony, but now they're just stored. There is still power in those items."

Hopi advisors emphasized the area's importance by pointing out additional place-names in the vicinity—Wunuqa (The One Standing Up) near Monument Valley, Nayavuwaltsa (Clay Gap Place) just to the east of Marsh Pass, and Kiiqöwala (Gap of the Ruins) just to the west of Marsh Pass and known as the entry place into and out of Kawestima (figure 2.7). This area is directly connected to the Hopi Mesas through

TABLE 2.2 A selection of Hopi place-names around
the study area recorded during NTP research

HOPI PLACE-NAME	ENGLISH EQUIVALENT	TOPOGRAPHIC DESCRIPTION
Kawestima	Snowy Place (Keresan language)	Tsegi Canyon and Marsh Pass (Betatakin or Keet Seel)
Kiiqöwala	Gap of the Ruins	Long House Valley
Komayusim	Koyemshi Place	Baby Rocks Mesa
Kuytaqa	Peeping Point	Distinctive landform on White Mesa
Kwanivi	One-Horn Society Mountain	Kendrick Mountain
Kyeekeltuy Kiiöam	New Fledgling/Initiates House	Salt Trail Shrine, south of The Gap
Lenaytupqa	Flute Canyon	Tsegi Canyon
Màasaw	Spirit-Being	Across from Baby Rocks
Maasitsmo	Gray Hills	Hills around U.S. 89/U.S.160 intersection
Malatstukwi	Thumb Point	Distinctive landform on White Mesa
Mupiiwa	Place of Rocks That Fold Like Waves	Comb Ridge
Na'uyva	Hidden Springs	Hidden Springs, south of The Gap
Naasiwam	Older Brother-Younger Sister Pair	Distinctive landform on White Mesa
Nayavuwaltsa	Clay Gap Place	Northern edge of Black Mesa
Palavayu	Red River	Little Colorado River
Qatoya	Horned Serpent Place	Piute Canyon
Qawingpi	Gray Mountain	Northern edge of Gray Mesa, near Cameron, Arizona
Qötsatuutuyqa	White Cliffs	White Mesa
So'itsiwpu	Star Point	Toward the north end of Echo Cliffs
Sowi'ingki	Antelope House Shrine	Hills north of San Francisco Peaks
Talastima	Place of the Tassels	Betatakin
Tao'ota	Rocks Like a River's Rapid	Comb Ridge
Tokoonavi	Black (basalt) Mountain	Navajo Mountain
Tokotsmo	Bobcat Hill	Shadow Mountain northwest of Cameron, Arizona
Totolospi	Hopi Board Game	Salt Trail Shrine, south of The Gap
Totsiwnamuru	Shoe Point	Northern tip of Gray Mesa
Tsu'ovi	Rattlesnake Place	Inscription House
Tuwvota	The Shield	Across from Baby Rocks
Wunuqa	The One Standing Up	Spire in Monument Valley
Wùukotutkwa	Big Wide Land	Kayenta to Chinle
Yotse'vayu	San Juan River	Ute River
Yupqovi	The Place Beyond	Toward Shiprock

FIGURE 2.6 CRATT talks about Hopi history at Kawestima, also known as Marsh Pass in Tsegi Canyon, Arizona (photo by Chip Colwell, October 13, 2006).

ancestral villages, pilgrimage trails, and religious practices. Wilton Kooyahoema explained to us that the Fire Clan migration route came from Tokoonavi (Navajo Mountain) to Kawestima to Orayvi. This migration route established the Fire Clan's eagle gathering area and directs the ritual practices of the Fire Clan. He continued, "In the migration story, they talk about how they got to Orayvi, the footprints. They talk about which areas they went through and that's how they got the eagle nesting areas. So they gave us the area from Blue Canyon to Kawestima to Munqapi. You've got your footprints there, so that's your area." Kooyahoema has made prayer feathers for Betatakin, which were at times left at the ancient village itself.

Among others, Flute Clan members from First Mesa believe that Lenaytupqa (Tsegi Canyon) is a stopping point along the ceremonial route that the *katsinam* (deified ancestral spirits) take from the San Francisco Peaks to the Hopi Mesas. These stopping points are traditionally recalled through a ceremony in March in which the Mudheads go from kiva to kiva—the Hopis' ceremonial structures—announcing the upcoming dances and the coming of the *katsinam*. During that announcement, they list each of the eighteen places that the *katsinam* will travel through, which includes Tsegi Canyon. As Leigh J. Kuwanwisiwma explained, "There is a continuity of mem-

FIGURE 2.7 Harold Dawavendewa stands north of Nayavuwaltsa, just to the east of Marsh Pass, in Arizona (photo by Chip Colwell, October 17, 2006).

ory of these places through stories, of this route from the Peaks to the kivas. And that's what we teach to our kids, these places."

In 1906, during the Orayvi split, the intention of those who left was to resettle Kawestima (Whiteley 1988:257). Wilton Kooyahoema explained, "After they got kicked out of Orayvi, they said the footprints are still fresh, so they could go back and live there. They planned to go, but people started building here at Hotvela, so they stayed." To commemorate the split, in September 2006, a group of Hopis undertook a run from Hotvela to Kawestima, which they called *piw kuktota* (literally making feet), reestablishing the spiritual and physical trail between the contemporary village and the ancient canyon.

The research team concluded that Kawestima should be protected under NEPA for its environmental value and that it is eligible for the National Register under criterion A because of its associations with events that have made a significant contribution to the broad patterns of Hopi history, namely clan migration. It is a highly significant place for many reasons, including its ancestral villages, shrines, place in Hopi history, and ongoing religious practices.

The proposed NTP would run to the south of Kawestima, along the northern edge of Black Mesa. Although the transmission line would not go directly through Kawestima, it would be visible from portions of that site, particularly at Marsh Pass.

Thus, advisors expressed concern that the transmission line would affect the area's natural viewshed, its aesthetic qualities, and the feelings of beauty and spiritual power it inspires. Advisor Sharon Sockyma added, "This is where we're going when we left Orayvi. I was always told to visit Kawestima, that it's a beautiful spot." Although there is currently construction through Marsh Pass, advisors said that there would be a cumulative impact should yet another transmission line transect the pass. Gilbert Naseyowma told us, "I'm afraid if they keep building here it will affect the beauty. I think we need to keep the beauty." Leigh J. Kuwanwisiwma explained that viewsheds are particularly important for communities that do not move often: "The viewshed is important to sedentary people because they are there a long time." If the beauty of Kawestima is ruined, Hopis cannot simply choose a new place to go.

HOMVÌIKYA (GRAND CANYON SALT PILGRIMAGE TRAIL)

This trail is a sacred *homvìikya* (pilgrimage trail, lit. corn meal route) that connects the Hopi village of Orayvi on Third Mesa and a natural salt mine on the Colorado River in the Grand Canyon. The salt mine is situated in a dangerous place so "long ago the War Twins had set up shrines and established rules to make the journey safe for the Hopi" (Simmons 1942:233). For generations, members of Hopi religious societies made the arduous journey to gather salt and to conduct various rituals (Hopkins 2012). Many anthropologists have documented the religious activities associated with pilgrimages to the salt mine, and Hopis have consistently told researchers of its contemporary importance (Colton 1964; Colton and Colton 1931; Eiseman 1959; Ferguson 1998:161–169; Ferguson and Anyon 2001:43; Ferguson and Dongoske 1994:63; Ferguson et al. 2007:22; Titiev 1937).

The sacredness of the journey is profound because "Hopis believe that the Grand Canyon is the abode of the spirits of the dead. Here the unseen spirits are believed to live in invisible pueblos and carry on their daily life like living Hopis in the world above" (Colton 1946:3). "The trail is really important," Ferrell Secakuku told us: "Salt is a form of life: it generates. By bringing salt from there it brings life here. The salt goes to the woman, the aunt. It represents that because women give life."

Along the pilgrimage route is a series of shrines and trail makers, some of which are named and evoke ancient events. During fieldwork for this project, we visited six of the Salt Pilgrimage Trail shrines. One is called Kyeekeltuy Kiiöam, which means "Fledgling House," referring to both the eaglets ritually gathering each spring and the new Wuwtsim initiates (considered fledglings) who are journeying to the salt mine for the first time. The next shrine is called Totolospi, which refers to a Hopi gambling game. This is the place, Hopis believe, where long ago Hásòokata (the Gambler) challenged the Pöqangwhoya (War Twins) to *totolospi* (figure 2.8). These shrines were

FIGURE 2.8 Leigh J. Kuwanwisiwma kneels next to the Totolospi shrine on the Grand Canyon Salt Pilgrimage Trail (photo by Chip Colwell, October 20, 2006).

specifically mentioned in the anthropological literature as early as 1912 (Ellis 1974:219). The point of referencing these other shrines distant from the NTP transmission line is that, while to non-Hopis they may seem to be discrete sites on the landscape, to Hopis these individual features constitute one extensive feature, the sacred *homviikya*. All of these parts make the whole, and thus damage to one shrine threatens damage to the entire pilgrimage route. As Leigh J. Kuwanwisiwma explained, "The trail is a whole. You impact one part, you impact everything. It's all connected, spiritually and physically. It's not just a trail—it's a pilgrimage trail. It's the difference between a *naapvö* (a foot trail) and a *homviikya*."

The NTP proponents have planned to construct a new tower less than 100 meters from the trail; a planned access road will intersect the trail and several planned staging areas are located adjacent to it. A shrine is located several hundred meters from a proposed staging area. This shrine, in Hopi is called a *tuutuskya* (offering place) and it also serves as a *tutukwmola* (trail marker) along the Salt Pilgrimage Trail. The circular shrine consists of a single course of sandstone blocks, some of which are placed vertically into the ground. Perhaps because this shrine is highly visible on the landscape, it is often dismantled by disrespectful non-Hopis. While such actions are as offensive as they are harmful, ultimately the Hopi believe that the power of the place remains. Nearby the shrine is a *tsongonongoyakni* (smoking circle), a space enclosed by sandstone blocks on which Hopis sit to engage in a ritual offering of smoked tobacco (Simmons 1942:237). Shrines, except in rare cases, are deemed to be immovable (Ellis 1994:104). The trail has been a major part of Hopi religious practices, and even when it not actively traveled, it remains an important landscape feature used to teach young Hopis about their history and culture (see Ferguson et al. 2009; Hedquist et al. 2015).

The Grand Canyon Salt Pilgrimage Trail is eligible for the National Register of Historic Places under criteria A and D. As a *homviikya*, it is associated with traditional practices used in the recognition, retention, and transmission of Hopi culture. If investigated archaeologically, it has the potential to yield important information about Hopi prehistory and history, Hopi land use, and Hopi religious practices. The trail is more than fifty years old, and the property has integrity of location, setting, feeling, and association.

Where the NTP will cross the trail, the trail has already been heavily affected by previous transmission line projects (two extant lines) and the development of dirt roads in the area. However, advisors insist that yet another transmission line will lead to a cumulative negative effect on the trail, which will detract from the *homviikya*'s feeling of sacredness that is essential to its integrity. Furthermore, more roads in the area may have the indirect impact of encouraging non-Hopis to settle in the area, further threatening the trail. The placement of a new tower and staging areas would appear to be very close to the trail and its associated parts and therefore could directly damage this historic and sacred *homviikya*.

TRADITIONAL PLACES FOR, BY, AND WITH HOPI PEOPLE

In a review of tribal heritage management programs in the American Southwest, Roger Anyon and his colleagues suggested that each tribe has worked to create and manage an approach to "fit its own needs, goals, and culture" (2000:130). For example, some tribes, like the Pueblo of Zuni and the Navajo Nation, started with a focus on historic preservation, rode the first wave of contract archaeology projects and even developed major archaeological projects off their reservations. In contrast, the Hopi Tribe's program started with a clear focus on cultural preservation and an approach to research that bridges anthropology's subfields (Anyon et al. 2000:130–131). We would suggest that there are at least six ways in which the HCPO provides an important model for cultural preservation:

1. It approaches land, culture, history, and heritage holistically
2. It tackles the impacts on Hopi culture far beyond the reservation boundaries
3. It converts cultural traditions and religious beliefs into political and legal action
4. It studies and manages cultural heritage using interdisciplinary methods
5. It pursues research that is fundamentally collaborative
6. It ensures that academic and applied knowledge are noncompeting goals

What we think is so central to the Hopi model is that the Hopi community's needs are the primary drivers of research. In the case of NHPA and NEPA compliance, the Hopi Tribe is empowered by overseeing the research funds and process; by having a Hopi administrative staff and CRATT, the Hopi people can assure that Hopi perspectives and interests are articulated throughout the research process (see Dongoske et al. 2015). George Nicholas and his colleagues (2008) have suggested that collaborative research can be framed as work done for, by, or with descendant communities. In a sense, the Hopi Tribe's approach to traditional cultural property research uniquely combines all three of these methods: it is research done *for* the Hopi people, it is research done *by* Hopi tribal members (such as coauthor Stewart Koyiyumptewa), and it is research done *with* Hopi traditionalists, specifically members of CRATT, who represent a broad range of mesas, villages, clans, and religious societies and possess the kinds of expertise needed to document traditional cultural properties.

Even projects on Hopi culture proposed by academics that require a permit through the HCPO are structured in a similar way. For example, the very first question that prospective researchers must answer in their proposals is about the project's benefits to the Hopi Tribe. The researcher must also convincingly address such issues as informed consent (at the individual, family, clan, village, and government levels); rights to privacy, confidentiality, and compensation; Hopi employment and training preference; ownership of data; and review and critique of the results by the Hopi Tribe before publication. These issues are reflective of broader discussions within the field about the ethics of anthropological and archaeological practice. For instance, informed consent is a vital ethical imperative that can help ensure that participants are empowered to enter into research fully understanding its purposes and risks (Colwell and Nash 2015; Fluehr-Lobban 2003; Schrag 2009).

This approach to research has been critiqued as bordering on the methods of a "police state" (Mails 1997:130) and causing some people at Hopi to see a researcher with a permit as the "HCPO's pet 'anthro'" (McCaffery 2012:251). But we see this method mainly fulfilling Leigh Kuwanwisiwma's (2008) vision of a tribal research program that insists upon equality, reciprocity, and respect. Most anthropologists at universities must submit their work to the ethical scrutiny of an institutional review board. The HCPO provides a mechanism for a similar level of scrutiny—but by the community.

Although there are obviously many times when conflict may potentially arise between HCPO staff, in its authority to control certain kinds of research, and researchers, in their desire for academic freedom, in our experience there are surprisingly few times when this has actually occurred. In practice, we would agree that "this tension is diffused by open discussion of the ethical systems of both anthropologists and Hopi in an attempt to find a middle ground acceptable to all parties" (Dongoske et al. 1994:56). Our view is that, if we consider Hopis not just as subjects but also as co-authors, then they should have involvement in writing their own story (Ferguson et al. 2015). The goal is to interrupt the historical imbalance of anthropological research, in which the scales of research are tipped away from the Hopi people and instead find a balance of mutual benefit.

REFERENCES CITED

Albert, Steve, and Chip Colwell-Chanthaphonh. 2007. *Hopi Cultural and Natural Resources Report for the Navajo Transmission Project*. Hopi Cultural Preservation Office, Kiq.tsmovi, Arizona.

Anyon, Roger, T. J. Ferguson, and John R. Welch. 2000. Heritage Management by American Indian Tribes in the Southwestern United States. In *Cultural Resource Management in Contemporary Society: Perspectives on Managing and Presenting the Past*, edited by Francis P. McManamon and Alf Hatton, pp. 120–141. Routledge, London.

Atalay, Sonya. 2012. *Community-Based Archaeology: Research with, by, and for Indigenous and Local Communities*. University of California Press, Berkeley.

Balenquah, Lyle. 2012. Connected by Earth: Metaphors from Hopi Tutskwa. In *Thinking Like a Watershed: Voices from the West*, edited by Jack Loeffler and Celestia Loeffler, pp. 45–66. University of New Mexico Press, Albuquerque.

Brew, J. O. 1979. Hopi Prehistory and History to 1850. In *Handbook of North American Indians*, edited by Alfonso Ortiz, vol. 9, pp. 514–523. Smithsonian Institution, Washington, D.C.

Brighton, Stephen A. 2011. Applied Archaeology and Community Collaboration: Uncovering the Past and Empowering the Present. *Human Organization* 70(4):344–354.

Colton, Harold S. 1946. Fools Names Like Fools Faces. *Plateau* 19(1):1–8.

———. 1964. Principal Hopi Trails. *Plateau* 36(3):91–94.

Colton, Mary Russell, and Harold S. Colton. 1931. Petroglyphs, The Record of a Great Adventure. *American Anthropologist* 33(1):32–37.

Colwell, Chip. 2016. Collaborative Archaeologies and Descendant Communities. *Annual Review of Anthropology* 45:113–127.

Colwell, Chip, and Stephen E. Nash. 2015. Repatriating Human Remains in the Absence of Informed Consent. *SAA Archaeological Record* 15(1):14–16.

Colwell-Chanthaphonh, Chip, and T. J. Ferguson. 2006. Memory Pieces and Footprints: Multivocality and the Meanings of Ancient Times and Ancestral Places Among the Zuni and Hopi. *American Anthropologist* 108(1):148–162.

———. 2008. *Collaboration in Archaeological Practice: Engaging Descendant Communities.* AltaMira Press, Lanham, Maryland.

Colwell-Chanthaphonh, Chip, T. J. Ferguson, Dorothy Lippert, Randall H. McGuire, George P. Nicholas, Joe E. Watkins, and Larry J. Zimmerman. 2010. The Premise and Promise of Indigenous Archaeology. *American Antiquity* 75(2):228–238.

Dongoske, Kurt E., T. J. Ferguson, and Michael Yeatts. 1994. Ethics of Field Research for the Hopi Tribe. *Anthropology News* 35(1):56.

Dongoske, Kurt E., Leigh Jenkins, and T. J. Ferguson. 1993. Understanding the Past Through Hopi Oral History. *Native Peoples* 6(2):24–31.

Dongoske, Kurt E., Theresa Pasqual, and Thomas F. King. 2015. The National Environmental Policy Act (NEPA) and the Silencing of Native American Worldviews. *Environmental Practice* 17(1):36–45.

Eiseman, Fred B., Jr. 1959. The Hopi Salt Trail. *Plateau* 32(2):25–32.

Ellis, Florence Hawley. 1974. The Hopi: Their History and Use of Lands. In *Hopi Indians*, pp. 25–278. Garland American Indian Ethnohistory Series. Garland, New York.

———. 1994. Pueblo Religious Patterns, Especially Types of Shrines and Areas for Collecting Herbs and Other Religious Necessities. In *Artifacts, Shrines, and Pueblos: Papers in Honor of Gordon Page*, edited by Meliha S. Duran and David T. Kirkpatrick, pp. 101–112. Archaeological Society of New Mexico, Albuquerque.

Ferguson, T. J. 1998. *Öngtupqa niqw Pisisvayu (Salt Canyon and the Colorado River): The Hopi People and the Grand Canyon: Final Ethnohistoric Report for the Hopi Glen Canyon Environmental Studies.* Hopi Cultural Preservation Office, Kiqötsmovi, Arizona.

———. 2009. Improving the Quality of Archaeology in the United States through Consultation and Collaboration with Native Americans and Descendant Communities. In *Archaeology and Cultural Resource Management: Visions for the Future*, edited by Lynne Sebastian and William D. Lipe, pp. 169–193. School for Advanced Research Press, Santa Fe.

Ferguson, T. J., and Roger Anyon. 2001. *Hopi Traditional Cultural Properties Along the Questar Southern Trails Pipeline.* Prepared by Heritage Management Research Consultants in collaboration with the Hopi Cultural Preservation Office. Hopi Cultural Preservation Office, Kiqötsmovi, Arizona.

Ferguson, T. J., G. Lennis Berlin, and Leigh J. Kuwanwisiwma. 2009. Kukhepya: Searching for Hopi Trails. In *Landscapes of Movement: Trails, Paths, and Roads in Anthropological Perspective*, edited by James E. Snead, Clark L. Erikson, and J. Andrew Darling, pp. 20–41. University of Pennsylvania Press, Philadelphia.

Ferguson, T. J., and Kurt E. Dongoske. 1994. *Navajo Transmission Project EIS Hopi Ethnographic Overview*. Hopi Cultural Preservation Office, Kiqötsmovi, Arizona.

Ferguson, T. J., and Stewart B. Koyiyumptewa. 2007. *Hopi Traditional Cultural Properties Investigation for the Black Mesa Project*. Prepared by Anthropological Research, LLC, in association with the Hopi Cultural Preservation Office. Hopi Cultural Preservation Office, Kiqötsmovi, Arizona.

Ferguson, T. J., Stewart B. Koyiyumptewa, and Chip Colwell-Chanthaphonh. 2007. *Hopi Traditional Cultural Properties along the US 160 Highway Corridor*. Prepared by the Hopi Cultural Preservation Office and Anthropological Research, LLC. The Hopi Tribe, Kiqötsmovi, Arizona.

Ferguson, T. J., Stewart B. Koyiyumptewa, and Maren P. Hopkins. 2015. Co-creation of Knowledge by the Hopi Tribe and Archaeologists. *Advances in Archaeological Practice* 3(3):249–262.

Fluehr-Lobban, Carolyn. 2003. Informed Consent in Anthropological Research: We Are Not Exempt. In *Ethics and the Profession of Anthropology: Dialogue for Ethically Conscious Practice*, edited by Carolyn Fluehr-Lobban, pp. 159–78. AltaMira Press, Walnut Creek, California.

Fuller, Reba. 1997. Aspects of Consultation for the Central Sierran Me-Wuk. In *Native Americans and Archaeologists: Stepping Stones to Common Ground*, edited by Nina Swidler, Kurt E. Dongoske, Roger Anyon, and Alan S. Downer, pp. 181–187. AltaMira Press, Walnut Creek, California.

Gumerman, George, Joëlle Clark, Elmer J. Satala, and Ruby Chimerica. 2012. Footprints of the Ancestors: Reengaging Hopi Youth with Their Culture. *Museums and Social Issues* 7(2):149–166.

Hedquist, Saul L., Stewart B. Koyiyumptewa, Wesley Bernardini, T. J. Ferguson, Peter M. Whiteley, and Leigh J. Kuwanwisiwma. 2015. Mapping the Hopi Landscape for Cultural Preservation. *International Journal of Applied Geospatial Research* 6(1):39–58.

Hedquist, Saul L., Stewart B. Koyiyumptewa, Peter M. Whiteley, Leigh Kuwanwisiwma, Kenneth C. Hill, and T. J. Ferguson. 2014. Recording Toponyms to Document the Endangered Hopi Language. *American Anthropologist* 116(2):324–331.

Hopkins, Maren P. 2012. *A Storied Land: Tiyo and the Epic Journey Down the Colorado River*. Master's thesis, School of Anthropology, University of Arizona, Tucson.

Kerber, Jordan E. (editor). 2006. *Cross-Cultural Collaboration: Native Peoples and Archaeology in the Northeastern United States*. University of Nebraska Press, Lincoln.

Koyiyumptewa, Stewart B., and Chip Colwell-Chanthaphonh. 2011. The Past Is Now: Hopi Connections to Ancient Times and Places. In *Movement, Connectivity, and Landscape Change in the Ancient Southwest*, edited by Margaret C. Nelson and Colleen Strawhacker, pp. 443–455. University Press of Colorado, Boulder.

Kuwanwisiwma, Leigh J. 2002. Hopi Understanding of the Past: A Collaborative Approach. In *Public Benefits of Archaeology*, edited by Barbara J. Little, pp. 46–50. University Press of Florida, Gainesville.

——. 2008. Collaboration Means Equality, Respect, and Reciprocity: A Conversation about Archaeology and the Hopi Tribe. In *Collaboration in Archaeological Practice: Engaging Descendant Communities*, edited by Chip Colwell-Chanthaphonh and T. J. Ferguson, pp. 151–169. AltaMira Press, Lanham, Maryland.

Kuwanwisiwma, Leigh J., and T. J. Ferguson. 2004. Ang Kuktota: Hopi Ancestral Sites and Cultural Landscapes. *Expedition* 46(2):25–29.

Lyons, Patrick D. 2003. *Ancestral Hopi Migrations.* Anthropological Papers of the University of Arizona 68. University of Arizona Press, Tucson.

Mails, Thomas E. 1997. *The Hopi Survival Kit: The Prophecies, Instructions and Warnings Revealed by the Last Elders.* Penguin Compass, New York.

McAnany, Patricia A., and Sarah M. Rowe. 2015. Re-visiting the Field: Collaborative Archaeology as a Paradigm Shift. *Journal of Field Archaeology* 40(5):499–507.

McCaffery, Nick. 2012. Re-presenting Hopis: Indigenous Responses to the Ethnographic Interview. In *The Interview: An Ethnographic Approach*, edited by Jonathan Skinner, pp. 245–260. Berg, London.

McManamon, Francis P. 1997. Notice of Intent to Repatriate Cultural Items in the Possession of the Peabody Museum of Archaeology and Ethnology, Harvard University, Cambridge, MA; Correction. *Federal Register* 67(48):11462.

Nicholas, George P., John R. Welch, and Eldon Yellowhorn. 2008. Collaborative Encounters. In *Collaboration in Archaeological Practice: Engaging Descendant Communities*, edited by Chip Colwell-Chanthaphonh and T. J. Ferguson, pp. 273–298. AltaMira Press, Lanham, Maryland.

Parker, Patricia L., and Thomas F. King. 1998. Guidelines for Evaluating and Documenting Traditional Cultural Properties. *National Register Bulletin* 38. U.S. Government Printing Office, Washington, D.C.

Reed, Paul F. 2004. *The Puebloan Society of Chaco Canyon.* Greenwood Press, Westport, Connecticut.

Schrag, Brian. 2009. Piercing the Veil: Ethical Issues in Ethnographic Research. *Science and Engineering Ethics* 15(2):135–160.

Schwartz, Douglas W. 1989. *On the Edge of Splendor: Exploring Grand Canyon's Human Past.* School of American Research, Santa Fe.

Silliman, Stephen W. (editor). 2008. *Collaborating at the Trowel's Edge: Teaching and Learning in Indigenous Archaeology.* University of Arizona Press, Tucson.

Simmons, Leo W. 1942. *Sun Chief: The Autobiography of a Hopi Indian.* Yale University Press, New Haven, Connecticut.

Smith, Claire H., and Martin Wobst (editors). 2005. *Indigenous Archaeologies: Decolonizing Theory and Practice*. Routledge, London.

Supernant, Kisha, and Gary Warrick. 2014. Challenges to Critical Community-Based Archaeological Practice in Canada. *Canadian Journal of Archaeology* 38:563–591.

Titiev, Mischa. 1937. A Hopi Salt Expedition. *American Anthropologist* 39(2):244–258.

Versaggi, Nina M. 2006. Tradition, Sovereignty, Recognition: NAGPRA Consultation with the Iroquois Confederacy of Soverign Nations of New York. In *Cross-Cultural Collaboration: Native Peoples and Archaeology in the Northeastern United States*, edited by Jordan E. Kerber, pp. 18–31. University of Nebraska Press, Lincoln.

Welch, John R., and T. J. Ferguson. 2016. Preservation Spotlight: Apache, Hopi, and Zuni Perspectives on Kinishba History and Stewardship. *Archaeology Southwest* 30(1):26–27.

Welch, John R., Dana Lepofsky, and Michelle Washington. 2011. Assessing Collaboration with the Sliammon First Nation in a Community-Based Heritage Research and Stewardship Program. *Archaeological Review from Cambridge* 26(2):171–190.

Whiteley, Peter M. 1988. *Deliberate Acts: Changing Hopi Culture Through the Oraibi Split*. University of Arizona Press, Tucson.

———. 2011. Hopi Place Value: Translating a Landscape. In *Born in the Blood: On Native American Translation*, edited by Brian Swann, pp. 84–108. University of Nebraska Press, Lincoln.

3

MAINTAINING HOPI STEWARDSHIP OF ÖNGTUPQA (THE GRAND CANYON)

MICHAEL YEATTS

THE GRAND CANYON, defined here as the entire stretch of the Colorado River between Glen Canyon Dam and the upper end of Lake Mead, is a place of national and international renown. While legislative attempts to protect the Grand Canyon began in 1882, it was not until 1908 that Theodore Roosevelt, under the 1906 Antiquities Act, designated it a national monument. Then, in 1919, it became the fifteenth national park in the United States, only three years after the formation of the National Park Service (Anderson 2000). In 1979, the Grand Canyon was recognized as a World Heritage Site.

Long before its national and international recognition, Öngtupqa (literally, salt canyon), as the Grand Canyon is called by the Hopi, was a place uniquely intertwined with the Hopi people, their ancestors, and their history. It was here that the original Hopi ancestors emerged into this, the Fourth World, and entered into a spiritual covenant with Màasaw, the caretaker of the world, to serve as stewards of the earth. In their formative travels, numerous clans that would ultimately coalesce to become the Hopi people lived in and passed through the Grand Canyon. The archaeological sites, petroglyph panels, trails, cairns, shrines, pottery, human graves, and other cultural materials seen on the landscape are viewed by the Hopi as their "footprints," a physical manifestation of their ongoing adherence to their covenant with Màasaw. And the Grand Canyon has similarly left its mark on the Hopi culture, its presence felt in ceremonies, traditional knowledge, and clan histories.

The Hopi relationship to the Grand Canyon is not static, only looking backward in time. Instead, it is ongoing and evolving, with stewardship responsibilities as important as ever. Because the spirits of the Hopi people, past, present, and future, assume their duties in the afterlife within the Grand Canyon, it is incumbent on each generation of Hopis to maintain the sanctity of the place. What follows is a discussion of a subset of work that has been undertaken by the Hopi Cultural Preservation Office (HCPO) in an effort to further that stewardship. It specifically focuses on activities that have been carried out as part of the Hopi Tribe's participation in federal compliance activities related to the Bureau of Reclamation's ongoing operations of Glen Canyon Dam.

1991–1996: GLEN CANYON DAM ENVIRONMENTAL IMPACT STATEMENT ERA

The construction of Glen Canyon Dam in the early 1960s fundamentally altered the surrounding ecosystem including both the landscape and the Colorado River, which was impounded to form Lake Powell. While the Bureau of Reclamation sponsored some environmental and archaeological work upstream of the dam, in Glen Canyon (Fowler 2011), no one gave much thought to possible effects that might occur downstream in the Grand Canyon once the dam came online in 1963. By the 1980s, however, people were beginning to recognize that there were downstream effects along the Colorado River, through the heart of the Grand Canyon (figure 3.1).

In 1991, the Hopi Tribe became a cooperating agency for an environmental impact statement that was being prepared by the Bureau of Reclamation for the operation of Glen Canyon Dam. Leigh J. Kuwanwisiwma, who had been hired a couple of years earlier as director of the nascent HCPO, was tasked by the Hopi Tribe to oversee the tribe's involvement in the program. He realized that participation in the production of the environmental impact statement and the associated technical studies afforded a new venue for the Hopi people to further their stewardship role, albeit in a less traditional form than had been practiced for millennia.

The first task undertaken by the Hopi Tribe was to conduct an archaeological survey of the lower portion of the Little Colorado River (LCR), from Blue Springs to its confluence with the main stem Colorado River (figure 3.2). From Hopi traditional knowledge (some of which had been recorded in various documentary sources), it was known that this area contained numerous culturally important locations including the Hopi place of emergence (Sipapuni) and places associated with the Hopi salt pilgrimage. Because the area was going to be the focus of concentrated research activity by biologists studying an endangered fish called the Humpback Chub, the Hopi Tribe wanted to ensure that that the researchers would avoid culturally sensitive areas. This inventory was conducted in 1991, just as the concept of a traditional cultural property (TCP) was becoming recognized in the historic preservation arena, but before the

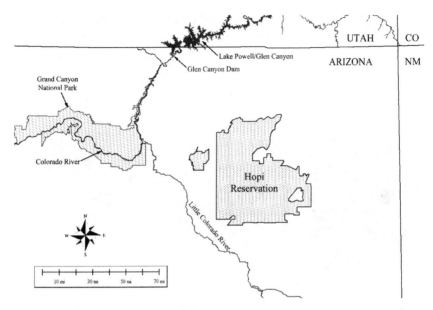

FIGURE 3.1 Grand Canyon National Park in relation to the Hopi Reservation.

National Historic Preservation Act (NHPA) was amended to include TCPs. Methodologically, the survey was approached as a standard archaeological inventory, but the vast majority of historic properties recorded were TCPs—places that were important foremost for the continuing roles they play in Hopi society rather than as archaeological sites, which at the time were valued primarily as objects for scientific study (Yeatts 1991).

As the LCR survey was wrapping up, the HCPO initiated a four-year ethnohistory research effort to document the myriad associations of the Hopi people with the Grand Canyon (figure 3.3). The underlying impetus for this effort was the need to identify the "affected environment" (in National Environmental Policy Act [NEPA] jargon) so that the various alternatives being considered for the future operations of Glen Canyon Dam could be analyzed and their effects on resources considered. This same information was also needed for a programmatic agreement that was concurrently being developed to meet the Bureau of Reclamation's NHPA (Section 106) responsibilities. Compliance with Section 106 was needed because any changes in Glen Canyon Dam operation as a result of the environmental impact statement decision were also considered to be a federal action requiring compliance under NHPA.

The Hopi ethnohistorical study, with T. J. Ferguson serving as principal investigator, continued through the development of the environmental impact statement.

FIGURE 3.2 Little Colorado River near its confluence with the Colorado River.

Hopi elders took numerous river trips to examine and identify areas and resources of cultural significance along the Colorado River in the Grand Canyon. A final report, completed in 1998 (Ferguson 1998), served as the basis of the Hopi sections in the final environmental impact statement (Bureau of Reclamation 1995). This report documented the essential role that the Grand Canyon has played in Hopi culture, including its role in the origin narrative and in events related to the commencement and continuation of Hopi ceremonial knowledge and practices, as well as its importance as a home for ancestral Hopi clans during their migrations, as an area for resource procurement and interaction with other tribal groups, and as the place for residence in the next life.

Because there was not a substantial body of cultural or environmental research regarding the Grand Canyon ecosystem or the existing and potential effects of the dam on the environment that could be used in developing the environmental impact

FIGURE 3.3 Hopi team conducting ethnohistorical research in the Grand Canyon.

statement, this information needed to be collected concurrently with the writing of the environmental impact statement. The need for information in nearly real time, coupled with the desire by the Bureau of Reclamation and the cooperating agencies for an open, collaborative approach to the development of the environmental impact statement, resulted in far deeper participation by the Hopi Tribe and other cooperating entities than was commonly seen in the development of such documents. Enhanced participation meant that the Hopi Tribe conducted its own research, participated in drafting language for inclusion in the environmental impact statement and the programmatic agreement, and represented itself at technical and public meetings. The ability of the Hopi Tribe to speak for itself as a true collaborator in the process resulted in progressive and forward-looking documents that fully embraced the concept of TCPs and resulted in the tribe's perspectives being accurately portrayed. Again, the environmental impact statement and programmatic agreement were being written at the time that the NHPA was being amended to incorporate TCPs, but there were no regulations describing how to address the identification and management of TCPs in a compliance situation. In lieu of federal regulations that would have addressed these issues, the programmatic agreement references National Park Service Bulletin 38 as guidance for the undertaking (Bureau of Reclamation 1994:3 [Stipulation 1.c.]).

1997–2002: ADAPTIVE MANAGEMENT
AND FURTHER RESEARCH

A Record of Decision, signed by the secretary of the interior in 1996, selected a new operational framework for Glen Canyon Dam and brought to a close the environmental impact statement process. The new operations at Glen Canyon Dam were anticipated to reduce the impacts of its operations on downstream resources through the Grand Canyon. Significantly, in the environmental impact statement, scientists and managers recognized that they could not and would probably never be able to fully model the intricacies of an ecosystem as complex as the Grand Canyon. Therefore, any imposed management action would likely have at least some unforeseen consequences. Rather than selecting an alternative, making changes, and walking away, which was the standard practice for most environmental impact statements conducted previously, the Record of Decision set in place a program to actively monitor the ecosystem, continue research to better understand what wasn't known, and to use this information to conduct *adaptive management*. The Hopi Tribe, along with twenty-five other stakeholders, became the Adaptive Management Work Group, a group that would make recommendations to the secretary of the interior on how to best manage Glen Canyon Dam. Leigh Kuwanwisiwma was named as the Hopi Tribe's first official representative to the group.

Among the first items identified by the Hopi Tribe as requiring further research in order to make informed decisions were the culturally important plant resources in the Grand Canyon. The ethnohistory research had hinted at the range of culturally important plants, but this was never a primary focus of the research. Therefore, in 1998, the Hopi Tribe began a two-year ethnobotany study to identify these plants so that their status could be tracked into the future (Lomaomvaya et al. 2001). A total of 141 plants were investigated during this research (figure 3.4). Cultural associations included use for clan or ceremonial functions, medicine, food, and other utilitarian purposes. Culturally important plants were found in all of the vegetation zones bordering the Colorado River including the perennially wet marsh zones, the occasionally watered riparian areas, and the desert habitats beyond the reach of river flows.

At the same time, mitigation activities called for under the programmatic agreement were begun. Monitoring of archaeological sites along the Colorado River by the National Park Service identified numerous locations where erosion was adversely affecting the integrity of cultural deposits. It was hypothesized that the vast reduction in the sediment load of the Colorado River (as sediment was trapped upstream in Lake Powell) and the lack of a large spring runoff due to impounded water were resulting in a system-wide sediment deficit that led to exposure and loss of archaeological sites that had been buried for hundreds or even thousands of years. Many of these sites

FIGURE 3.4 Hopi team conducting ethnobotanical research in the Grand Canyon.

are associated with the Hopi ancestors who resided in Öngtupqa during their clan migrations. Therefore, when the Park Service proposed testing and limited excavation at some of these sites, the Hopi Tribe took an integral role in the work. Hopi Cultural Preservation Office staff helped develop excavation strategies and participated in the field efforts and documentation of the findings (Leap and Yeatts 1998, 1999; Leap et al. 1999a, 1999b; Yeatts 1998, 2000; Yeatts and Leap 1996, 1997)

In 1996, an experimental, relatively short-term high flow was released from Glen Canyon Dam in an attempt to mimic, in a small way, the high spring runoff that occurred before the dam was built. One product of a high spring runoff was the deposition of new sediment along the shorelines of the river. If a similar result could be attained with a higher than normal release of water from the dam, it was postulated that this might benefit archaeological site preservation by replacing some of the sediment that was being lost. To the Hopi Tribe, stabilizing the ancestral archaeological sites was of the highest priority—preservation of sites in place was viewed as the preferred management philosophy. When the high-flow experiment was conducted, the Hopi Tribe conducted research to ascertain whether sediment was deposited in proximity to a number of archeological sites (Yeatts 1996). The results demonstrated that sediment could be deposited in proximity to at least some of the archaeological sites and that it was retained over the next year (Yeatts 1997). Whether this will lead to better long-term preservation of the archaeological sites was and still is an open question.

The work conducted by the Hopi Tribe during the development of the environmental impact statement and the early years of the Adaptive Management Program demonstrates that Hopi cultural interests cover the full range of resources in the Grand Canyon ecosystem. For the Hopi Tribe, cultural resources encompass far more than archaeological sites and TCPs as they have been defined in the NHPA. Cultural resources include all those interacting components of the ecosystem that played a part in creating the Hopi culture and still shape it today. These include physical resources, but perhaps more importantly, there are intangible linkages that tie Hopi people to their landscape, reach back into their history, and guide their direction into future.

2003–PRESENT: DEVELOPMENT AND IMPLEMENTATION OF A HOPI LONG-TERM MONITORING PROGRAM

In a real sense, monitoring is a key component of any type of sustainable management and the backbone of adaptive management. Without some form of feedback, whether formal or informal, there is no way of assessing whether stewardship responsibilities are being achieved. With this understanding and drawing on the knowledge gained from the Hopi ethnohistorical and ethnobotanical work and activities occurring under the programmatic agreement (such as testing and excavation at archaeological sites), a Hopi long-term monitoring program was designed. The guiding philosophy was to implement an approach that would address the Hopi stewardship responsibilities in a culturally appropriate manner that would accommodate the cultural and logistical constraints of working in the Grand Canyon. This would include acknowledgement of cultural restrictions on entry into the Grand Canyon by Hopi or other people who were not initiated, minimization of the impacts of monitoring activities on the resources, and recognition of the nonuniform distribution of traditional knowledge among Hopi tribal members. Further, the monitoring program needed to bridge the divide between a Western science-based system of understanding nature and the more humanistic and integrative Hopi worldview in which people are part of the ecosystem through both physical and spiritual interaction (figure 3.5). The initial step in this process was to evaluate the monitoring program that was already in place at the Grand Canyon Monitoring and Research Center (GCMRC), the federal entity designated to lead the monitoring and research aspects of the Adaptive Management Program and to identify its relevance to addressing Hopi resource monitoring needs (Huisinga and Yeatts 2003). While the monitoring program at the GCMRC was robust in its ability to track numbers of certain species and to measure the numerous biological attributes and physical and chemical parameters of the ecosystem, it mostly lacked the human component associated with the resources under study and certainly did not incorporate the knowledge and values of the Hopi people. To ameliorate this shortcoming, the HCPO developed a monitoring approach that drew from both the data collected by scientists employing a Western-science based methodology and the traditional knowledge of the Hopi people to interpret those data. The resulting program, which was formally adopted in 2007, incorporates the following methodologies (Yeatts and Huisinga 2006):

- It utilizes an approach based on social science survey methodology to record observations about the health of culturally important resources in the Grand Canyon from a Hopi perspective.
- It doesn't require a large number of Hopis to enter the Grand Canyon. Because of the spiritual danger that is present in the Grand Canyon, only certain initiated male members of Hopi religious societies are supposed to enter the canyon.
- It incorporates data collected by both Hopi researchers and other researchers.
- It assumes that interpretation of data, rather than data collection, is the most appropriate mechanism for incorporating traditional Hopi understanding of

FIGURE 3.5 Leigh Kuwanwisiwma leads a discussion about petroglyphs on a boulder in the Grand Canyon.

the ecosystem and determining whether stewardship responsibilities are being achieved (that is, whether the system is healthy from a Hopi cultural perspective).

- It includes provisions for the Hopi Tribe's ownership of cultural information, which is reviewed by the Hopi Tribe to ensure that accurate information is published and that sensitive esoteric knowledge is utilized appropriately and safeguarded when necessary.

As of 2016, more than 250 surveys have been completed under the Hopi Long-Term Monitoring Program. The health of culturally important resources (including plants, birds, animals, fish, archaeological sites, springs, sacred sites, and other historic locations), the interactions among these resources, and the ongoing relationship between the Grand Canyon and the Hopi have all been assessed from a Hopi perspective and data have been presented annually to the federal managers of Glen Canyon Dam and the National Parks along the Colorado River.

DISCUSSION

What has been learned from more than twenty years of participation by the Hopi Tribe in the management activities associated with the Grand Canyon and the operation of the Glen Canyon Dam, particularly as it relates to cultural resource management?

First, from the perspective of the Hopi people, the Grand Canyon is relatively healthy. This reflects recognition that the federal management philosophy for the Grand Canyon has changed and that natural and biological resources are being more highly valued for their own sake. It also is a direct result of the Hopis currently playing an active role in management decisions and being able to better exercise their stewardship responsibilities.

With regard to the management of TCPs, unfortunately little has changed in the time that the Hopi Tribe has been involved. While there is broader recognition and understanding of TCPs, there is no optimum solution for incorporating them into a regulatory framework. What is clear is that the Section 106 process, as currently defined in federal regulations, is a poor fit for adequately managing TCPs. The attributes that make a TCP important are often fundamentally different from those that the Section 106 process was established to handle. A quick tally of those items that are considered cultural resources by the Hopi Tribe in the Grand Canyon reveals that very few fit neatly within the current historic preservation framework. Most are defined at best by fuzzy boundaries, and their cultural significance is not isolated to a single discrete location. Some cultural resources, such as animals, do not remain in one location or, like plant communities, they evolve through time. More challenging is that some aspects of cultural resources are intangible. Finally, because these resources still serve an integral role within Hopi culture, their significance to the Hopi people can and likely will continue to change through time as the Hopi culture itself changes.

Integration of cultural values into the regulatory framework has been most successful when it has occurred within the NEPA process. Even then cultural values have been successfully integrated only when the tribe has been directly involved in all phases of program planning, including development of relevant research questions and methodologies, definition of culturally significant resources from the unique Hopi perspective, and full participation in the outcomes of a decision-making process.

In 2012, a new environmental impact statement was jointly initiated by the Bureau of Reclamation and the National Park Service to further modify the operations of Glen Canyon Dam. This environmental impact statement drew on the information that has been accumulated over more than twenty years of monitoring and research. The Hopi Tribe again served as a cooperating agency to advance its stewardship role and to ensure that its traditional knowledge and values are incorporated into the overall decision-making process. While direct Hopi involvement was considerably less than in the 1995 environmental impact statement, effort was once again made to recognize and incorporate the unique Hopi relationship to the Grand Canyon. Information gained from Hopi research and through the Hopi Long-Term Monitoring Program was used to guide the process. A new programmatic agreement is also being developed to address cultural resource compliance needs. Management of the environmental impact on TCPs is still of major concern, and the difficulty of developing an approach reaffirms the inadequacy of the current historic preservation process for these types of resources. The environmental impact statement process was completed in late 2016 and development of a new programmatic agreement was completed in 2017. The Hopi Tribe will continue to be an active participant in the Adaptive Management Program that will guide operation of Glen Canyon Dam over the next twenty years, in both management and monitoring of its culturally important resources.

REFERENCES CITED

Anderson, Michael F. 2000. *Polishing the Jewel: An Administrative History of Grand Canyon National Park*. Monograph 11. Grand Canyon Association, Grand Canyon Village, Arizona.

Bureau of Reclamation. 1994. *Programmatic Agreement on Cultural Resources*. Upper Colorado Region Bureau of Reclamation, Salt Lake City, Utah.

———. 1995. *Operation of Glen Canyon Dam: Final Environmental Impact Statement*. Upper Colorado Region Bureau of Reclamation, Salt Lake City, Utah.

Ferguson, T. J. 1998. *Öngtupqa Niqw Pisisvayu (Salt Canyon and the Colorado River): The Hopi People and the Grand Canyon*. Hopi Cultural Preservation Office, Kiqötsmovi, Arizona.

Fowler, Don D., 2011, *The Glen Canyon Country, A Personal Memoir*. University of Utah Press, Salt Lake City.

Huisinga, Kristin, and Michael Yeatts. 2003. *Sooysoy Himu Naanamiwiwyungwa: An Analysis of the Grand Canyon Monitoring and Research Center's Terrestrial Ecosystem Monitoring Program and the Development of a Hopi Long-Term Plan*. Report on file at Grand Canyon Monitoring and Research Center, Flagstaff, Arizona.

Leap, Lisa M., and Michael Yeatts. 1998. *Proposed Data Recovery and Site Management at C:13:010, Grand Canyon National Park*. River Corridor Monitoring Project Report No. 54. Report on file at Grand Canyon National Park, Flagstaff, Arizona.

———. 1999. *Proposed Data Recovery at AZ C:13:099 and AZ C:13:100, Palisades Delta, Grand Canyon, Arizona*. Report on file at Grand Canyon National Park, Flagstaff, Arizona.

Leap, Lisa M., Michael Yeatts, and Jennifer L. Kunde. 1999a. *Data Recovery at Four Sites Along the River Corridor, Grand Canyon National Park, AZ*. River Corridor Monitoring Project Report No. 61. Report on file at Grand Canyon National Park, Flagstaff, Arizona.

———. 1999b. *Data Recovery Proposed for C:13:010, Feature 24*. River Corridor Monitoring Project Report No. 62. Report on file at Grand Canyon National Park, Flagstaff, Arizona.

Lomaomvaya, Micah, T. J. Ferguson, and Michael Yeatts. 2001. *Öngtuvqava Sakwtala, Hopi Ethnobotany in the Grand Canyon*. Manuscript on file at the Hopi Cultural Preservation Office, Kiqötsmovi, Arizona.

Yeatts, Michael. 1991. *A Cultural Resources Inventory of the Lower Little Colorado River, Coconino County, Arizona*. Hopi Cultural Preservation Office, Kiqötsmovi, Arizona.

———. 1996. *High Elevation Sand Deposition and Retention from the 1996 Spike Flow: An Assessment for Cultural Resources Stabilization*. Final report submitted to the Grand Canyon Monitoring and Research Center, Bureau of Reclamation, Flagstaff, Arizona.

———. 1997. *High Elevation Sand Retention Following the 1996 Spike Flow*. Final report submitted to the Grand Canyon Monitoring and Research Center, Bureau of Reclamation, Flagstaff, Arizona.

———. 1998. *1997 Data Recovery at Five Sites in the Grand Canyon, Final Report*. River Corridor Monitoring Project Report No. 60. Report on file at Grand Canyon National Park, Flagstaff, Arizona.

———. 2000. *Testing at Site AZ:C:09:051 (GRCA), Grand Canyon National Park*. Report on file at the Bureau of Reclamation, Upper Colorado River Office, Salt Lake City, Utah.

Yeatts, Michael, and Kristin Huisinga. 2006. *A Hopi Long-Term Monitoring Program for Öntupqa (the Grand Canyon)*. Report on file at the Bureau of Reclamation, Upper Colorado River Office, Salt Lake City, Utah.

Yeatts, Michael, and Lisa M Leap. 1996. *Proposal for Data Recovery at Six Sites in the Grand Canyon During FY 1997*. River Corridor Monitoring Project Report No. 45. Report on file at Grand Canyon National Park, Flagstaff, Arizona

———. 1997. *Proposed Testing at AZ:C:09:051 (GRCA)*. River Corridor Monitoring Project Report No. 49. Report on file at Grand Canyon National Park, Flagstaff, Arizona.

4

TUNGWNIWPI NIT WUKWLAVAYI (NAMED PLACES AND ORAL TRADITIONS)

Multivocal Approaches to Hopi Land

SAUL L. HEDQUIST, MAREN P. HOPKINS,
STEWART B. KOYIYUMPTEWA, LEE WAYNE
LOMAYESTEWA, AND T. J. FERGUSON

H OPI CULTURE INTEGRATES varied understandings of Hopitutskwa (Hopi land) and its history. Unique connections to different components of the Hopitutskwa landscape are shaped, for example, by lived experience; gender; and village, clan, and society membership. These connections are exemplified through the many ways Hopis remember, interact with, and honor their land.

Hopi views of the land are not singular or unidimensional; they are the cumulative product of numerous unique clan histories and personal experiences (Bernardini 2005; Dongoske et al. 1997; Fewkes 1900; Hopkins 2012). As clans with diverse historical trajectories settled on the Hopi Mesas, they brought with them the knowledge and rights to use different shrines and resources. Consequently, various perceptions and cultural practices regarding Hopitutskwa developed as these groups maintained (and continue to maintain) distinct claims to different components of the landscape (Jenkins et al. 1994:8; Kuwanwisiwma and Ferguson 2009:90; Whiteley 1989). Differential access to knowledge in Hopi society—regulated through social and religious protocols such as initiated membership in religious societies—further shapes how the Hopi people understand past events and places (Hopkins 2012).

Drawing upon our collaborative research, we will discuss Hopi perspectives of the land and its meaning. We will focus on three interrelated sources of variability: (1) conceptual understandings of the form and extent of Hopitutskwa; (2) knowledge of and experience with named places on the landscape; and (3) oral historical traditions of different clans and religious societies, exemplified through varied renderings of the Hopi story of Tiyo. These examples underscore the complex and dynamic nature of Hopi land.

HOPITUTSKWA

The concept of Hopitutskwa is embedded in Hopi history and religion (Jenkins et al. 1994:1; Kuwanwisiwma and Ferguson 2009:90; Whiteley 1989). At its greatest extent, Hopitutskwa encompasses all places where Hopi ancestors once resided and everywhere there is a spiritual attachment associated with religious practices (Jenkins et al 1994; Kuwanwiswma and Ferguson 2014:143). Following their pact with the deity Màasaw, Hopi ancestors migrated throughout the Fourth World (present world), leaving their metaphorical and physical "footprints" as they journeyed to find their ultimate destination on the Hopi Mesas (figure 4.1). Today these footprints—known in the Hopi language as *itaakuku*—are recognized as ancestral villages, artifact scatters, petroglyphs and pictographs, and other archaeological sites. Along with other cultural features, Hopi footprints constitute landmarks by which Hopi people verify their clan histories and religious beliefs (Jenkins et al. 1994:2; Kuwanwiswma and Ferguson 2014). These places are commemorated through ongoing ceremonies, prayers, and pilgrimages.

Variation in the histories, oral traditions, and cultural practices among clans, villages, and religious societies lead to important differences in how Hopitutskwa is understood (Kuwanwisiwma and Ferguson 2014:142). Today, Hopis living on Second and Third Mesa, for instance, conceptualize Hopi land using different frames of reference and regional scales (Jenkins et al. 1994:8–9). Historical and contemporary depictions of Hopitutskwa derive in large part from hand-drawn maps prepared to assert or defend Hopi religious and political rights (Kuwanwisiwma and Ferguson 2014:135).

One such map, drawn in 1930 by Hopi artist Fred Kabotie and village leaders from Second Mesa, accompanied several Hopi petitions to the commissioner of Indian affairs and the U.S. Senate in the 1930s (figure 4.2). At this time the federal government was establishing new reservation boundaries, notably in the Navajo-Hopi Boundary Bill enacted into law in 1934 (48 Stat. 960), and in the establishment of grazing districts in 1937, including District Six for exclusive Hopi use. In 1951 a slightly modified version of Kabotie's map of Hopitutskwa was used by the traditional leaders of Songòopavi village on Second Mesa to depict its aboriginal land claim presented in Docket 210 of the Indian Claims Commission. Songòopavi's claim was eventually withdrawn when village leaders learned that the Indian Claims Commission would only award a monetary payment for lands taken by the United States and not actually return the land.

Kabotie's depiction of Hopitutskwa outlines a series of ten linked shrines that are described as having "boardered [*sic*] the Hopi people from every direction, [marking and designating] . . . the Hopis' tribal land boundary lines" for centuries (Komalentewa

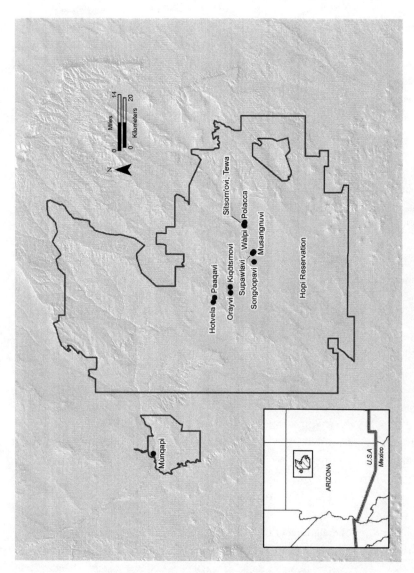

FIGURE 4.1 Hopi Reservation and contemporary villages.

UTAH

Navajo Mt.

Ky-westima   Lolomai Point

Point
Sublime

Moencopi   • Chinle
        •
Grand Canyon   Cameron   HOPI
                                  VILLAGES
                                      •• •Keams
Little Colorado R.   Canyon

San Francisco Pts.   Lupton

Flagstaff   • Winslow
    Sedona   Holbrook
       Mormon
        Lake
    Eagle Shrine   Woodruff
                                         Butte

ARIZONA

                PHOENIX
                   ●

                        HOPI VILLAGES

                        Tewa
                        Sichomovi   — First Mesa
                        Walpi

                        Mishongnovi
                        Shipaloci   — Second Mesa
                        Shungopovi

                        Kyakotsmovi
                        Bakabi
                        Hotevilla   — Third Mesa
                        Oraibi.
                        Moencopi

*map to
accompany the
Hopi Petition of April 8, 1930
drafted by Fred Kabotie and
and Shungopavi.*

FIGURE 4.2 Hand-drawn map of Hopitutskwa prepared by Hopi artist Fred Kabotie and others (Komalentewa and others 1930).

et al. 1930; see also Ferguson 1998:61; Jenkins et al. 1994:4; Kuwanwisiwma and Ferguson 2014). This route is traversed in a ceremonial pilgrimage or *homviikya* to a course of shrines where sacred cornmeal is deposited (Hopi Dictionary Project 1998:93), conducted periodically by members of the village of Songòopavi (figure 4.3). The route includes shrines at Toko'navi (Navajo Mountain), Kòoninhahàwpi (Havasupai Descent Trail), Tusaqtsomo (Bill Williams Mountain), Hoonàwpa (Bear Springs), Yotse'hawhàwpi (Apache Descent Trail), Tsimòntukwi (Woodruff Butte), Namituyqa (Lupton Point), Nayavuwaltsa (Lolomai Point), and Kawestima (Tsegi Canyon area) (see Jenkins et al. 1994; Kuwanwisiwma and Ferguson 2014; Page and Page 1982; Whiteley 1989, 2011). One of the religious leaders who conducted this pilgrimage in the late twentieth century explained that the shrines visited on the *homviikya* are used to pay homage to a greater domain of Hopi stewardship (Jenkins et al. 1994:8; Kuwanwisiwma and Ferguson 2009:92). In this view, the *homviikya* is thought to encircle the traditional core or "plaza" of the Hopi homeland (Jenkins et al. 1994; Kuwanwisiwma and Ferguson 2014:143).

On Third Mesa, however, Hopitutskwa is not specifically conceptualized as an area demarcated by boundary shrines. Instead, it is understood as the area encompassing all places associated with or visited by clans and religious societies in the maintenance of their spiritual responsibilities (Kuwanwisiwma and Ferguson 2014:144). For example, as described by Jenkins and colleagues (1994:9),

> Toko'navi [Navajo Mountain] . . . is a recognized sacred mountain but it is a sacred mountain of the Rattlesnake Clan. When the Rattlesnake Clan was accepted into Orayvi they supported the Village Chief's spiritual stewardship by maintaining their shrine on Toko'navi but this shrine is not something that the Orayvi Chief says belongs to Orayvi. This shrine will always be recognized in relation to how the Rattlesnake clan contributed their religious sites to the Bear Clan's spiritual stewardship. Other clans have shrines in other areas that are important to them, and thus to their village.

The Third Mesa view of Hopitutskwa can be depicted by mapping the spatial relationships between villages and associated places (Leigh J. Kuwanwisiwma in Hedquist et al. 2014). This is shown schematically in figure 4.4, where a series of radial lines connects the Hopi Reservation with named locations on the Hopi landscape. Spokes signify connections between villages and named places associated with spiritual responsibilities and historical land use. These spokes collectively depict the extent of Hopitutskwa, resulting in a different and more expansive rendering than the outline connecting the ten pilgrimage shrines that are visited during the Songòopavi *homviikya*.

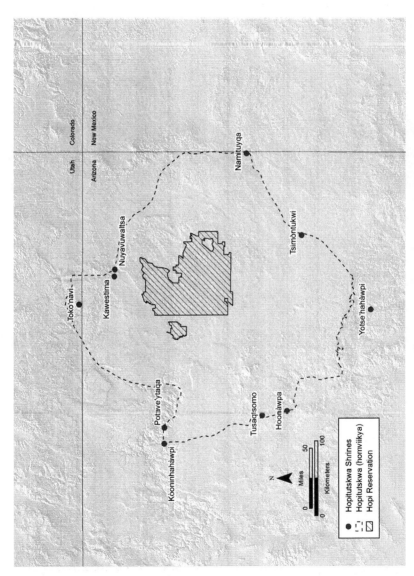

FIGURE 4.3 Hopitutskwa depicted as a *homviikya* associated with a series of shrines.

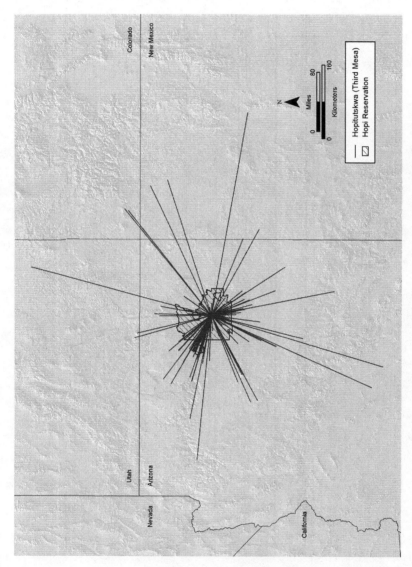

FIGURE 4.4 Hopitutskwa depicted by radial lines connecting the Hopi Reservation and approximately 300 named locations.

Different conceptions of Hopitutskwa discourage the use of a single static boundary to depict Hopi land (Kuwanwisiwma and Ferguson 2014). There are multiple ways to represent the Hopi landscape in different cultural contexts and legal settings. Nonetheless, in the process of mapping Hopi lands for political petitions and the Indian Claims Commission, the symbolic uses of Hopitutskwa associated with the Songòopavi *homviikya* as a spiritual expression of Hopi ties to the land became conflated with its legal use as a geopolitical boundary (Jenkins et al. 1994:3; Kuwanwisiwma and Ferguson 2014:135). For example, the Indian Claims Commission (1974), which rendered its opinion in 1970, used a single cartographic boundary to define Hopi aboriginal territory (figure 4.5). This area, smaller than that enclosed by the outline in Kabotie's 1930 map, encompasses only the area that the federal government determined to be exclusively used and occupied by the Hopi Tribe when the United States first established the Hopi Reservation in 1882. The boundary thus denotes a snapshot in time, one that conflicts with the expansive and complex temporality of the ancestral Hopi landscape. It provides a "singular visual statement" (Colwell-Chanthaphonh and Hill 2004:177) predicated on Western geographic values favoring static definable entities that can be measured, described, depicted, and arranged in linear time (Ferguson and Colwell-Chanthaphonh 2006:28; Zedeño 1997; Zedeño et al. 1997). This notion differs from the Hopi concept of spatial and temporal continuity that connects Hopi people and places, both past and present (Koyiyumptewa and Colwell-Chanthaphonh 2011; Kuwanwisiwma 2008:157).

In the United States, geopolitical boundaries have important legal implications that influence land use patterns and the management of cultural resources (Ferguson and Anyon 2001; Jenkins et al. 1994). The Indian Claims Commission's depiction of Hopi land is often used by government officials and museum personnel when determining whether to consult with the Hopi Tribe about archaeological resources and other culturally important properties (Kuwanwisiwma and Ferguson 2014:144–145). Some officials incorrectly assume that the Hopi Tribe does not have legitimate interests in lands and resources beyond its judicially determined aboriginal territory (Ferguson and Anyon 2001:109–111). As Jenkins and colleagues note, "The establishment of a narrowly circumscribed interpretation of Hopitutskwa diminishes the legitimate interests of the Hopi Tribe in the much larger area within which Hopi ancestors set their footprints, an area many Hopis also consider to be Hopitutskwa" (1994:9). Today the Hopi Cultural Preservation Office (HCPO) is reluctant to inscribe a single cartographic boundary denoting the geographic limit of its historical interest (Ferguson and Anyon 2001). According to Hopi cultural advisors, religion and faith have no boundaries; boundaries and associated legal notions of land ownership are a product of federal intervention (Jenkins et al. 1994:4).

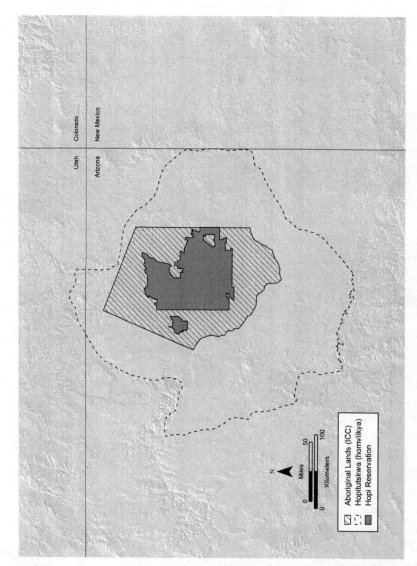

FIGURE 4.5 Hopi Reservation and aboriginal territory determined by the Indian Claims Commission.

HOPI PLACE-NAMES

Hopi knowledge and use of place-names further demonstrates the complex and variously perceived nature of Hopi land. Hopitutskwa, in its various conceptualizations, includes numerous named locations or salient places that explicate Hopi history and culture (Hedquist et al. 2014; Whiteley 2007, 2011). Toponyms (place-names) mark sacred locations, landforms associated with deities, historical events, springs, trails, and ancestral sites among other features (Ferguson et al. 2009; Ferguson et al. 1995; Ferguson and Loma'omvaya 2011:147; Kuwanwisiwma and Ferguson 2009:90; Whiteley 2011). Names are strongly tied to experiences of place (Ferguson and Koyiyumptewa 2007:5). For Hopis, place-names provide important means of localizing, commemorating, and transmitting traditional knowledge. Components of the land are remembered and honored through a variety of means, including visitation, story, song, and ritual, all of which are indexed by place-names (Whiteley 2007, 2011). Toponyms provide "metonyms of narrative," evoking images of the named location, as well as associated emotions, moral values, experiences, and stories (Young 1987:4; see also Basso 1996; Cruikshank 1990; Thornton 1997, 2008). The Hopi past and present are shaped by the way the land is remembered and discussed (Ferguson and Loma'omvaya 2011; see also Küchler 1993; Morphy 1995; Young 1987).

In 2010, the HCPO, American Museum of Natural History, and University of Arizona initiated a three-year collaborative project to record Hopi toponyms and document the endangered Hopi language (Hedquist et al. 2014). The Hopi Place Names Project involved investigating the linguistic performance of place-names and associated narratives using digital audio and video recordings and constructing a geographic information systems database of named locations (Hedquist et al. 2015). Interviews with fifteen tribal members (twelve men and three women) representing ten clans from seven villages on First, Second, and Third Mesa (including Munqapi) resulted in the documentation of nearly three hundred place-names within and beyond the Hopi Reservation (figure 4.6). Figure 4.6 includes *tutskwanawit* (landforms), *paahu* (water), *kiikiqö* (ancestral villages), *kitsokinawit* (contemporary settlements), and other locations such as eagle-gathering areas, farms and gardens, grazing areas, and plant and animal collection areas. For additional discussion, see Hedquist et al. (2014) and Whiteley (2011).

While the project was initiated for the purpose of language preservation, it also shows the many ways that Hopis reference and relate to their land. Interviews were generally unguided; research participants were simply asked to provide information about places and place-names they deemed important in their lives. Resulting narratives involved both general and localized discussions of the landscape and its meaning.

Springs (e.g., Hoonàwpa and Munaqvi), landforms (e.g., Nuvakwewtaqa, Nuvatukya'ovi, and Öngtupqa), and ancestral locations were commonly mentioned during

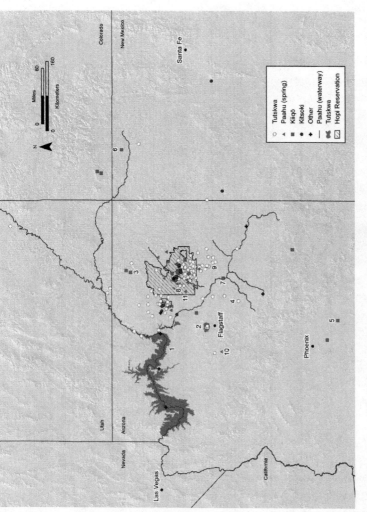

FIGURE 4.6 Toponyms documented through the Hopi Place Names Project. Places are coded by Hopi geographic domain, including *tutskwa* (topography or landform), *paahu* (natural water, e.g., spring or waterway), *kiiqö* (ancestral village), and *kitsoki* (contemporary settlement). Numbered locations are (1) Öngtupqa (Grand Canyon), (2) Nuvatukya'ovi (San Francisco Peaks), (3) Kawestima (Betatakin [Navajo National Monument]), (4) Nuvakwewtaqa (Chavez Pass), (5) Naasavi (Casa Grande [Casa Grande National Monument]); (6) Hoo'ovi (Aztec Ruin [Aztec Ruins National Monument]), (7) Homol'ovi (ancestral village near Winslow), (8) Yongyatsayvi (Padilla Mesa), (9) Tuutukwi (Hopi Buttes), (10) Hoonàwpa (Bear Springs), and (11) Munaqvi (Sand Springs).

interviews (see figure 4.6 for examples). Ancestral villages were prevalent in narratives of clan migration histories. For Hopis, referencing places such as Homol'ovi, Kawestima, Hoo'ovi, and Naasavi recalls and commemorates the ancestral past and preserves cultural memory over time (Bradley 1998:85–100; Ferguson and Colwell-Chanthaphonh 2006:30). Multiple interviewees emphasized the importance of learning the names of ancestral locations; to know *hisathiniwtipu*— how things happened in the past.

Diverse combinations and uses of toponyms during interviews revealed personal connections reflecting unique experiences with or knowledge of the environment (Hedquist et al. 2014; see also Colwell-Chanthaphonh and Ferguson 2006:159; Rodman 1992). Differences in the uses of place-names often correlated, for example, with gender and village, clan, or society membership. As an interviewee from Supawlavi explained, "each community knows its own places" (Hedquist et al. 2014).

While individual narratives demonstrate widely varying place-related experiences and perceptions, all contribute to a comprehensive community (i.e., Hopi) network of person-place relationships. For Hopis, personal experiences with particular components of the land are placed in a context of collective place-related knowledge that spans many generations. Individuals rely on the experiences and knowledge of others to gain and maintain a more holistic understanding of the greater Hopi landscape. Individual perspectives, experiences, and histories in turn contribute to a dynamic cumulative community understanding of the land and its meaning. In this regard, Hopitutskwa comprises a complex amalgam of personal experiences, history, and culture.

STORIED LANDSCAPES: THE NARRATIVES OF TIYO

Storytelling is another form of mapping and commemorating the land that offers diverse views of Hopitutskwa. Hopi accounts of Tiyo, the boy from Toko'navi (Navajo Mountain), provide an example of how the Hopi people use storied landscapes to preserve and perpetuate geographical and historical knowledge. These oral narratives recount the journey of a young man who traveled from Toko'navi down the Colorado River to the Sea of Cortez and beyond, to the land of the Snake People (figure 4.7). These stories are important pieces of Hopi spatial discourse that encapsulate elements of religious, historical, and folk knowledge, revealing how differences in personal worldviews and epistemological frameworks influence the Hopi people's relationship with the land.

An analysis of thirty-four accounts of Tiyo's journey, documented since 1894, identified eighty-seven locations through place-names and descriptive geography that are

FIGURE 4.7 Tiyo's journey down the Colorado River as depicted by Fred Kabotie. Image displayed at Desert View Tower, Grand Canyon National Park. Photograph by T. J. Ferguson, August 26, 2005.

associated with meaningful cultural information. These accounts were derived from biographies and autobiographies of Hopi people and from ethnographic and ethno-historic records (Ferguson 1998; Fewkes 1894; Secakuku 2006; Stephen 1891; Voth 1903; Yava 1978). Recent collaborative research conducted for federal land management purposes at Glen Canyon National Recreation Area, Grand Canyon National Park, and Barry M. Goldwater Range contributed to the ethnographic literature used in the analysis. This research is important because it situates contemporary Hopi knowledge and cognition of land use in tangible locations within the physical environment (Anyon 1999; Ferguson 1998; Hopkins et al. 2013, 2017).

The story of Tiyo is ubiquitous among Hopis. The authority to hear and retell it, however, is structured through the concepts of *wiimi*, *navoti*, and *tuuwutsi*—types of traditional knowledge to which access is determined by one's social and religious standing. *Wiimi* is the knowledge of the priesthoods, *navoti* is the knowledge of initiated clan members, and *tuuwutsi* is information for all Hopis (Balenquah and

Talaswaima 2011). Abbreviated versions of the Tiyo narratives provide an outline of events that includes the boy's departure from Toko'navi, his arrival at the ocean and subsequent encounter with the Snake People, and his return home to Toko'navi with a Rattlesnake maiden. These narratives recount Hopi values and instill Hopi worldviews, but lack specific details. The most comprehensive accounts of Tiyo's journey were narrated by Rattlesnake Clan members and offer details about the young man's encounters with various people and deities during his journey to the ocean, places he visited on his way back to Toko'navi, and villages Rattlesnake Clan members settled during their migrations to the Hopi Mesas after leaving Toko'navi. These accounts are encrypted with information that is still used in the religious practices of the Rattlesnake Clan. The relationship between general and specific knowledge conveyed by the Tiyo narratives represents Hopitutskwa as a shared yet differentiated landscape that simultaneously binds together and creates important distinctions in Hopi society (Ferguson and Colwell-Chanthaphonh 2006:29).

The area covered by the Tiyo narratives offers an additional perspective on what Hopitutskwa represents to the Hopi people, an area extending far beyond the boundaries of the Hopi Reservation and judicially determined aboriginal lands (figure 4.8). Toko'navi is the northernmost location mentioned in the various accounts and the place most frequently cited as a starting point of Tiyo's journey. In some accounts, Wuhkokiekeu, an ancient settlement located at Toko'navi, was named as the residence of Tiyo's family (Courlander 1971:82–95; Yava 1978:55–61). The people of Toko'navi were described as the Puma people, a group who migrated from the north (Fewkes 1894:107). Another version states that the people arrived from the west, where they resided with the Paiutes for some time before journeying to Toko'navi (Courlander 1971:82; Yava 1978:55). Ferrell Secakuku (2006:38), a Rattlesnake Clan member, explained that the people of Toko'navi were reminded by the mountain's natural red cliff faces of their former home, Palatkwapi, and this is the reason why they settled there. Alternate departure points for Tiyo's journey have also been suggested, including Wupatki (Walter Hamana in Ferguson 1998:111), Canyon Diablo (Max Taylor in Ferguson 1998:111), and a location near Holbrook (Herschel Talashoma in Ferguson 1998:111–119), all of which are located along the Little Colorado River.

The southernmost destination for Tiyo's journey was sometimes interpreted as South America; however, most accounts refer to central Mexico or Mesoamerica as being the land of the Snake People. An area northwest of the Grand Canyon, possibly near today's Lake Mead, is described as the westernmost geographical point in the stories. Fewkes (1894:106–119) and Stephen (1929:35–50, 1936:636–7) recount a version of the story that lists "So-tcap'-tü-kwi" (a location near Santa Fe) or "Wu-kó-bai-ya" (the Rio Grande) as places in the east where the Rattlesnake Clan had social connections. Hoo'ovi and Yupköyvi (Chaco Canyon) in northwestern New Mexico were the

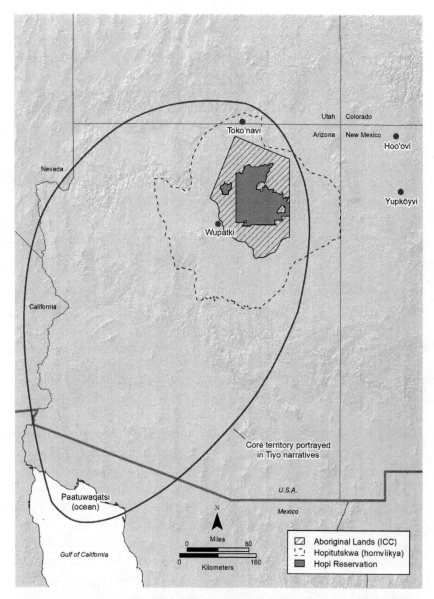

FIGURE 4.8 The core territory represented in the Tiyo narratives extends far beyond the Hopi Reservation and judicially determined Hopi aboriginal lands.

easternmost locations listed as part of the Rattlesnake Clan's migrations. Some of the storytellers provided specific details of places Tiyo visited during his journey, including the types of trees and color of the rocks, indicating familiarity with the terrain.

The historical details provided in both general and specific versions of this story form a geographic dictionary of sorts that explains how Hopis perceive their traditional landscape; these are the reasons why Hopitutskwa is meaningful to Hopis. Furthermore, the events that occurred in the past continue to influence the Hopi peoples' actions in the present. As one member of the Butterfly Clan explained, "even though [this story] may not be part of one's clan history, it is still part of Hopi heritage in a broad sense. It is shared so that Hopis will appreciate and understand why important places need to be protected and preserved, and paid attention to and respected" (Secakuku 2011).

CONCLUSION

Hopitutskwa is a vast and variable concept that expresses polysemic meanings for different users, both Hopi and non-Hopi, at multiple geographic scales or frames of reference. Hopi relationships with the land are deeply phenomenological and based in the lived experience of individual members of the tribe, as modulated by gender and social status associated with village, clan, and religious identities. A universal understanding of Hopi land cannot be extrapolated from individual perspectives, which may be highly localized. A Hopi farmer from the village of Hotvela (Third Mesa), for example, may not be familiar with farming areas around the village of Walpi (First Mesa), a type of knowledge that is generally village-specific.

For Hopis, like other traditional societies, cultural knowledge necessitates a spatial context—it becomes superficial or diluted through secular decontextualized references (see Pearce and Louis 2008:109). Place naming and storytelling provide two means for localizing, commemorating, and transmitting traditional knowledge (Whiteley 2007, 2011). Knowledge of places and associated cultural information varies widely among Hopis, a product of different experiences, perceptions, and societal positions associated with structured systems of knowledge. Relationships between general and specific place-related references in oral traditions constitute shared yet differentiated landscapes that simultaneously bind together and create important distinctions in Hopi society (Ferguson and Colwell-Chanthaphonh 2006:29). Likewise, place-names evoke both shared and personal experiences with the land, providing mnemonic devices or touchstone references for common, clan-specific, and autobiographical narratives (Cruikshank 1990; Thornton 1997).

Discussions of different places provide insights into the many ways Hopis remember, interact with, and honor their land. While the term *Hopi* identifies one group of people, it is the various subcategories within the group, such as clans, religious societ-ies, and autonomous villages, that embody Hopitutskwa in its own right. Each group, as well as individuals within those groups, has unique insights into the meaning and history of Hopi land. However, Hopis also maintain a general appreciation for the physical environment that reflects a collective worldview anchored in spiritual beliefs and cultural values.

For the Hopi people, understanding and documenting varied views of the land-scape carry wide-ranging benefits, foremost of which is the preservation of historical and place-related knowledge for future generations—"itam hapi naap itàa sinmuy nit tsaatsakwmuy amungem it naavotit nàasaslalwa" (we are preparing this knowledge for our own Hopi people and children). This knowledge also provides a means of com-municating the importance of specific places to non-Hopi audiences, thus informing targeted studies of cultural affiliation and traditional land use, as well as facilitating the implementation of culturally sensitive land management strategies (see Chapin et al. 2005; Ferguson and Anyon 2001; Ferguson and Colwell-Chanthaphonh 2006; Mark et al. 2010; Pearce and Louis 2008; Thornton 1997).

ACKNOWLEDGMENTS

We thank Leigh J. Kuwanwisiwma for his help and guidance in conducting research with the Hopi Tribe over many years, and the Hopi Cultural Resources Advisory Task Team for graciously sharing its knowledge of Hopi culture and history.

REFERENCES CITED

Anyon, Roger. 1999. *Migrations in the South: Hopi Reconnaissance in the Barry M. Goldwater Range*. Prepared by Anthropological Research, LLC, in collaboration with the Hopi Cul-tural Preservation Office. Hopi Cultural Preservation Office, Kiqötsmovi, Arizona.

Balenquah, Riley, and Leonard Talaswaima. 2011. Interviewed by T. J. Ferguson and Maren Hopkins at Page, Arizona, July 1, 2011. Manuscript on file at the Hopi Cultural Preservation Office Archives, Kiqötsmovi, Arizona.

Basso, Keith H. 1996. *Wisdom Sits in Places: Landscape and Language Among the Western Apache*. University of New Mexico Press, Albuquerque.

Bernardini, Wesley. 2005. *Hopi Oral Tradition and the Archaeology of Identity*. University of Arizona Press, Tucson.

Bradley, Richard. 1998. *The Significance of Monuments: On the Shaping of Human Experience in Neolithic and Bronze Age Europe*. Routledge, London.

Chapin, Marc, Zachary Lamb, and Bill Threlkeld. 2005. Mapping Indigenous Lands. *Annual Review of Anthropology* 34:619–638.

Colwell-Chanthaphonh, Chip, and J. Brett Hill. 2004. Mapping History: Cartography and the Construction of the San Pedro Valley. *History and Anthropology* 15(2):175–200.

Colwell-Chanthaphonh, Chip, and T. J. Ferguson. 2006. Memory Pieces and Footprints: Multivocality and the Meanings of Ancient Times and Ancestral Places Among the Zuni and Hopi. *American Anthropologist* 108(1):148–162.

Courlander, Harold. 1971. *The Fourth World of the Hopis: The Epic Story of the Hopi Indians as Preserved in Their Legends and Traditions.* Crown, New York.

Cruikshank, Julie. 1990. Getting the Words Right: Perspectives on Naming and Places in Athapaskan Oral History. *Arctic Anthropology* 27(1):52–65.

Dongoske, Kurt E., Michael Yeatts, Roger Anyon, and T. J. Ferguson. 1997. Archaeological Cultures and Cultural Affiliation: Hopi and Zuni Perspectives in the American Southwest. *American Antiquity* 62(4):600–608.

Ferguson, T. J. 1998. *Öngtupqa niqw Pisisvayu (Salt Canyon and the Colorado River): The Hopi People and the Grand Canyon.* Manuscript on file at the Hopi Cultural Preservation Office, Kiqötsmovi, Arizona.

Ferguson, T. J., and Roger Anyon. 2001. Hopi and Zuni Cultural Landscapes: Implications of History and Scale for Cultural Resources Management. In *Native Peoples of the Southwest: Negotiating Land, Water, and Ethnicities,* edited by L. Weinstein, pp. 99–122. Bergin and Garvey, Westport, Connecticut.

Ferguson, T. J., G. Lennis Berlin, and Leigh J. Kuwanwisiwma. 2009. Kukhepya: Searching for Hopi Trails. In *Landscapes of Movement: Trails, Paths, and Roads in Anthropological Research,* edited by J. E. Snead, C. L. Erickson, and J. A. Darling, pp. 20–41. University of Pennsylvania Press, Philadelphia.

Ferguson, T. J., and Chip Colwell-Chanthaphonh. 2006. *History Is in the Land: Multivocal Tribal Traditions in Arizona's San Pedro Valley.* University of Arizona Press, Tucson.

Ferguson, T. J., Kurt Dongoske, Mike Yeatts, and Leigh Jenkins. 1995. Hopi Oral History and Archaeology, Pt. 1: The Consultation Process. *SAA Bulletin* 13(2):12–15.

Ferguson, T. J., and Stewart B. Koyiyumptewa. 2007. *Hopi Traditional Cultural Properties Investigation for the Black Mesa Project.* Prepared by Anthropological Research, LLC, in association with the Hopi Cultural Preservation Office. Hopi Cultural Preservation Office, Kiqötsmovi, Arizona.

Ferguson, T. J., and Micah Loma'omvaya. 2011. Nuvatukya'ovi, Palatsmo, niqw Wupatki: Hopi History, Culture, and Landscape. In *Sunset Crater Archaeology: The History of a Volcanic Landscape: Prehistoric Settlement in the Shadow of the Volcano,* edited by Mark Elson, pp. 143–186. Anthropological Papers 37. Center for Desert Archaeology, Tucson.

Fewkes, Jesse Walter. 1894. The Kinship of the Tusayan Villagers. *American Anthropologist* 7(4):394–417.

———. 1900. Tusayan Migration Traditions. *Nineteenth Annual Report of the Bureau of American Ethnology for the Years 1897–1898*, Pt. 2, pp. 573–634. Government Printing Office, Washington, D.C.

Hedquist, Saul L., Stewart B. Koyiyumptewa, Wesley Bernardini, T. J. Ferguson, Peter M. Whiteley, and Leigh J. Kuwanwisiwma. 2015. Mapping the Hopi Landscape for Cultural Preservation. *International Journal of Applied Geospatial Research* 6(1):39–58.

Hedquist, Saul L., Stewart B. Koyiyumptewa, Peter M. Whiteley, Leigh J. Kuwanwisiwma, Kenneth C. Hill, and T. J. Ferguson. 2014. Recording Toponyms to Document the Endangered Hopi Language. *American Anthropologist* 116(2):324–331.

Hopi Dictionary Project. 1998. *Hopi Dictionary/Hopìikwa Lavàytutuveni: A Hopi-English Dictionary of the Third Mesa Dialect*. University of Arizona Press, Tucson.

Hopkins, Maren P. 2012. *A Storied Land: Tiyo and the Epic Journey Down the Colorado River*. Master's thesis, School of Anthropology, University of Arizona, Tucson.

Hopkins, Maren P., T. J. Ferguson, and Stewart B. Koyiyumptewa. 2013. *Hopisinmuy Wu'ya'mat Hisat Yang Tupqa'va Yeesiwngwu (Hopi Ancestors Lived in These Canyons): Hopi History and Traditions at Glen Canyon National Recreation Area and Rainbow Bridge National Monument*. School of Anthropology, University of Arizona, Tucson. Colorado Plateau CESU Cooperative Agreement H1200-09-0005. Manuscript on file at the Hopi Cultural Preservation Office, Kiqötsmovi, Arizona.

Hopkins, Maren P., Stewart B. Koyiyumptewa, Saul L. Hedquist, T. J. Ferguson, and Chip Colwell. 2017. Hopisinmuy Wu'ya'mat Hisat Yang Tupqa'va Yeesiwngwu (Hopi Ancestors Lived in These Canyons). In *Legacies of Space and Intangible Heritage: Archaeology, Ethnohistory, and the Politics of Cultural Continuity in the Americas*, edited by Fernando Armstrong-Fumero and Julio Hoil Gutierrez, pp. 33–52. University Press of Colorado, Boulder.

Indian Claims Commission. 1974. Commission Findings on the Hopi Indians. In *Hopi Indians*, pp. 387–424. Garland, New York.

Jenkins, Leigh, T. J. Ferguson, and Kurt Dongoske. 1994. A Reexamination of the Concept of Hopitutskwa. Paper presented at the Annual Meeting of the American Society for Ethnohistory, Tempe, Arizona.

Komalentewa and others. 1930. Petition to the Commissioner of Indian Affairs (through Reservation Superintendent Edgar K. Miller), April 8, 1930, including map drawn by Fred Kabotie and other men of Shungopavi. BIA Central Classified Files 21141-29-056-Hopi, Record Group 75. National Archives, Washington, D.C.

Koyiyumptewa, Stewart B., and Chip Colwell-Chanthaphonh. 2011. The Past Is Now: Hopi Connections to Ancient Times and Places. In *Movement, Connectivity, and Landscape Change in the Ancient Southwest*, edited by Margaret C. Nelson and Coleen Strawhacker, pp. 443–455. University Press of Colorado, Boulder.

Küchler, Susanne. 1993. Landscape as Memory: The Mapping of Process and Its Representation in a Melanesian Society. In *Landscape Politics and Perspectives*, edited by B. Bender, pp. 85–106. Berg, Oxford, England.

Kuwanwisiwma, Leigh J. 2008. Collaboration Means Equality, Respect, and Reciprocity: A Conversation About Archaeology and the Hopi Tribe. In *Collaboration in Archaeological Practice: Engaging Descendent Communities*, edited by C. Colwell-Chanthaphonh and T. J Ferguson, pp. 151–169. AltaMira Press, Lanham, Maryland.

Kuwanwisiwma, Leigh J., and T. J. Ferguson. 2009. *Hopitutskwa* and *Ang Kuktota*: The Role of Archaeological Sites in Defining Hopi Cultural Landscapes. In *The Archaeology of Meaningful Places*, edited by B. J. Bowser and M. N. Zedeño, pp. 90–106. University of Utah Press, Salt Lake City.

———. 2014. Hopitutskwa: The Meaning and Power of Maps. In *Mapping Native America: Cartographic Interactions Between Indigenous Peoples, Government, and Academia*, vol. III, edited by D. G. Cole and I. Sutton, pp. 132–147. CreateSpace Independent Publishing Platform (Amazon).

Mark, David M., Andrew G. Turk, and David Stea. 2010. Ethnophysiography of Arid Lands: Categories for Landscape Features. In *Landscape Ethnoecology: Concepts of Biotics and Physical Space*, edited by L. Main Johnson and E. S. Hunn, pp. 27–45. Berghahn Books, New York.

Morphy, Howard. 1995. Landscape and the Reproduction of the Ancestral Past. In *The Anthropology of Landscape: Perspectives on Space and Place*, edited by E. Hirsch and M. O'Hanlon, pp. 184–209. Clarendon Press, Oxford, England.

Page, Susanne, and Jake Page. 1982. *Hopi*. Abrams, New York.

Pearce, Margaret Wickens, and Rene Paulani Louis. 2008. Mapping Indigenous Depth of Place. *American Indian Cultural and Research Journal* 32(3):107–126.

Rodman, Margaret C. 1992. Empowering Place: Multilocality and Multivocality. *American Anthropologist* 94(3): 640–656.

Secakuku, Ferrell H. 2006. *Hopi and Quetzalcoatl, Is There a Connection?* Master's thesis, Department of Anthropology, Northern Arizona University, Flagstaff.

Secakuku, Susan. 2011. Interviewed by Maren Hopkins at Second Mesa, September 15, 2011. Manuscript on file at the Hopi Cultural Preservation Office, Kiqötsmovi, Arizona.

Stephen, Alexander M. 1891. Wiki Tells His Tradition, Owing to His Deafness, Wikyatiwa and Masiumtüwa Assist Him. Fewkes Collection No. 4408, 2–5. National Anthropological Archives, Smithsonian Institution, Washington, D.C.

———. 1929. Hopi Tales. *Journal of American Folk-Lore* 42:1–72.

———. 1936. *Hopi Journal of Alexander M. Stephen*. Edited by Elsie Clews Parsons. 2 vols. Columbia University Press, New York.

Thornton, Thomas F. 1997. Anthropological Studies of Native American Place Naming. *American Indian Quarterly* 21(2):209–228.

———. 2008. *Place and Being Among the Tlingit*. University of Washington Press, Seattle.

Voth, H. R. 1903. The Snake Legend. In *The Mishongnovi Ceremonies of the Snake and Antelope Fraternities* by George A. Dorsey and H. R. Voth. Anthropological Series Vol. III(3), pp. 349–353. Field Columbian Museum 66, Chicago.

Whiteley, Peter. 1989. Hopitutskwa: An Historical and Cultural Interpretation of the Hopi Traditional Land Claim. Expert Witness Report for the Hopi Tribe in Masayesva vs. Zah vs. James (1934 Reservation Case). U.S. District Court, Phoenix, Arizona.

———. 2007. Salient Places: Notes toward a Typology of Hopi Toponyms. Manuscript on file, Hopi Cultural Preservation Office, Kiqötsmovi, Arizona.

———. 2011. Hopi Place Value: Translating a Landscape. In *Born in the Blood: On Native American Translation*, edited by B. Swann, pp. 84–108. University of Nebraska Press, Lincoln.

Yava, Albert. 1978. *Big Falling Snow, a Tewa-Hopi Indian's Life and Times and the History and Traditions of His People*. Edited and annotated by Harold Courlander. Crown, New York.

Young, M. Jane. 1987. Toward an Understanding of "Place" for Southwestern Indians. *New Mexico Folklore Record* 16:1–13.

Zedeño, M. Nieves. 1997. Landscapes, Land Use, and the History of Territory Formation: An Example from the Puebloan Southwest. *Journal of Archaeological Method and Theory* 4 (1):67–103.

Zedeño, M. Nieves, Diane Austin, and Richard Stoffle. 1997. Landmark and Landscape: A Contextual Approach to the Management of American Indian Resources. *Culture & Agriculture* 19(3):123–129.

5

VISUAL PROMINENCE
AND THE STABILITY OF
CULTURAL LANDSCAPES

WESLEY BERNARDINI

The bare vastness of the Hopi landscape emphasizes the visual impact of every plant, every rock, every arroyo. . . . So little lies between you and the sky. So little lies between you and the earth.

SILKO, "LANDSCAPE, HISTORY, AND THE PUEBLO
IMAGINATION," *ANTAEUS*, 1986

The Hopi landscape is a living theater.

WHITELEY, "HOPI PLACE VALUE: TRANSLATING A
LANDSCAPE," *BORN IN THE BLOOD: ON NATIVE
AMERICAN TRANSLATION*, 2011

FOR THOSE WHO have visited an archaeological site with Leigh Kuwanwisiwma and other Hopi Cultural Preservation Office (HCPO) advisors, the scene is familiar (figure 5.1). The HCPO group gathers at a high point and begins looking at distant landmarks, talking in Hopi and pointing. Unlike archaeologists, whose gaze is typically fixed on the ground, HCPO advisors scan the horizon. After a period of private conversation, a member of the HCPO group calls over to the archaeologist to interpret and summarize the discussion.

On visits to some well-known archaeological sites like Chavez Pass or Homol'ovi II, HCPO advisors have recounted well-documented migration stories that match accounts given to archaeologists like Fewkes and Mindeleff almost a century ago. But some site visits have involved places previously unknown to the HCPO group—either because the ancestral village was too small or short-lived for oral traditions about it to survive the centuries or because the advisors were not members of the clan that held the relevant information. In these cases, the HCPO advisors were still able to offer ideas about the clans who once occupied the site, but they candidly noted that they were not recounting memorized oral traditions. Instead, they were pooling their cultural knowledge about places on the landscape and comparing it to the

FIGURE 5.1 Leigh Kuwanwisiwma and Hopi cultural advisors visiting an archaeological site in Arizona. Photograph by T. J. Ferguson, August 23, 2005.

visual information available from the vantage point of the ancestral village. Using a logical process both inductive and deductive, the group identified socially significant landforms—sometimes with effort, given that these features were being viewed from an unfamiliar angle or from a great distance. They then situated their vantage point on a mental map crisscrossed with the migration pathways of dozens of different clans, oriented the entire map with reference to the Hopi mesas, and finally inferred the clan ancestors who must have moved through that location.

This chapter will reflect on the epistemology that enables HCPO advisors to interpret landscapes far removed in time and space from contemporary Hopi villages. In particular, the focus will be on a central paradox of Pueblo history and cosmology: Pueblo peoples are deeply grounded in their local landscapes, but their histories were dominated by movement that constantly shifted the definition of *local*.

The analytical approach applied in this chapter is explicitly that of the Southwestern School of Landscape Archaeology. A fundamental premise of this approach is that Native American intellectuals are "interlocutors with distinct epistemological stances who have their own contributions to make toward the theorization of cultural landscapes" (Fowles 2010:453). Hopi epistemology is leveraged to guide and facilitate interpretation of a geographic information system (GIS) analysis of ancient landscapes.

PUEBLO PERSPECTIVES ON THE LANDSCAPE

As Alfonso Ortiz (1972:17–25) showed in his analysis of Tewa ritual space, in contemporary Pueblo thought the village is often considered to be the center of the world where the six primary axes (up, down, north, south, east, and west) converge. Each village is surrounded by a nested set of landscape features that mark cardinal directions, sacred places, and boundaries, giving physical definition to the notion of centeredness. The horizon often symbolizes the boundary between known and unknown, safe and dangerous, familiar and foreign (Tuan 1974), and it organizes the year by the movement of the sun (McCluskey 1977; Zeilik 1985). Whiteley (2011) described how contemporary Hopi religious practice "draws the powers of life into the center from the periphery" by ritually visiting, dramatizing, and singing named localities on the landscape. It is in this sense that the Hopi landscape is a "living theater" of Hopi action and imagination (Whiteley 2011:91, 105).

Rundstrom (1995; see also Pearce and Louis 2008) used the term *process cartography* to contrast the incorporative, embodied nature of such Indigenous mapping with the inscriptive, result-based nature of Western mapping. Interestingly, there is a recent movement in Western GIS toward place-based rather than space-based cartography, in which a map would emphasize relational links between named places rather than Euclidean distances in x y coordinate space (e.g., Goodchild 2011). The motivation for this switch from "spatial to platial" approaches is to avoid the false precision of coordinate space and to better operationalize the place-based nature of human wayfinding (turn left at the Eiffel Tower as opposed to turn left at latitude y, longitude x). That is, Pueblo mental maps are not designed to locate objects in Cartesian space but are rather stages upon which action and history occurs. This contrast matches that drawn by Zedeño (2000) between the space-bound landscape approach that typifies archaeology, which defines an arbitrary space (a study area or region) and locations within it, and Indigenous relational and place-based approaches. Indigenous cognitive maps tend to consist of a network of relationships among landforms, each of which is understood relative to other landforms.

This contrast helps to explain a puzzling paradox of Puebloan cosmologies: the anchoring of ritual practice to the landscape despite the frequent shifts in ancestral Puebloan village locations. Archaeological evidence suggests that, despite their large size and sturdy construction, most ancestral Puebloan villages were occupied for little more than a generation or two before populations dispersed to reform new villages (Bernardini 2005). Movement was so common among precontact agricultural Puebloan populations that Fox (1967:24) described them as "urbanized nomads." But locally anchored cosmologies can be reconciled with dynamic movement if we allow that the principle of anchoring outweighed the details of any one landscape. In fact, Naranjo (1995:249) clarified that "specific [geographic] boundaries are not the important elements because as the people moved, their mountain boundaries also moved. The idea was to have boundaries to create a place—to fix a place—temporarily within a larger idea of movement."

We can further resolve the paradox by recognizing that, while cognitive maps are heavily informed by one's lived bodily experience with the landscape, their range can be extended by information transmitted across space (social interaction) and especially over time (oral tradition). Schachner (2011:435), for example, suggested that we might trace a change in the nature of socially significant connections between points on the landscape to a shift in settlement patterns between circa AD 900 and 1300. Across that interval, populations in the American Southwest contracted into fewer larger villages, leaving behind ever more ancestral places. Whereas previously most connections may have been between groups across *space* (e.g., an outlying great house to Chaco Canyon), by the fourteenth century important connections were increasingly being made between points in *time*—between contemporary and ancestral villages and landscapes. Physical movement on the landscape was restricted after Spanish contact, but connections to ancestral places were preserved through oral tradition and pilgrimage (Bernardini 2008).

Fowles (2011) encouraged archaeologists to understand ancestral Puebloan migration specifically in relation to Indigenous perceptions of space and place. He argued that, from a Puebloan perspective, "movement to and from one's village or within a community's existing cosmic boundaries was not 'migration' nor were temporary excursions to foreign lands. Rather, a 'migration' was when the center of the world shifted, when new cosmic landmarks were adopted" (Fowles 2011:note 2). Thus, we could define migration in Pueblo terms as "a residential move that leads to the establishment of a new spiritual center or middle place as well as the redefinition of a group's major cosmological boundaries" (Fowles 2011:52).

ANALYZING PRE-HISPANIC PUEBLOAN VISUAL LANDSCAPES

This chapter employs a method for operationalizing an Indigenous spatial lens that can identify likely cosmological landmarks. With this method, it is possible to suggest the boundaries of ancestral Puebloan visual landscapes and identify the migrations that would have been necessary to transcend these boundaries (e.g., Bernardini and Peeples 2015). A robust literature in spatial cognition suggests that people organize their spatial knowledge about an environment through a hierarchy of landmarks (Allen and Kirasic 1985; Couclelis et al. 1987; Tversky 1993). The main methodological challenge in ancient landscapes, when actors cannot be queried about their cognitive maps, involves the quantification of visual prominence—that is, identification of the landforms that would likely have been visual anchors (Golledge 1978) for local cosmologies.

A number of approaches from geographic information science have been suggested, but most employ a global measure of prominence: how big a bump does a mountain make on the planet's surface as seen from a planar perspective (e.g., Podobnikar 2012)? What is needed, however, is a more local measure—an assessment of the prominence of a landform not from the air but from the particular vantage point of a Pueblo village. Measuring local prominence is difficult because the same landform can look different depending on which direction one is viewing it from and from what distance.

The GIS-based method of calculating local prominence employed in this chapter is outlined in greater detail elsewhere (Bernardini et al. 2013) and summarized briefly here (figure 5.2). For each viewing location, points on the horizon skyline are analyzed to determine their relative importance in characterizing the shape of the skyline. Points that project farther above a flat horizon and that rise steeply relative to their neighbors receive higher prominence values. A horizon skyline is progressively simplified until only the most prominent points remain. The mountains that comprise the most prominent vertices would have been the most visually conspicuous parts of the local skyline. Prominence values were calculated in this manner for a database of 1,116 sites consisting of fifty rooms or more across the Southwest dating from AD 1200 to 1700, resulting in prominence values for about 171,000 total landforms.

The social significance of a landform is a function of both its visual qualities and the number of people who can see it. As with the proverbial tree in the forest, a mountain must first be seen before it can be interpreted as prominent. To factor the number of people who could view a peak at a given point in time into its prominence measure, prominence values were multiplied by the number of people living at each site who could see a given peak. These *population prominence* values were then summed for each peak to obtain the peak's social prominence within the broader region. This was done for all peaks for each fifty-year interval from AD 1200 to AD 1700.

CASE STUDY: PATKI CLAN MIGRATION

Hopi traditional knowledge about migration is held individually by each Hopi clan, which curates songs and stories about the ancestral villages and landscapes it once

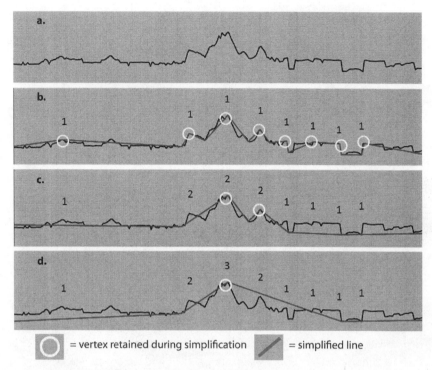

○ = vertex retained during simplification ╱ = simplified line

FIGURE 5.2 Illustration of the line simplification method for calculating prominence: (a) a horizon skyline mapped in profile; (b) the skyline simplified at a 1° elevation angle; (c) the skyline simplified at a 2° elevation angle; (d) the skyline simplified at a 3° elevation angle.

inhabited (e.g., Fewkes 1900). Migration patterns recounted in Hopi traditional knowledge are complex and nonlinear; when plotted together, the movements of Hopi clans produce a reticulate or braided stream pattern of connections among sites (Bernardini 2005; Terrell 2001). Even the traditions of a single clan are amalgamations of the experiences of many composite subclans (Bernardini 2008). Yet the apparent disarray of Hopi clan traditions need not be an indication of their inaccuracy. In fact, the social units and patterns of movement recorded in Hopi clan migration traditions better match the archaeological record than do the geographic regions and migration models conventionally used by many archaeologists. For example, while archaeologists traditionally use the culture area or the village as the unit of social identity or movement, the spatial distribution of totemic petroglyphs and patterns of long-distance exchange suggest that small social units, perhaps analogous to contemporary clans, acted independently of either of these larger analytical units (e.g., Bernardini 2005).

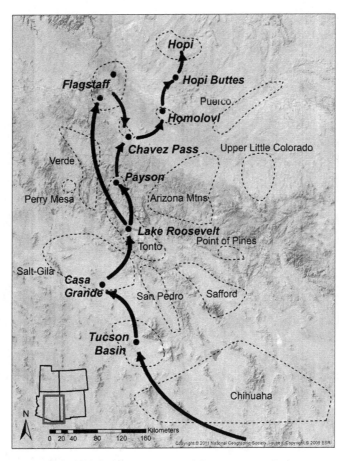

FIGURE 5.3 The Patki Clan migration pathway (after Ferguson and Lomaomvaya 1999: figure 27).

A case study of Patki (Water) Clan migration traditions (figure 5.3) is used to explore the definition of migration as "a residential move that leads to the establishment of a new spiritual center or middle place as well as the redefinition of a group's major cosmological boundaries" (Fowles 2011:52). The migration traditions of the Patki Clan have been recorded repeatedly over the last one hundred years, creating one of the better documented Hopi migration accounts (see Ferguson and Lomaomvaya 1999). The case study will use movements described in Patki Clan traditions to consider when and where movements occurred that would have broken a line-of-sight connection with a prominent visual anchor and to identify new landforms that may have been adopted in their place.

Most Patki Clan accounts begin in Palatkwapi, the "Red-Walled City" (Hopi Dictionary Project 1998:383), whose location is uncertain but may have been as far south as central Mexico (Waters 1963:68). From Palatkwapi the Patki Clan moved north first to the Tucson valley, next to Casa Grande in the Phoenix Basin, and then through Wukoskyavi, the area near Roosevelt Lake (Ferguson and Lomaomvaya 1999). From here some Patki people went toward Payson, Arizona, and then to Chavez Pass, while others went to Pasiovi (Elden Pueblo) and Wupatki near Flagstaff, Arizona, before rejoining their clan-mates at Chavez Pass (Fewkes 1900; Siweumptewa 1998). From Chavez Pass, Patki Clan members moved to Homol'ovi, then to the Hopi Buttes, and finally into villages on First and Second Mesa (Nequatewa 1967:100–101).

The Patki Clan migration crossed at least nine major archaeological regions (Chihuahua, Tucson Basin, Phoenix Basin, Tonto, Verde, Chavez Pass, Flagstaff, Homol'ovi, Hopi Buttes, and Hopi Mesas), each containing villages that were occupied primarily between AD 1200 and AD 1400/1450 (Adams and Duff 2004). By AD 1400/1450, most of these regions were largely depopulated, with the notable exception of the Hopi Mesas. Changes in population density across Arizona between AD 1200 and AD 1450 leave little doubt that many people did indeed migrate north and east toward destinations in the Hopi and Zuni regions and to points farther east along the Rio Grande (Hill et al. 2004).

The Patki Clan pathway transcends huge environmental and topographic variability: the Basin and Range Province of southern Arizona, characterized by closely spaced north-south trending mountain ridges; the transitional zone of central Arizona, characterized by eroded, low rolling hills; and the Colorado Plateau of northern Arizona, a high flat plain punctuated by tall isolated mountains. The distinctive topographic qualities of each physiographic zone provided different contexts for grounding cosmologies in the landscape, including the distance to the horizon, the local relief of landforms above the surrounding terrain, and the relative clustering or isolation of tall landforms.

Using the GIS method outlined above, population prominence values were calculated for all points on the horizons of villages along the Patki Clan migration pathway. The analysis identified five peaks that would have dominated local horizons along this pathway: Wasson Peak, San Tan Mountain, the Superstition Mountains, the Four Peaks, and the San Francisco Peaks. The visual significance of each of these landforms will be explored in more detail below.

In the Tucson Basin, the horizon would have been dominated by Wasson Peak, the highest point in the Tucson Mountains (figure 5.4). At 1,400 meters Wasson Peak is only half the height of the rolling Santa Catalina and Rincon Mountains to the east, but its isolation in the middle of the Tucson Basin makes it a more visually striking part of the horizon from the perspective of Tucson Basin villages. All of the large

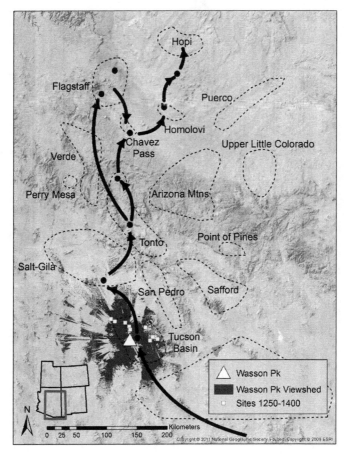

FIGURE 5.4 The visual landscape in the Tucson Basin showing Wasson Peak, its viewshed, and sites occupied between AD 1250 and AD 1400 with a prominent view of Wasson Peak.

sites in the Tucson Basin between AD 1200 and AD 1400 were located to the north of Wasson Peak; therefore, this landform would almost certainly have been assigned meanings relating to the southern cardinal direction. The modest elevation of Wasson Peak and the basin and range topography, with closely spaced north-south trending mountain ranges, largely limited the range over which Wasson Peak was visible as a prominent landform to the Tucson Basin.

Movement to Casa Grande on the eastern side of the Phoenix Basin would have caused a significant disruption in the visual landscape of ancestral Paki Clan migrants (figure 5.5). Wasson Peak would no longer have been visible. In its place, two nearby peaks and one distant peak (or cluster of peaks) would have dominated the horizon:

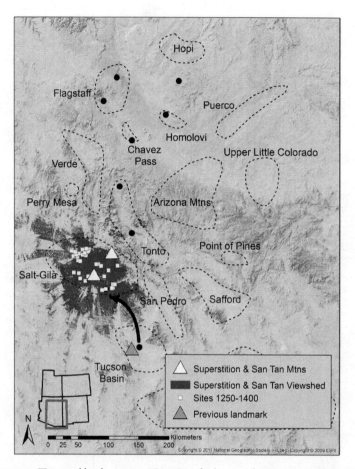

FIGURE 5.5 The visual landscape near Casa Grande showing the Superstition Mountains and San Tan Mountain, their viewsheds, and sites occupied between AD 1250 and AD 1400 with a prominent view of these peaks.

the local San Tan Mountains and Superstition Mountains and the more distant Four Peaks. Although the San Tan Mountains rise only 250 meters above the valley floor, they are tall and steep enough to break the line of sight to the east for sites located within the eastern Phoenix Basin. From Casa Grande, the San Tan Mountains would have dominated the western horizon, although there were contemporaneous sites located on all sides of this landform. The San Tan Mountains were accessible—low and close enough to villages that religious practices could happen *on* them. The Superstition Mountains to the northeast of the basin are only slightly higher (450 meters), but they were still a high point on the western edge of the range that dramatically projected into the horizon, possibly marking the summer solstice sunset. The San Tan

Mountains and the western prominence of the Superstition Mountains were strictly local prominences, visible only from viewpoints in the Phoenix Basin.

Thirty kilometers further northeast behind the Superstitions are the Four Peaks, a dramatically steep-sided cluster of four prominences. These peaks are much higher (2,300 meters) and are often snowcapped in the winter. They are tall enough to project into the northeastern skyline of the Phoenix Basin and would have constituted the most significant "big mountain" visible from the basin. The Four Peaks would also have been visible to sites to the northeast in the Tonto Basin, making them the first landform on the Patki Clan migration pathway to have had visual prominence across multiple regions. Having visual anchors in common across multiple regions could have meant that spatially separated populations shared common aspects of their cosmology, united in their use of a common landform to mark directions and measure time on solar calendars.

The next step in the Patki Clan migration, to the Lake Roosevelt/Tonto Basin area, would have involved both continuity and disruption of previous visual landscapes (figure 5.6). The movement would have broken visual contact with the peaks in the Phoenix Basin (the San Tan Mountains and the western prominence of the Superstition Mountains), the previous eastern and northeastern prominences. But the movement would have also increased proximity to the Four Peaks—previously visible as distant projections on the northeastern horizon but now the dominant landform on the western horizon. This change in proximity and placement on the horizon must have involved changes in the social significance attributed to the Four Peaks. They likely took on new and deeper meanings, made more powerful because the Four Peaks cluster was the one part of the horizon that could still be connected to the previous visual landscape of the Phoenix Basin.

When a portion of the Patki Clan moved from the Lake Roosevelt region to the area around Payson, Arizona, they entered the broken landscape of the transitional zone physiographic province. This rolling terrain provides few distinctive landforms on local horizons and inhibits line of sight to larger landforms that lie beyond it. Residents of this area would have had no significant visual contact with the Four Peaks nor could they see larger landforms to the north like the San Francisco Peaks. From a visual perspective, this region is isolated from more striking landscapes to the north and south. The impact of movement into the transitional zone on local cosmologies was likely significant, involving breaking contact with the Four Peaks landmark that may have anchored generations of ancestors. The local landscape provided no remotely comparable landform for substitution.

In contrast, movement of another portion of the Patki Clan from Lake Roosevelt to the Flagstaff area brought it into visual contact with the single most prominent landform in all of Arizona, the San Francisco Peaks (Nuvatukya'ovi; figure 5.7). This is the largest landform in the state at 3,850 meters, rising over 1,800 meters from the surrounding

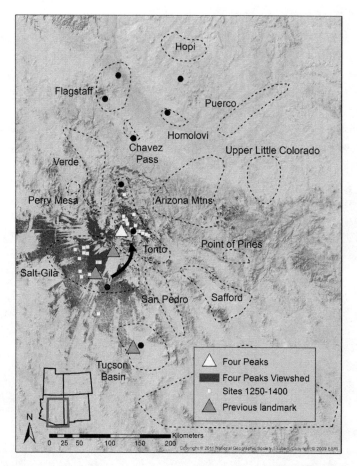

FIGURE 5.6 The visual landscape near Lake Roosevelt showing the Four Peaks, their viewshed, and sites occupied between AD 1250 and AD 1400 with a prominent view of the Four Peaks.

plateau, visible up to 150 km away. Snowcapped almost half of the year, Nuvatukya'ovi is the most significant peak to the Hopi Tribe. It is the residence of the *katsinam*, Hopi ancestors who travel in the form of clouds and rain to sustain life on the Hopi Mesas.

Movement from the Flagstaff and Payson areas to Chavez Pass brought travelers to one of the primary "staging areas" (Bernardini 2005) from which clans would negotiate entrance into a village on the Hopi Mesas. Although Chavez Pass lies at the very northeast edge of the transition zone province, from high points near the pass the San Francisco Peaks are clearly visible. For migrants from the south, this would be the first village horizon they had experienced that would have brought them into visual contact with the San Francisco Peaks. For migrants moving south from the Flagstaff area, the

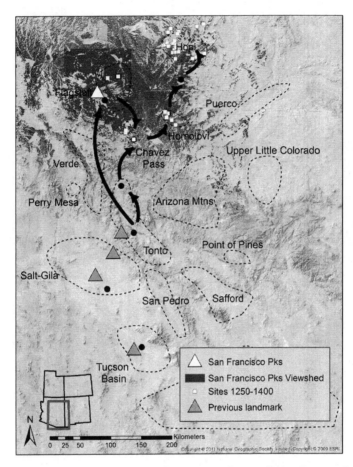

FIGURE 5.7 The visual landscape in northern Arizona showing the San Francisco Peaks, their viewshed, and sites occupied between AD 1250 and AD 1400 with a prominent view of the San Francisco Peaks.

ability to maintain visual connection to the San Francisco Peaks would have enabled some continuity in their social constructions of the landscape. All immigrants arriving at Chavez Pass, regardless of differences in language, religion, and material culture, would have been united in their common visual orientation to the San Francisco Peaks.

The next step of the migration, from Chavez Pass to the Homol'ovi region, took migrants to a flat expanse of the Colorado Plateau from which the distant San Francisco Peaks were visible from many (though not all) village locations. Some sites, like Homol'ovi III, were built on top of small landforms that may have been specifically chosen to enable a view to the peaks (Adams 2002:137). A kiva in the plaza of Homol'ovi II contained a mural of the San Francisco Peaks, attesting to its importance to the residents of that village (Adams 2002:161). From the Homol'ovi area the Hopi Buttes (a cluster of extinct volcanic cores) would also have been visible to the northeast. These are distinctive points on the horizon, but most rise only a few hundred feet above the local terrain and their clustering reduces the visual impact of any one landform.

The final steps of the migration, to the area of the Hopi Buttes and then to the Hopi Mesas proper, maintained visual contact with the San Francisco Peaks from almost all villages occupied between AD 1200 and AD 1400–1500. In the Hopi Mesas region thirty of thirty-four sites (88%) occupied between AD 1250 and AD 1300 had a view of the San Francisco Peaks, likely a reflection of deliberate choices in site location to optimize this view.

DISCUSSION

Although the Patki Clan migration tradition is likely a composite of experiences by multiple small social units, the different visual landscapes experienced along its path nevertheless provide an idea of the visual changes that might have been experienced by ancestral Puebloan migrants. Routes north through Arizona required movement through a number of discrete geologic areas, beginning with the bowl-like landscapes of the Tucson and Phoenix Basins. The horizons of these landscapes were formed by relatively low nearby landforms that encircled the basins, creating a relatively small-diameter visual landscape. Movement north from these basins into the broken terrain of the transitional zone physiographic province quickly severed visual contact with most prominent points on these earlier horizons, requiring a nearly total reset of cosmological landscape reference points. In Fowles's definition, these were significant migrations. Movements among villages in the transitional zone, even if distances were not great, were also often sufficient to break visual contact with the low landforms of the region, suggesting that many of these relocations could also be considered migrations from a visual perspective.

A turning point in the northward migrations of ancestral Puebloan groups would have come when they reached Chavez Pass, a place from which, for the first time, they lived within daily sight of the San Francisco Peaks. The continuous prominence of the San Francisco Peaks for northern Arizona populations for more than eight hundred years and across hundreds of square kilometers must have been a kind of social glue for the ancestral Puebloan populations who shared that view. When individuals and groups gathered in villages like those in the Chavez Pass or Homol'ovi areas or on the Hopi Mesas, many would have brought with them personal visual experiences of the peaks and also the multigenerational knowledge of culture that had been generated about the peaks. Although not all of this information would necessarily have been compatible—with different names, different languages, and different ritual associations—the common visual orientation of populations in northern Arizona toward the San Francisco Peaks must have helped to unite people when they found themselves living together.

The persistence of the San Francisco Peaks as a visual anchor must have facilitated continuity and stability in the cultural construction of the northern Arizona landscape. Such stability is in vivid contrast to the short-lived and/or local nature of visual anchors in central and southern Arizona from which many residents of the Hopi originally derived. We might even suggest that the stability of the visual landscape around the Hopi Mesas—the fact that populations for 100 kilometers and eight hundred years were oriented around the same dominant landform—could have been part of what made the Hopi Mesas a successful destination for migrants in the late prehistoric period. In contrast to many of the places from which migrants had come, like the Arizona Mountains, Upper Little Colorado River, Verde Valley, or Tonto Basin, the landscape around the Hopi Mesas provided a common visual framework around which diverse village and regional populations could orient themselves.

CONCLUSION

This chapter began with a reflection on the epistemology of Hopi cultural advisors that enables them to reconcile present and past social landscapes. Puebloan ancestors must have engaged in the same practice as migrations carried them beyond sight of familiar landmarks and into view of new ones. The substitution or reinterpretation of landmarks within a cosmological framework must have required negotiation among co-residents, with the outcomes of these negotiations favoring some groups and histories over others. The complexity of these changes can only be suggested here, but it is hoped that the model outlined in this chapter has provided a method of identifying the times and places where such changes must have occurred. Now that we know where to look, we may find evidence to deepen our understanding of the evolution of social landscapes in the archaeological record and in traditional knowledge.

REFERENCES CITED

Adams, E. Charles. 2002. *Homol'ovi: An Ancient Hopi Settlement Cluster*. University of Arizona Press, Tucson.

Adams, E. Charles, and Andrew I. Duff. 2004. Settlement Clusters and the Pueblo IV Period. In *The Protohistoric Pueblo World, A.D. 1275–1600*, edited by E. Charles Adams and Andrew I. Duff, pp. 3–16. University of Arizona Press, Tucson.

Allen, Gary L., and Kathleen C. Kirasic. 1985. Effects of Cognitive Organization of Route Knowledge on Judgement of Macrospatial Distances. *Memory and Cognition* 13:218–227.

Bernardini, Wesley. 2005. *Hopi Oral Tradition and the Archaeology of Identity.* University of Arizona Press, Tucson.

Bernardini, Wesley. 2008. Identity as History: Hopi Clans and the Curation of Oral Tradition. *Journal of Anthropological Research* 64(4):483–509.

Bernardini, Wesley, Alicia Barnash, Mark Kumler, and Martin Wong. 2013. Quantifying Visual Prominence in Social Landscapes. *Journal of Archaeological Science* 40:3946–3954.

Bernardini, Wesley, and Matthew Peeples. 2015. Sight Communities: The Social Significance of Shared Visual Landmarks. *American Antiquity* 80(2):215–235.

Couclelis, Helen, Reginald G. Golledge, Nathan Gale, and Waldo Tobler. 1987. Exploring the Anchor-Point Hypothesis of Spatial Cognition. *Journal of Environmental Psychology* 7:99–122.

Ferguson, T. J., and Micah Lomaomvaya. 1999. *Hoopoq'uaqam niqw Wukoskyavi (Those Who Went to the Northeast and Tonto Basin): Hopi-Salado Cultural Affiliation Study.* Hopi Cultural Preservation Office, Kiqötsmovi, Arizona.

Fewkes, Jesse W. 1900. Tusayan Migration Traditions. *Nineteenth Annual Report of the Bureau of American Ethnology for the Years 1897–1898*, Pt. 2, pp. 573–634. Government Printing Office, Washington, D.C.

Fowles, Severin. 2010. The Southwest School of Landscape Archaeology. *Annual Review of Anthropology* 39:453–468.

———. 2011. Movement and the Unsettling of the Pueblos. In *Rethinking Anthropological Perspectives on Migration*, edited by G. Cabana and J. Clark, pp. 45–67. University Press of Florida, Gainesville.

Fox, Robin. 1967. *The Keresan Bridge: A Problem in Pueblo Ethnology.* London School of Economics Monographs on Social Anthropology, No. 35. Athlone, London.

Golledge, R. 1978. Representing, interpreting, and using cognized environments. *Papers in Regional Science* 41(1):169–204.

Goodchild, Michael F. 2011. Formalizing Place in Geographic Information Systems. In *Communities, Neighborhoods, and Health*, edited by Linda M. Burton, Susan P. Kemp, ManChui Leung, Stephen A. Matthews, and David T. Takeuchi, pp. 21–33. Springer, New York.

Hill, J. Brett, Jeffery J. Clark, William H. Doelle, and Patrick D. Lyons. 2004. Prehistoric Demography in the Southwest: Migration, Coalescence, and Hohokam Population Decline. *American Antiquity* 69(4):689–716.

Hopi Dictionary Project. 1998. *Hopi Dictionary/Hopìikwa Lavàytutuveni, A Hopi-English Dictionary of the Third Mesa Dialect.* University of Arizona Press, Tucson

McCluskey, Stephen. 1977. The Astronomy of the Hopi Indians. *Journal for the History of Astronomy* 8:174–195.

Naranjo, Tessie. 1995. Thoughts on Migration by Santa Clara Pueblo. *Journal of Anthropological Archaeology* 14:247–250.

Nequatewa, Edmund. 1967. *Truth of a Hopi: Stories Relating to the Origin, Myths and Clan Histories of the Hopi.* Northland Press and the Museum of Northern Arizona, Flagstaff.

Ortiz, Alfonzo. 1972. *The Tewa World: Space, Time, Being, and Becoming in a Pueblo Society.* University of Chicago Press, Chicago.

Pearce, Margaret W., and Renee P. Louis. 2008. Mapping Indigenous Depth of Place. *American Indian Culture and Research Journal* 32.(3):107–126.

Podobnikar, Tomaz. 2012. Detecting Mountain Peaks and Delineating Their Shapes Using Digital Elevation Models, Remote Sensing and Geographic Information Systems Using Autometric Methodological Procedures. *International Journal of Remote Sensing.* 4:784–809.

Rundstrom, Robert A. 1995. GIS, Indigenous Peoples, and Epistemological Diversity. *Cartography and Geographic Information Systems* 22(1):45–57.

Schachner, Gregson. 2011. Ritual Places and Landscapes: Connecting Southwest Peoples Across Time and Space. In *Movement, Connectivity, and Landscape Change in the Ancient Southwest,* edited by Margaret Nelson and Colleen Strawhacker, pp. 423–441. University Press of Colorado, Boulder.

Siweumptewa, LaVern. 1998. Interview of LaVern Siweumptewa by Micah Lomaomvaya, December 4, 1998. Notes on file at Hopi Cultural Preservation Office, Kiqötsmovi, Arizona.

Silko, Leslie M. 1986. Landscape, History, and the Pueblo Imagination. *Antaeus* 57:83–94.

Terrell, John. 2001. The Uncommon Sense of Race, Language, and Culture. In *Archaeology, Language, and History: Essays on Culture and Ethnicity,* edited by John Terrell, pp. 11–31. Bergin and Garvey, Westport, Connecticut.

Tuan, Yi-Fu. 1977. *Space and Place: The Perspective of Experience.* University of Minnesota Press, Minneapolis.

Tversky, Barbara. 1993. Cognitive Maps, Cognitive Collages, and Spatial Mental Models. In *Spatial Information Theory: A Theoretical Basis for GIS,* edited by Andrew U. Frank and Irene Campari, pp. 14–24. Springer-Verlag, Berlin.

Waters, Frank. 1963. *Book of the Hopi.* Penguin Books, New York.

Whiteley, Peter M. 2011. Hopi Place Value: Translating a Landscape. In *Born in the Blood: On Native American Translation,* edited by Brian Swann, pp. 84–108. University of Nebraska Press, Lincoln.

Zedeño, Maria N. 2000. On What People Make of Places: A Behavioral Cartography. In *Social Theory in Archaeology,* edited by Michael Schiffer, pp. 97–111. University of Utah Press, Salt Lake City.

Zeilik, Michael. 1985. Sun Shrines and Sun Symbols in the U.S. Southwest. *Archaeoastronomy* 9:86–96.

6

THE HOMOL'OVI
RESEARCH PROGRAM

Enriching Hopi History Through Collaboration

E. CHARLES ADAMS

A FORTUITOUS CONVERGENCE OF circumstances resulted in my exposure to Hopi history from its ancient roots to the present. This story follows two threads—my work at Homol'ovi and my work with the Hopi. It is framed by my awareness that Hopi is a philosophy of life practiced by people occupying the mesas. Homol'ovi is a description that Hopi apply to the area that is now Winslow, Arizona, and it translates as "place of hills or small mounds," describing the many buttes that dominate the landscape east and north of Winslow. Occupation of Homol'ovi goes back thousands of years and we have radiocarbon dates showing the first use of maize in the area at 185 BC, followed by small pit house villages first appearing about AD 600 and continuing to past AD 1200. The primary focus of archaeologists and Hopi has been the seven large late villages occupied from roughly AD 1260 to AD 1400.

HOMOL'OVI: THEN AND NOW

In 1856, Lt. A. W. Whipple first documented Homol'ovi villages when he reported wood sticking out of the larger pueblos with walls standing higher than a human (Whipple:1856). The first published work at the Homol'ovi cluster villages was by Jesse Walter Fewkes in 1896, resulting in two reports (Fewkes 1898, 1904). Fewkes was hired by John Wesley Powell, director of the Bureau of American Ethnology, to conduct archaeology and ethnology in the Southwest and was prolific in his publication of Hopi ethnography and archaeology. Fewkes (1898) noted that Mormon settlers, who established two forts near Homol'ovi in 1876, used stone from Homol'ovi I to build their forts. A century later, in the 1960s and 1970s, vandalism, focused on burial areas, reached epidemic levels with heavy equipment destroying kivas, rooms, and entire room blocks (Adams 2002). Many of the villages were on state land and local ranchers thought they had the right to make decisions about resources on these lands.

Fewkes learned of the existence of villages at Homol'ovi from Hopi at First Mesa while excavating Sikyatki Pueblo in 1895. His reports document oral histories of the clans who once lived at Homol'ovi and include data from his excavations in cemeteries at Homol'ovi I and Chevelon as well as limited testing at Homol'ovi II and III. The only other documented excavations at Homol'ovi I and Chevelon were conducted by George Dorsey, J. A. Burt, and Charles L. Owen from 1897 to 1900 for the Field Museum of Natural History, Chicago, with no published report.

Fewkes also documented Hopi visits to their ancestral villages to collect water and turtles for ceremonies on the mesas. In addition to First Mesa, Second and Third Mesa Hopi also have ancestral clans who once resided at Homol'ovi and brought important ceremonies to the villages where they reside today.

Since 1985, Richard C. Lange and I have codirected the Homol'ovi Research Program (HRP) at the Arizona State Museum (ASM) with fieldwork ending in 2006. During this time excavations were conducted at Homol'ovi I–IV and Chevelon pueblos (figure 6.1). In addition, Lange surveyed thirty square miles and recorded four hundred sites. Two field house sites and a small outlier pueblo to Homol'ovi I were also excavated.

In the mid-1990s, Bruce and Lisa Huckell surveyed two sections west of Chevelon Canyon, documented nine new preceramic sites, and excavated a Basketmaker II (early agricultural) pit house site, dated to 750 BC by ASM. In addition, two former graduate students on the project conducted research: William H. Walker, New Mexico State University, at Jackrabbit Pueblo in 1997 and Lisa C. Young, University of Michigan, at two pre Homol'ovi village sites in 1998 and 2006–08.

HOPI: THEN AND NOW

In 1975 I completed my doctorate at the University of Colorado, Boulder, and was given the unique opportunity by the Museum of Northern Arizona (MNA) to direct an ethnoarchaeological project at Wàlpi Pueblo, First Mesa. First Mesa Consolidated Villages received a $350,000 grant from the United States Department of Commerce to preserve and renovate deteriorating sections of Wàlpi, which included most of the village. The National Historic Preservation Act of 1966 required that any remodeling be documented through photographs and drawings. In addition, the grant required

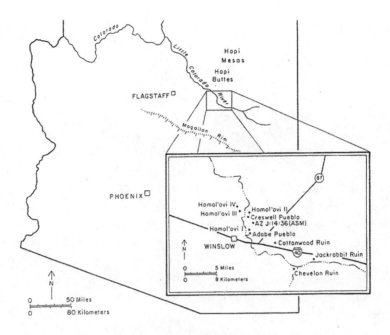

FIGURE 6.1 Map of Homol'ovi Pueblos (drawing by Ronald Beckwith).

archaeological documentation to preserve artifacts that might be recovered as part of the restoration. Thus, the Walpi Archaeological Project was created at MNA and I spent eighteen months in the field from November 1975 through April 1977 directing excavations at Wàlpi (figure 6.2).

In addition to holding frequent conversations with the all-Hopi crew about the objects I removed from excavations in more than seventy structures dating from the 1680s to the present, Jenny Adams and I hosted quarterly open house events in the First Mesa Community Center featuring a show-and-tell component of the interesting and significant objects we had recovered since the previous gathering. Members from all First Mesa villages came to view the objects and tell us their Hopi name and purpose. We learned much about the subtleties of objects we thought we knew. As a result of this successful collaboration, I received permission to take artifacts off the Hopi Reservation to the MNA for further analysis. which continued until 1982. In addition to eight volumes describing the Wàlpi material, a synthetic volume was produced as well as several articles and monographs (Adams 1982; Adovasio and Andrews 1985; Ahlstrom et al.1978). However, First Mesa religious leaders ultimately decided that the synthetic volume should not be published and that all reports could have only limited distribution. This decision was a result of the change in leadership at

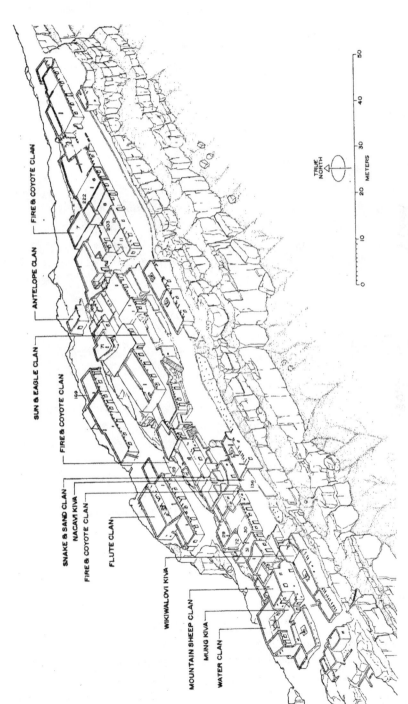

FIGURE 6.2 Walpi Pueblo as it appeared in 1975 (courtesy Museum of Northern Arizona).

First Mesa; individuals party to the original agreement were no longer involved and new leaders were reticent to approve an agreement that they didn't fully understand. I wrote of the collaborative process developed during my work on the Hopi Reservation in *Ethics and Values in Archaeology* (Adams 1984). This chapter outlines the ethos I practice to this day in my work with the Hopi People: listen, work cooperatively, and share knowledge.

When I worked at Wàlpi, responsibility for matters of archaeology and ethnography resided with the vice chairman's office. As luck would have it, the vice chairman was Alvin Dashee from First Mesa. Dashee's connections with First Mesa village leaders and the Hopi Tribe were essential to the success of the project and made my life much easier because trust between the villages and tribal government was not strong even then. The vice chairman continued to handle cultural resource matters in 1978 when Stanley Honanie replaced Dashee as vice chairman, reporting to Abbott Sekaquaptewa, who continued as chairman. After serving his term as vice chairman, Honanie took on the difficult task of developing land for the Hopi Tribe in the newly acquired former Joint-Use Area. In both roles he was a strong advocate for the Hopi Tribe, protecting the Homol'ovi villages and ultimately creating Homolovi [*sic*] State Park.

In 1987 the Hopi Tribal Council approved a tribal historic preservation plan calling for the creation of a Hopi Cultural Preservation Office (HCPO). This office came into being in 1989 with Leigh Jenkins (Kuwanwisiwma) as director. The passage of the Native American Graves Protection and Repatriation Act (NAGPRA) in 1990 transformed the relationship between the Hopi Tribe and the University of Arizona. As a result of NAGPRA, similar legislation was passed by the Arizona Legislature (ARS 41–844 and 41–865), implementing rules in June 1991 to protect human remains on state and private lands from unwarranted disturbance. This in turn resulted in the development of formal agreements between the ASM/HRP and the HCPO on the treatment of human remains beginning in 1993.These agreements include four elements that Leigh initiated at the HCPO: (1) development of procedures for reinterring human remains with which the Hopi asserted affiliation, (2) creation of the Cultural Resources Advisory Task Team (CRATT) of elders and religious leaders from all three mesas and the upper and lower villages of Munqapi, (3) identification of one or more individuals to conduct interment ceremonies, and (4) work with local agencies to identify appropriate areas for reinterring human remains and associated objects.

An important part of the burial agreements between ASM and HCPO was to develop a plan for the handling and treatment of human remains that were not from burials. Beyond the recovery of remains from three burials at Homol'ovi III, no other buried human remains were recovered from the excavation of 178 structures during twenty years of fieldwork. However, the ASM did find many other varieties of human remains that generally fell into four categories:

1. Articulated full or nearly full skeletons (usually small children or neonates), which did not have accompanying burial goods and were found on the floor or in the fill of structures.
2. Skeletons that were products of prehistoric reburial that never had accompanying grave goods and were found on the floor or in the fill of structures.
3. Articulated elements of human skeletons, often feet or hands.
4. Isolated human bone, usually phalanges or teeth.

With this variability in mind, the ASM and HCPO worked closely on wording of the agreements for treatment of human remains. The ASM was allowed to continue work in structures where articulated elements and isolated human bone were recovered after removing the bone. Initially, the agreement required placing human remains in paper bags. These were stored in a cardboard box and left at Homolovi State Park. The plan initially called for all recovered remains, which at the time were mostly from Homol'ovi II, to be reburied in a designated area within the park with a ceremony to be conducted by Dalton Taylor (Hopi elder and member of CRATT). However, the reburial never happened, and the remains ultimately were transported to the ASM to await a decision from the HCPO

As this scenario was unfolding, the ASM and HCPO shifted their policy on the treatment of human remains, an agreement which was revised every five years. The 1998 agreement allowed us to continue to remove isolated and articulated elements of human remains from structures to allow for additional excavation; the remains were to be placed in a paper bag and left in a secure location in our field trailer before being returned to the fill of the excavation unit when it was backfilled with its original fill. We continued to do basic nondestructive analysis by recording element, condition, and anomalies of the remains. The bones were sometimes sketched, but were not photographed.

This procedure illustrates the importance of being flexible and building trust and communication among various constituencies to make agreements work while protecting the interests of both sides. Trust and communication were greatly enhanced by inviting Leigh, HCPO staff, and members of CRATT to visit the excavations and witness firsthand the work we were doing. After a tour of the excavations, Hopi visitors were invited to ask questions and a lively discussion ensued, much of it in Hopi among the CRATT members and with Leigh and other members of HCPO.

One of our most interesting discussions with Leigh and CRATT concerned burning of kivas at Homol'ovi II. During our excavations at Homol'ovi II from 1991 to 1995, we noted burned roofs in seven kivas we excavated or tested. This pattern stood in stark contrast to excavations of room block structures, of which only one of thirty-four had evidence of burning (Adams 2002). When CRATT visited with Leigh in 1992, I was eager to explore the meaning of this pattern. As we visited three kivas we were excavating, two of which had complete articulated human skeletal remains, I pointed out our evidence of kiva burning and inquired if Hopi history had examples of such a pattern or if there was an explanation for the pattern we were observing.

After considerable conversation in Hopi among the CRATT members, Leigh summarized their conclusions by stating that, since Hopi never burn their kivas, it is likely that they were burned by Apaches. At this point I noted that, although one kiva contained the bodies of three individuals, the bodies were covered with large sandstone blocks before the roof was burned. I pointed out that only one domestic structure had been burned. Next, I remarked that there was no evidence of Apaches being in this part of the Southwest when the kivas were burned. Finally, I pointed out that kivas at Homol'ovi III had also been burned and that I knew of others in Arizona that had suffered the same fate. After looking at more details of the burned roofs, the Hopi elders huddled once again for a much longer discussion. Leigh summarized the discussion as follows: "Hopi sometimes burn kivas." They were unwilling to discuss details, which I respected, but the message for me was that archaeology could not only challenge the knowledge of archaeologists but it could also encourage Hopi religious leaders to share information among themselves to deepen the pool of traditional knowledge that could be shared.

Leigh has brought professionalism and structure to HCPO during his twenty-eight years as director. He knows the state and federal laws and has created a strong voice for Native American involvement in all aspects of the federal and state processes for handling fieldwork and repatriation issues. He has projected the Hopi voice to every corner of Arizona on the basis of the Hopi oral tradition of widespread migration, claiming affiliation with nearly every pre-Hispanic group in this state and in bordering regions on the east, north, and northeast.

Working at Hopi is always about developing personal relationships and creating opportunities for sharing views steeped in Hopi knowledge and value systems. I first experienced this when I lived at First Mesa during the Walpi Project in the mid-1970s. These relationships included the First Mesa crew and Hopi tribal officials. I built on those relationships in the 1980s and 1990s to form a collaboration with Hopi people from many villages and stations in Hopi life. With Leigh these relationships deepened and strengthened. It is essential to know a person in a Hopi sense before engaging in depth. Relationships are built over time, and trust is fostered through experiences, not words. I was always deeply honored when Leigh took time to share his accumulated knowledge and Hopi philosophy. These conversations contributed enormously to my view of archaeology and its societal and cultural value that can be shared and enjoyed by all.

As I learned from those who taught me at First Mesa, it is a privilege to receive this knowledge and with that privilege comes responsibility for obtaining approval before writing or publishing it. This knowledge affects my view of the world, the field, and the archaeological record. More than most non-Hopi people, I see archaeology as a Hopi and the archaeological record and I are better for it.

THE SPIRITUAL WORLD

When I first came to Hopi in 1969 with my mentor David A. Breternitz and witnessed a *katsina* dance at Lower Munqapi village, I was presented with the opportunity to place people and activities into the context of a living pueblo. As a result, I began to animate my perception of all the archaeological sites I have encountered. In addition, experiencing the use of Munqapi's plaza as a sacred space sparked my fascination with the liminal aspect of the human experience.

The next and most significant stage of my journey took place during the eighteen months I lived at First Mesa and worked at Wàlpi (Adams 1982). Here I was offered the opportunity to work with traditional religious and clan leaders who were willing to share details about the use history of still-standing rooms in Wàlpi, as well as the spaces between rooms. Few of the rooms were still in use, yet nearly all still had active roles in the community, either maintained for occasional use or holding religious objects requiring weekly if not daily care. Still other rooms, some of which had not been in use for more than one hundred years, had deep deposits filled with objects; members of the community maintained knowledge of these places and their contents. Some of these rooms had designated ceremonial uses and contained objects much different from those in more domestic spaces, including many intact heirloom objects, usually rare or unusual and perishable. Many of the objects had distinctive decorative styles, often depicting maize, water-associated insects, animals, or birds. Finally, the closure of these rooms was distinctive. Often doors had been sealed, sometimes the floors were buried, and in one case an emetic was used to protect the living from the powerful ceremonies and ritual that once invoked these objects and were still harmful to the uninitiated.

As I moved through the village and documented room use and ownership, I discovered that more than a quarter of the standing structures at Wàlpi, twenty-two of eighty-five, had direct association with the performance of ceremonies or the storage or disposal of ceremonial objects, excluding kivas (Adams 1978). The knowledge given me by religious practitioners from Wàlpi as I studied and produced reports on the research through 1982 reminded me that most Southwest archaeologists, myself included, were not seeing or were misinterpreting a huge portion of the archaeological record that we were responsible for recovering and interpreting. This misconception stems from the Western view that, when a structure is no longer used, it is abandoned and filled with trash. In contrast, the Hopi see former homes and their contents as preserving history and memory of the family or social group. Rooms at Wàlpi were not just depositories for everyday trash from residents in the village. Objects and the deposits themselves were frequently selected for placement in specific rooms. This means that "trash-filled" rooms at Wàlpi and in ancient settlements throughout the Pueblo Southwest have social meaning.

When I came to the ASM in 1985 to direct the HRP, it was the chance of a lifetime to connect what I had witnessed at Wàlpi with ancestral Hopi settlements off the Hopi Reservation. I began excavations at Homol'ovi III, a forty- to fifty-room village, because it seemed manageable logistically and in terms of getting a foothold on the vast Homol'ovi archaeological record (figure 6.3). We found a rich and complex history of a small hamlet that at various times during the past one hundred years had been used as a year-round community, a field house, and a seasonal farming village for Homol'ovi I (Adams 2001). We located and excavated four small kivas as well as a rectangular great kiva; uncovered evidence of turkey raising; located the first remains of adobe bricks; and discovered a cemetery containing macaws, turkeys, and neonates. The great kiva and one small kiva plus parts of several rooms had been burned. There were obvious signs of reuse and remodeling within the rooms and in the small complex plaza area.

There was abundant evidence of formal closure of structures and features through burning and burial. For example, the kiva at Homol'ovi III (structure 31), built about AD 1360, was used and decommissioned by the occupants of the farming village. When the kiva was no longer used, its roof was removed and whole or nearly whole objects sorted by material class were deposited in flat layers in the fill of this small structure. There was a layer of locally made pottery, a layer of ground stone, a layer of articulated animals, and so forth. These artifacts not only represented decisions made by people who used this kiva as to the proper way to terminate its use, but they also represented biographies of objects as viewed by those who used them.

Although I was now able to recognize these patterns, interpreting their meaning was more complicated. Help came from five sources: (1) the rich Hopi ethnographic record; (2) conversations with fellow anthropologists and archaeologists; (3) conversations with graduate students working at Homol'ovi; (4) frequent Hopi visitors to our fieldwork, including CRATT; and (5) conversations with Leigh. Fortunately for me, Leigh decided that I was hopelessly naive and needed intervention and a course correction and that my desire to go deeper into the religious record of ancient Hopi

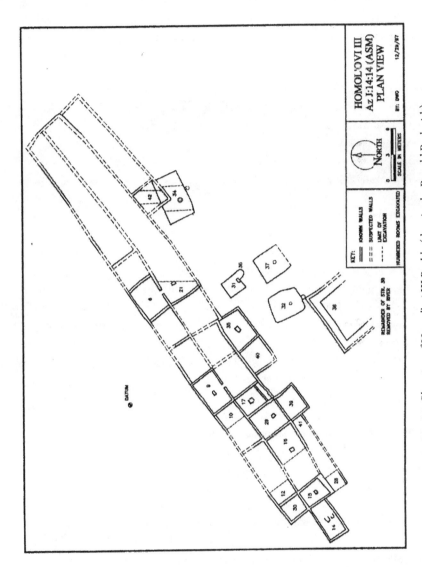

FIGURE 6.3 Plan view of Homol'ovi III Pueblo (drawing by Ronald Beckwith).

communities needed mentoring. Wesley Bernardini (2012) has recently shared aspects of Leigh's worldview. My experience with Leigh taught me about the source and purpose of Hopi knowledge, theories about the relationships between people of the past and present, ceremonies in the Third World and this world, and the essential need to maintain balance in and among all domains of human existence.

Today the project continues to focus on deposits and the formation of the archaeological record. One particularly noteworthy pattern observed at the Homol'ovi sites was the infusion of ash into deposits used to fill structures (Adams 2002, 2016a). Cross-culturally—including at Hopi—ash is associated with rituals of purification or protection (Parsons 1939; Titiev 1944; Whiteley 1998). For example, during two winters working at Wàlpi, I was marked with ash on my forehead to help protect me during Wuwtsim (Parsons 1939). Kiva ash and ash from the Hopi New Fire Ceremony (Fewkes 1900) at First Mesa were also carefully disposed in appropriate areas. These patterns indicate that ash was actively used in ritual contexts at Hopi and transformed into a sacred element.

In Homol'ovi villages, reminiscent of these Hopi rituals, ash was used to seal deposits, with many kivas used for ash disposal. Ash deposits at Homol'ovi are often associated with planned closure events as evidenced by accumulated ash cones created when a structure's roof was still intact (figure 6.4). Ash is also used when a structure is repurposed rather than closed (Adams 2016b; Adams and Fladd 2017; Fladd 2012). In either case, ash marks a change in the nature of the space. Finally, ash was deposited in structures in multiple ways. Evidence suggests that these structures were singularized due to their long-term roles in the history of the community, making them repositories of social memory. The manipulation of ash to form deposits and layers in these structures suggests that, as in Hopi practice today, ash was used to purify these spaces and to protect living members of the community.

My attempts to interpret Hopi history through the archaeological record, from the deep past to the present, have been made possible through the generosity of generations of Hopi people from all walks of life who have shared and encouraged me to attempt comparisons between the past and the present. Their mentoring reminds me of my primary responsibility as a teacher and mentor, which is to encourage all of my students to read and incorporate knowledge from ethnographic sources in their research at Homol'ovi. Many of my students have worked with Hopi or other descendent groups in their research. They are expected to share their publication, thesis, or dissertation with the HCPO, ideally in person. However, neither the HCPO nor any Hopi individual bears responsibility for the resulting interpretations. Finally, *kwakwha* (thank you) to Leigh, members of HCPO and CRATT, and others for your patience in teaching me over these past forty years,

FIGURE 6.4 Profile view of an ash cone in Kiva 901 from Chevelon (photo by E. Charles Adams).

REFERENCES CITED

Adams, E. Charles. 1978. Walpi Archaeological Project, Phase I. Manuscript on file, Museum of Northern Arizona, Flagstaff.

——. 1982. Walpi Archaeological Project: Synthesis and Interpretation. Manuscript on file, Arizona State Museum Library, Tucson.

——. 1984. Archaeology and the Native American: A Case at Hopi. In *Ethics and Values in Archaeology*, edited by Ernestine Green, pp. 236–242. Free Press, New York.

——. 2002. *Homol'ovi: An Ancient Hopi Settlement Cluster*. University of Arizona Press, Tucson.

——. 2008. What We Have Learned. In *Chevelon: Pueblo at Blue Running Water*, edited by E. Charles Adams, pp. 405–442. Manuscript on file, Homol'ovi Lab, Arizona State Museum, Tucson.

——. 2016. Closure and Dedication Practices in the Homol'ovi Settlement Cluster, Northeastern Arizona. *American Antiquity* 81:42–57.

Adams, E. Charles (editor). 2001. *Homol'ovi III: A Pueblo Hamlet in the Middle Little Colorado River Valley*. Arizona State Museum Archaeological Series 193. University of Arizona, Tucson.

Adams, E. Charles, and Samantha G. Fladd. 2017. Composition and Interpretation of Stratified Deposits in Ancestral Hopi Villages at Homol'ovi. *Archaeological and Anthropological Sciences* 9:1101–1114.

Adovasio, J. M., and R. L. Andrews. 1985. *Basketry and Miscellaneous Perishable Artifacts from Walpi Pueblo, Arizona*. Ethnology Monographs 7. University of Pittsburgh, Pittsburgh.

Ahlstrom, Richard V. N., Jeffrey S. Dean, and William J. Robinson. 1978. *Tree-Ring Studies of Walpi Pueblo*. Laboratory of Tree-Ring Research, University of Arizona, Tucson.

Bernardini, Wesley. 2012. North, South, and Center: An Outline of Hopi Ethnogenesis. In *Religious Transformation in the Late Pre-Hispanic Pueblo World*, edited by Donna M. Glowacki and Scott Van Keuren, pp. 196–220. University of Arizona Press, Tucson.

Fewkes, Jesse Walter. 1898. Preliminary Account of an Expedition to the Pueblo Ruins Near Winslow, Arizona, in 1896. *Annual Report for the Smithsonian Institution for 1896*, pp. 517–540. Smithsonian Institution, Washington, D.C.

——. 1900. New Fire Ceremony at Walpi. *American Anthropologist* 2:79–138.

——. 1904. Two Summers' Work in Pueblo Ruins. *Twenty-second Annual Report of the Bureau of American Ethnology for 1899–1900*, pp. 3–196. Smithsonian Institution, Washington, D.C.

Fladd, Samantha G. 2012. *Social Shifts and Structure Use: Population Movement at Homol'ovi I*. Master's thesis, School of Anthropology, University of Arizona, Tucson.

Greene, Ernestine (editor). 1984. *Ethics and Values in Archaeology*. Free Press, New York.

Parsons, Elsie Clews. 1939. *Pueblo Indian Religion*. 2 vols. University of Chicago Press, Chicago.

Titiev, Mischa. 1944. *Old Oraibi: A Study of the Hopi Indians of Third Mesa*. Papers of the Peabody Museum of American Archaeology and Ethnology, Vol. XXII(1). Harvard University, Cambridge, Massachusetts.

Whipple, Amiel Weeks. 1856. *Reports of Explorations and Surveys to Ascertain the Most Practicable and Economical Route for a Railroad from the Mississippi River to the Pacific Ocean*, Vol. 3. Government Printing Office, Washington, D.C.

Whiteley, Peter M. 1998. *Rethinking Hopi Ethnography*. Smithsonian Institution, Washington, D.C.

7

THE DAVIS RANCH SITE

A Kayenta Immigrant Enclave and
a Hopi Footprint in Southeastern Arizona

PATRICK D. LYONS

THINKING BACK ON my more than twenty years of working with tribal representatives, in the contexts of collaborative research and legally mandated consultation, one moment stands out as a powerful convergence of oral accounts of ancient migrations and the tangible evidence that comprises the archaeological record. In May 2002, as a participant in the San Pedro Ethnohistory Project, I witnessed the strong emotional response of Hopi research team member Harold Polingyumptewa (Sand Clan, Hotvela) to the remains of an excavated fourteenth-century kiva at the Davis Ranch Site, some 380 kilometers (236 miles) south of the Hopi Mesas (Ferguson and Colwell-Chanthaphonh 2006:125). All of the Hopi members of the research team said that they felt a special connection to the site, but Harold's reaction was palpable. He climbed down into the depression that used to be the kiva, sat down, and smoked while praying to his ancestors. Before climbing out, he sprinkled cornmeal.

Located in the San Pedro River Valley of southeastern Arizona, the Davis Ranch Site (AZ BB:11:7[AF]; AZ BB:11:36[ASM]) was excavated by Rex Gerald in 1957 under the auspices of the Amerind Foundation, and although a draft report was completed in 1958, the data have never been published. This site, as well as the nearby and contemporaneous Reeve Ruin (AZ BB:11:12[AF]; AZ BB:11:26[ASM]), yielded abundant and compelling evidence of immigrants from the Kayenta region of northeastern Arizona and southeastern Utah. Indeed, the evidence supporting a Kayenta presence at the Davis Ranch Site surpasses, both in quantity and quality, that recovered from the Maverick Mountain phase deposits at Point of Pines (the Southwest's classic case study of how to reliably infer ancient migrations; Haury 1958).

In this chapter, I report on a recently completed multiyear reanalysis of the Davis Ranch Site data. I also place the Davis Ranch Site—identified by Hopi colleagues as a *kúuku* (ancestral Hopi village; literally, footprint; Hopi Dictionary Project 1998:161, 820)—in the wider context of late-pre-Hispanic ancestral Hopi migrations and the Salado phenomenon (Lyons 2003; Lyons and Clark 2012; Lyons et al. 2011).

REX GERALD AND HIS EXCAVATIONS

Rex Ervin Gerald received his BA in anthropology from the University of Arizona in 1951 and his MA in anthropology from the University of Pennsylvania in 1957. He attended the University of Arizona Point of Pines Field School in 1946, 1948, 1949, and 1956. In 1957, he joined the staff of the Amerind Foundation, filling its "first and only" predoctoral research position (Fenner 1977:325). Gerald was to excavate the Davis Ranch Site—located across the San Pedro River from the Reeve Ruin, excavated by Charles Di Peso (1958) in 1956—and to publish the results (figure 7.1).

Gerald (1958b) finished a 238-page draft report of his excavations and analyses in 1958. Although bits and pieces of the data were disseminated (Burt 1961; Di Peso 1958; Gerald 1958a, 1975), the manuscript was never completed or published. Differences between Gerald's results and interpretations and Di Peso's expectations regarding the dating and cultural affiliation of the Davis Ranch Site (also see Gerald 1968) seemingly contributed to Gerald's departure from the Amerind Foundation in 1958 and his abandonment of the site report. In that same year, Gerald became director of the Centennial Museum at Texas Western College (now the University of Texas at El Paso). In 1975, Gerald was awarded a PhD in anthropology by the University of Chicago, based mainly on analyses of pollen and ceramics from the Davis Ranch Site and the Reeve Ruin.

THE DAVIS RANCH SITE REVISITED

I first became aware of Gerald's manuscript and the collections from the Davis Ranch Site in 1999 and visited the Amerind Foundation to examine both. In 2004, along with colleagues William J. Robinson and Gloria J. Fenner, I began a reanalysis of the collections. The goal was to complete Gerald's 1958 manuscript while placing his results in the larger context of what was currently known about Kayenta migration into the southern Southwest and the role that Kayenta immigrants played in the development and spread of Roosevelt Red Ware (Salado Polychrome pottery). In 2006, funding to support the reanalysis was generously provided by the Southwestern Foundation for Education and Historical Preservation.

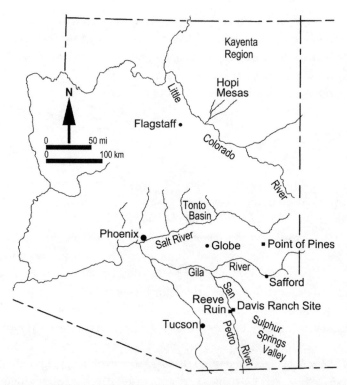

FIGURE 7.1 Map of Arizona showing the locations of archaeological sites and other places mentioned in the text. Base map drawn by Ronald J. Beckwith.

The Amerind Foundation curates the following documentary materials relevant to the project: a copy of Gerald's 1958 manuscript, his original field notebook, 200 black and white photographs (many duplicated as color slides), catalog cards for 236 artifacts, a catalog of 128 stone objects (many not curated), a 4- x 12-foot chart of sherd counts and percentages by type and provenience, the site map drafted for publication, files Gerald had in his possession at the time of his death (1990) that had been returned by the Centennial Museum, and correspondence relevant to the 1957 excavation and the original artifact analyses. The artifact collection available for study includes one hundred boxes of sherds; fifty whole, reconstructible, or partially reconstructible vessels identified by Gerald; flaked and ground stone tools; bone tools; shell; and other items. Also present at the Amerind Foundation are complete or partial sets of human remains representing twenty-one individuals.

As mentioned above, many items in the stone catalog were not kept, especially the larger objects, such as metates. At least one specialist report is missing. Hugh C.

Cutler of the Missouri Botanical Garden received ten or more macrobotanical items for identification. Correspondence indicates that Cutler examined the material, but a final report has not been located and the items apparently were not returned. Finally, pollen samples collected during the 1957 excavations were submitted to the Geochronology Laboratory at the University of Arizona for analysis and subsequently misplaced. As a result, Gerald returned to the site in 1965 to collect pollen from different proveniences. Field notes associated with this work have not yet been located. The 1965 samples were processed by James Schoenwetter (1965), who submitted a report to Gerald. The 1957 samples eventually resurfaced and were sent to Schoenwetter, but he was unable process them due to other commitments and returned them to Gerald in El Paso, where they later disappeared.

THE OCCUPATIONAL SEQUENCE AND ARCHITECTURAL REMAINS AT THE DAVIS RANCH SITE

The main occupation of the site occurred during the Hohokam Classic period, between ca. AD 1275/1300 and 1390, although evidence of much earlier components is present. Two shallow pit structures were most likely built and used during the Early Agricultural period (the San Pedro and Cienega phases, ca. 1200 BC–AD 150) and four pit structures probably date to the Hohokam Colonial period (AD 750–950)/ Sedentary period (AD 950–1150) transition. The Classic period component consists primarily of three architectural units listed here in stratigraphic order, from oldest to youngest: four pit houses and an associated kiva, a block of nine contiguous rooms, and a compound that later enclosed the room block and separated it from the kiva (figure 7.2). The compound has at least twenty-six rooms appended to its interior.

An isolated group of nine rooms is also present about 100 meters northeast of the compound and may represent, at least in part, an aborted attempt at Classic period platform mound construction. A three-room and a four-room unit lie within a few meters of the exterior of the southern compound wall. Their locations suggest that they postdate the compound wall, and their ephemeral nature, as well as their extremely small rooms (compared to those of the room block and the compound), suggest that they are not associated with the Classic period occupation.

Gerald excavated the kiva and twenty-one rooms, as well as ten pit houses, in their entirety and test-trenched another seventeen rooms and several extramural areas. He grouped pit houses based on shape, size, features, stratigraphy, horizontal spatial relationships, and ceramic associations, identifying four as Classic period structures

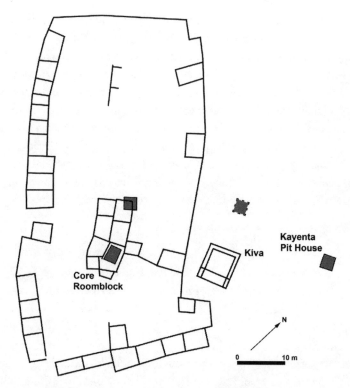

FIGURE 7.2 Map of the main Classic period component at the Davis Ranch Site. The shape of the pit house with the dashed outline is indeterminate.

and four as dating to the Colonial or Sedentary period. He did not place the last two houses, which are round, except to indicate that they predated the accumulation of trash rich in Maverick Mountain Series pottery (Lyons 2012, 2013) dating to the AD 1200s and 1300s as well as Colonial and Sedentary period Hohokam pottery dating from the late AD 700s to the mid-1100s.

THE REANALYSIS

Between 2004 and 2013, Fenner, Robinson, and I reexamined all the artifacts from the site as well as all the available documentary materials with the goal of adding the results of this reanalysis to Gerald's unfinished manuscript. We focused special attention on the decorated pottery from the site, which had been sorted by type, and sometimes by vessel part, rather than by provenience. After re-sorting the sherds and laying them out in trays by context, we embarked on an ambitious search for mends and matches in order to identify as many vessels as possible. The objectives were two-fold: to produce more meaningful counts than usually result from ceramic studies and to obtain as much stylistic information as possible so that intrasite chronological patterns might easily be discerned. Placing the site's architecture in comparative context and updating the typological information applied to flaked and ground stone tools were also priorities. This work continued through 2015 with the assistance of Claire S. Barker, Donna P. Cook, Samantha G. Fladd, and Jaye S. Smith.

As a result, it has been possible to make a number of inferences that Gerald could or did not. Among these are the presence of an Early Agricultural period occupation, the notion that a group of pit houses at the site was built and occupied by Kayenta immigrants who later built the pueblo (similar to what is documented at Point of Pines; see Haury 1958; Lindsay 1987), and the conclusion that the protohistoric Piman speakers of the San Pedro Valley—the Sobaipuri—briefly visited the site, perhaps on more than one occasion. The ceramic dating of the site's Classic period occupation has also been refined. Finally, Patricia Crown's (1994) seriation of Roosevelt Red Ware, based on styles of painted decoration, was tested and this powerful chronological tool was found to complement the vessel-form-based seriation that I later developed (Lyons 2004, 2013). These topics and others are addressed in a book currently under review (Lyons 2017).

THE EARLY AGRICULTURAL PERIOD OCCUPATION

Two shallow pit structures at the site were most likely built and used during the Early Agricultural period. As early as the 1940s, researchers had begun to recognize shallow, round or oval houses associated with the preceramic San Pedro phase (Sayles 1945:1–4), but the architecture of the Early Agricultural period (the San Pedro and Cienega phases) remained poorly understood until the 1980s and 1990s (Huckell 1995; Mabry 1998). Gerald's writings do not indicate whether he considered the possibility that the round houses at the Davis Ranch Site were preceramic.

Based on stratigraphic evidence, these houses must predate the deposit he referred to as the Northeast Trash and therefore should predate the pit houses occupied by those who generated this refuse. The absence of clearly associated artifacts hinders any attempt to assign a precise date to these structures. However, their size and shape, as well as the nature of their walls, suggest construction and use during the Early Agricultural period (see Huckell 1995:figure 3.8; Mabry 1998).

Furthermore, characteristic Early Agricultural period projectile points have been recovered from the site. Gerald had not identified them as preceramic or Early Ceramic period in age, even though one is an excellent example of the well-known San

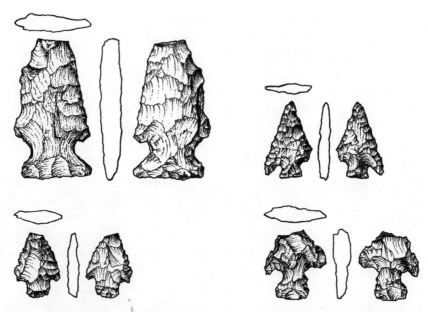

FIGURE 7.3 Top row (left to right): San Pedro Point (Amerind Foundation catalog no. D/93a; 4.5 cm long), Cienega Short Point (D/3b; 2.4 cm long). Bottom row (left to right): Cienega Stemmed Point (D/32; 2.1 cm long), Cienega Long Point (D/154g; 2.2 cm long). Drawings by Allen Denoyer.

Pedro Point (Sayles 1941:plate XVIc, d) and others, though not named until the 1980s, were known by the 1950s to postdate the San Pedro phase and predate the Hohokam and Mogollon sequences (e.g., Haury 1950, 1957; Martin et al. 1952). Three specimens were identified as Cienega Points (figure 7.3): one Cienega Short, one Cienega Long, and one Cienega Stemmed (Huckell 1988; Sliva 2005:95–98, figure 3.16). Additional evidence includes two fragments of knobbed stone trays. One was recovered from an intrusive pit in one of the round houses and the other was found near the same structure. Such objects are known to occur in Cienega phase contexts in the Tucson Basin and the Cienega Valley (Ferg 1998).

KAYENTA PIT HOUSES AND THE KIVA

The four Classic period pit houses form an arc around the kiva; the two that have intact hearths and whose orientation can be determined appear to face the kiva. Three of the four are square or nearly so and lack projecting lateral entryways. This form is dominant among late Kayenta pit houses (e.g., Geib 1985; Geib and Collette 2011; Harrill 1986; Schroedl 1989). The shape of the fourth could not be determined.

FIGURE 7.4 Newly identified, partially reconstructible perforated plate from the kiva at the Davis Ranch Site (Perforated Plate Vessel No. 1; 26-cm diameter). Photograph by Patrick D. Lyons, courtesy of the Amerind Foundation.

One of these pit houses is outfitted with a Kayenta entrybox (Ambler et al. 1964:24–25, figure 9; Dean 1981[1969]:27–28; Lindsay et al. 1968:7–8) and a partly slab-lined hearth, and another has a northern style slab-lined hearth. The third has a basin-shaped clay-lined hearth, and the floor features of the fourth were destroyed by subsequent construction activities. The floors of two of these structures yielded fragments of perforated plates (figure 7.4), and three had perforated plate fragments in their fill. One of these, however, was excavated in such a way that fill and floor contexts were not consistently distinguished as artifacts were recovered. Maverick Mountain Series pottery was recovered from the floors of three of these pit houses and was present in the fill deposits of all four. Perforated plates and Maverick Mountain Series pottery are telltale markers of Kayenta immigrants (Lindsay 1987; Lyons and Lindsay 2006). Together, these four pit houses and the kiva appear to represent the initial Kayenta occupation at the site.

The kiva at the Davis Ranch site is subterranean and nearly rectangular, being slightly constricted at the southern end (figure 7.5). It is outfitted with a raised platform

FIGURE 7.5 The kiva at the Davis Ranch Site. Photograph by Rex E. Gerald, courtesy of the Amerind Foundation.

on its southern end and benches along the east, north, and west walls. Floor features include a ventilator shaft that is L-shaped in cross-section, a deflector, a hearth, a pit that has been interpreted as a combination foot drum/sipapu, ladder holes, and at least four sets of loom-anchor holes. Its total area, including floor, platform, and benches, is nearly 50 m². This structure is similar in all respects to late pre-Hispanic kivas in the Kayenta region, on the Hopi Mesas, and in the Little Colorado River Valley.

The kiva was decommissioned in the mid AD 1300s. At this point, ritual deposits were left on the floor, including a concentration of eighty raptor bones representing the skulls, wings, legs, and feet of at least three red-tailed hawks and/or Swainson's hawks and one black hawk. The roof was then partially dismantled and collapsed. Later, domestic trash began to accumulate in the depression and eventually the kiva was reused as a cemetery. Ten individuals were interred there in six single burials and two multiple burials.

A SOBAIPURI PRESENCE

A handful of sherds of Whetstone Plain (Di Peso 1953:154–156; Masse 1980, 1981)—the pottery characteristic of the Sobaipuri—is present in the Davis Ranch Site assemblage, as are three Sobaipuri Points (Brew and Huckell 1987; Justice 2002:272–274;

Mabry 1999; Seymour 2009, 2011). Sobaipuri houses (oval to round, domed, brush huts with stone foundations) left very subtle traces in the archaeological record, but Amerind Foundation personnel had become adept at finding them, as demonstrated by Di Peso's (1953) excavations at Gaybanipitea (AZ EE:8:5[AF]; AZ EE:8:15[ASM], identified as Pitaitutgam by Seymour [1989]). Di Peso (1953:54) had been involved in the project at the Davis Ranch Site and had inferred that it represented the historic Sobaipuri village of Cusac, yet no diagnostic Sobaipuri architecture had been located. A later examination of the site by personnel from Archaeology Southwest (then the Center for Desert Archaeology) also failed to turn up any protohistoric houses (Clark and Lyons 2012).

CLASSIC PERIOD CERAMIC CHRONOLOGY

The reanalysis of the painted ceramics from the site, including more than 9,000 sherds and 20 whole, reconstructible, or partially reconstructible vessels of Roosevelt Red Ware and nearly 400 sherds and 4 whole vessels of Maverick Mountain Series types, has resulted in improved dating of the Classic period occupation. The presence of Pinto Polychrome, Pinto Black-on-red, Maverick Mountain Black-on-red, and Maverick Mountain Polychrome suggests an occupation beginning in the very late AD 1200s or the very early 1300s. The presence of the entire Roosevelt Red Ware stylistic sequence (as defined by Crown [1994]) indicates continued occupation through the late 1300s. Corroborating evidence is available in the form of recently defined Roosevelt Red Ware types: Cliff Polychrome, Nine Mile Polychrome, and Phoenix Polychrome (Lyons 2004, 2013). Cliff Polychrome initially appeared ca. 1360, whereas Nine Mile and Phoenix Polychrome have a start date of 1375. The apparent absence of later types, such as Los Muertos Polychrome, Dinwiddie Polychrome, and Cliff White-on-red, suggests that the Classic period occupation ended by about AD 1390.

ROOSEVELT RED WARE TYPOLOGICAL
AND STYLISTIC SERIATION

Because the burials within and near the kiva can be placed in stratigraphic sequence, and because many were associated with painted pottery vessels, a rare opportunity is available to evaluate the seriation of the newly defined Roosevelt Red Ware types (table 7.1). Burial 9 is the earliest in the kiva area, having been partly disturbed by and thus predating the kiva's construction. Funerary objects associated with this burial included two painted vessels: a Gila Polychrome bowl and a Tucson Polychrome jar. Burial 8, the second oldest stratigraphically speaking, was associated with two painted vessels, both Gila Polychrome bowls. Burial 5, next in the sequence, was interred with a

TABLE 7.1 Painted vessels associated with burials from within and near the kiva at the Davis Ranch Site in stratigraphic order (top row is most recent) and sorted by style, based on Crown (1994).

BURIAL	CATALOG NO.	TYPE	FORM	STYLE	STAGE
4	D/200	Phoenix Polychrome	bowl	Roosevelt	3
	D/203	Gila Polychrome	bowl	Roosevelt	3
	D/192	Gila Polychrome	jar	Pinedale	5
	D/193	Gila Polychrome: Salmon Variety	bowl	Pinedale	5
	D/201	Gila Polychrome	bowl	Pinedale	5
	D/202	Cliff Polychrome	bowl	Pinedale	5
	D/205	Cliff Polychrome	bowl	Pinedale	5
	D/196	Cliff Polychrome	bowl	Pinedale	4
	D/194	Gila Polychrome	bowl	Gila	—
5	D/207	Gila Polychrome	bowl	Gila	—
8	D/209	Gila Polychrome	bowl	Pinedale	5
	D/210	Gila Polychrome	bowl	Pinedale	5
9	D/214	Gila Polychrome	bowl	Roosevelt	1
	D/215	Tucson Polychrome	jar	—	—

single painted vessel, a Gila Polychrome bowl. The latest interment in the kiva, Burial 4, was accompanied by nine painted vessels: four Gila Polychrome bowls, three Cliff Polychrome bowls, one Phoenix Polychrome bowl, and one Gila Polychrome jar. The distribution of types just discussed is entirely consistent with the expectations of the typological seriation.

Other burials at the site associated with painted vessels provide corroborating evidence based on their stratigraphic relationships to architectural units such as the compound wall. Furthermore, the Roosevelt Red Ware stylistic seriation presented by Crown (1994:79–89) was found to be consistent with the stratigraphic sequence. The earliest interment is associated with a vessel painted in an early style (Roosevelt Style: Stage 1), those of medial age are associated with vessels painted in styles from the middle of the Roosevelt Red Ware sequence (Gila Style, and Pinedale Style: Stage 5), and the latest burial is associated with vessels painted in a style at the late end of the sequence (Roosevelt Style: Stage 3). This means that combining typological and stylistic data holds great potential for refining the chronology of sites throughout the southern Southwest with assemblages dominated by Roosevelt Red Ware.

THE DAVIS RANCH SITE IN THE
CONTEXT OF KAYENTA MIGRATIONS
AND THE SALADO PHENOMENON

The Davis Ranch Site is one of many in central and southern Arizona, as well as southwestern New Mexico, to yield abundant traces of immigrants from the Kayenta region and evidence linking these groups to both the origin and the spread of Roosevelt Red Ware—the ceramic component of the Salado phenomenon. This site is unique, however, in terms of the number of lines of evidence present. Architectural markers include the kiva, the occasional use of stacked-stone masonry, room block spatial organization, Kayenta entryboxes, slab-lined fireboxes, a mealing bin, and the use of high-altitude wood species for roofing. Ceramic indicators also abound, including perforated plates, Maverick Mountain Series types, a babe-in-cradle figurine, and palynological evidence of Rocky Mountain beeweed (presumably used as pottery paint; Schoenwetter 1965). Perhaps most important to linking Kayenta immigrants with the production of Roosevelt Red Ware is the fact that the site yielded examples of bowls combining aspects of the Maverick Mountain Series and Roosevelt Red Ware. Most of these exhibit interiors decorated in the manner of Roosevelt Red Ware and exteriors decorated in the style of Tucson Polychrome. Such vessels cover an impressive span of the Roosevelt Red Ware typological and chronological sequence, including specimens classifiable as Pinto Polychrome (early), Gila Polychrome (middle to late), and Cliff Polychrome (late).

The Davis Ranch Site's ground and flaked stone assemblages also bear witness to the origin of its inhabitants. Northern-style slab metates, faceted manos, manos with pecked finger-grips, grooved abraders, and shaft smoothers/straighteners are present, as is a Bull Creek Point characteristic of sites in northern Arizona (Justice 2002:268–270). Finally, four of the individuals interred in the kiva were buried in a flexed position, as were five individuals recovered from other parts of the site. Flexed inhumation was the dominant burial practice in the Kayenta region during the thirteenth century, immediately before depopulation (Lindsay 1969:386), and Classic period inhumations in southern Arizona are typically extended.

Excavations and analyses conducted between 1999 and 2012 by Archaeology Southwest (then the Center for Desert Archaeology) focused on twenty-nine Classic period sites in the Lower San Pedro Valley and provided an opportunity to place the Davis Ranch Site in comparative context (Clark and Lyons, 2012). This entailed new fieldwork at both the Davis Ranch Site and Reeve Ruin and illuminated strong patterns distinguishing the inhabitants of these sites and other suspected immigrant enclaves from local groups.

First and foremost, the Davis Ranch Site, Reeve Ruin, and nearby sites with architectural markers of Kayenta immigrants stand out from others in terms of the presence and abundance of perforated plates and Maverick Mountain Series types. Indeed, 94 percent of the perforated plates and more than 80 percent of the Maverick Mountain Series pottery recovered were found at these sites. In addition, the same sand tempers locally available to these groups were used to manufacture all of the perforated plates in the valley-wide sample, as well as 97 percent of the Maverick Mountain Series vessels and more than 80 percent of the Roosevelt Red Ware vessels. The immigrant inhabitants of the Davis Ranch Site produced much of the valley's Roosevelt Red Ware, supplying it to local groups, presumably in some sort of exchange relationship.

Kayenta enclaves in the San Pedro Valley are also distinguished by the presence of abundant raptor remains like those recovered from the kiva at the Davis Ranch Site, discussed above. This most likely reflects a greater need among immigrants for feathers, presumably used in the manufacture of prayer sticks and other objects used in rituals.

Equally notable is the fact that the Davis Ranch Site boasts by far the highest standardized count of obsidian in the valley (except for a site with a very small sherd sample). Indeed, use of obsidian in the San Pedro increased nearly twentyfold with the arrival of Kayenta groups during the Aravaipa phase (AD 1250/1275–1300/1325). Energy dispersive x-ray fluorescence sourcing of this material and regional distributional data indicate that virtually all of it came into the valley through relationships among Kayenta immigrants in the San Pedro and Kayenta immigrants who settled near obsidian sources in the Safford Basin and the Mule Creek area (Clark et al. 2012). This, as well as the striking consistency of Roosevelt Red Ware (in terms of shape, technology, and painted decoration), is evidence of a network linking dispersed enclaves of northerners and their descendants—an indication that we can model the dynamics of Kayenta migration and the development of Roosevelt Red Ware pottery through reference to the process of diaspora (Lyons and Clark 2012).

THE DAVIS RANCH SITE AS A HOPI FOOTPRINT

Leigh J. Kuwanwisiwma and T. J. Ferguson (2004:26) define *footprints* as "monuments that provide proof of ancestral [Hopi] migration and land stewardship" and include among them archaeological sites, petroglyphs and pictographs, pottery, stone tools, and other objects left as offerings (also see Kuwanwisiwma and Ferguson 2009). The Davis Ranch Site, as a result of having been included in the San Pedro Ethnohistory Project (Ferguson and Colwell-Chanthaphonh 2006), has been identified by Hopi research team members as a footprint. Hopi colleagues who visited the site and examined the excavated collections made this identification and placed the pueblo in the context of Hopi oral accounts describing ancient migrations, in part through reference to *navoti* (historical understandings transmitted from generation to generation).

As discussed above, the Hopi members of the research team perceived a strong relationship between themselves and the inhabitants of the Davis Ranch Site and Reeve Ruin. Our colleagues pointed to the masonry architecture, kivas, and Roosevelt Red Ware found at these sites, as well as the large expanses of land available nearby for agriculture, as indicators of a connection between themselves and Hopi ancestors who, they deduced, once lived there (Ferguson and Colwell-Chanthaphonh 2006:123–146). Paralleling the inferences of archaeologists, and based on *navoti*, they concluded that kivas in southern Arizona are an indication of the presence of Hopi ancestors who came to the San Pedro from the north. This, they reported, was because Hopi ancestors lacked kivas during their early migrations in the south; these groups acquired kivas in the north. They also noted important similarities (in terms of shapes, colors, and painted motifs) among Hopi pottery, Kayenta pottery, and Roosevelt Red Ware.

Wiimi (sacred objects and knowledge associated with their use) was also employed in the process of identifying the Davis Ranch Site as a footprint. Because of the sensitive nature of many aspects of Hopi sacred knowledge, much could not be shared in the context of the ethnohistory study. Nonetheless, pigments and other items from the site—some of which had been recovered from the kiva or from burials—were identified as examples of substances and objects used in religious practices linking the people of the Davis Ranch Site and the Hopi people of the present day.

SUMMARY AND CONCLUSION

The Davis Ranch Site was a "persistent place" utilized by many different groups over the centuries, during the Early Agricultural period, the Hohokam Colonial/Sedentary transition, the Hohokam Classic period, and the Protohistoric period. Occupation and use of this location were likely related to its hydrology—near the confluence of Buehman Canyon, Redfield Canyon, and the San Pedro River, and downstream from "the narrows," where bedrock forces the water table upward.

Investigation of the main occupation of the site, the Classic period component, produced evidence of immigrants from the Kayenta region in the form of architectural traits and features, aspects of ceramic technological style and decorative style, flaked and ground stone tools, burial traditions, and patterns of faunal exploitation and obsidian procurement quite different from those associated with sites in the valley inhabited by long-time participants in the Hohokam regional system. Pottery from the Davis Ranch Site and evidence of its local production clearly tie Kayenta immigrants to the origin and spread of Roosevelt Red Ware. Indeed, if Salado studies had begun in southeastern rather than central Arizona—in the context of the record from the San Pedro Valley, the Aravaipa Valley, the Sulphur Springs Valley, and the Safford Basin, rather than the Globe-Miami area and the Tonto and Phoenix basins—the Salado phenomenon would not be nearly so puzzling to archaeologists as it has been. There would have been a notion of a Salado "heartland" south of the Gila rather than north of the Salt (Lyons and Lindsay 2006).

The ceramic assemblage at the Davis Ranch Site is also important on a regional scale because it lends strong support to Crown's (1994) Roosevelt Red Ware stylistic seriation. Combining these styles with recent refinements to Roosevelt Red Ware typology holds great promise for increasing temporal resolution in central and southern Arizona, southwestern New Mexico, northern Sonora, and northern Chihuahua. Future investigations focused on Crown's (1994) styles and the regional differences that developed in the Roosevelt Red Ware tradition just before its end (ca. 1450) will likely shed more light on ancestral Hopi migrations and provide better ways for researchers to bridge archaeology and Hopi oral tradition.

Finally, recent ethnohistorical research at the site and with its collections has resulted in Hopi collaborators identifying the Davis Ranch Site as an ancestral village, a place that Hopi ancestors passed through during their migrations before arriving at the Hopi Mesas. The links identified by archaeologists and our Hopi colleagues, binding archaeological constructs such as Kayenta Anasazi and Salado to real people (groups of Hopi ancestors and the present-day Hopi people), call attention to challenges and opportunities in research on the Salado phenomenon and ancestral Hopi migrations, as well as determinations of cultural affiliation pursuant to the Native American Graves Protection and Repatriation Act (Dongoske et al. 1993, 1997; Ferguson 2003; Ferguson and Loma'omvaya 1999).

REFERENCES CITED

Ambler, J. Richard, Alexander J. Lindsay Jr., and Mary Anne Stein. 1964. *Survey and Excavations on Cummings Mesa, Arizona and Utah, 1960–1961*. Glen Canyon Series No. 5. Museum of Northern Arizona Bulletin No. 39. Northern Arizona Society of Science and Art, Flagstaff.

Brew, Susan A., and Bruce B. Huckell. 1987. A Protohistoric Piman Burial and a Consideration of Piman Burial Practices. *The Kiva* 52(3):163–191.

Burt, William H. 1961. A Fauna from an Indian Site near Redington, Arizona. *Journal of Mammalogy* 42(1):115–116.

Clark, Jeffery J., and Patrick D. Lyons. 2012. How, Where, and What We Excavated. In *Migrants and Mounds: Classic Period Archaeology of the Lower San Pedro Valley*, edited by Jeffery J.

Clark and Patrick D. Lyons, pp. 67–210. Anthropological Papers No. 45. Archaeology Southwest, Tucson.

Clark, Jeffery J., and Patrick D. Lyons (editors). 2012. *Migrants and Mounds: Classic Period Archaeology of the Lower San Pedro Valley*. Anthropological Papers No. 45. Archaeology Southwest, Tucson.

Clark, Jeffery J., Patrick D. Lyons, J. Brett Hill, Stacey Lengyel, and Mark Slaughter. 2012. Of Migrants and Mounds. In *Migrants and Mounds: Classic Period Archaeology of the Lower San Pedro Valley*, edited by Jeffery J. Clark and Patrick D. Lyons, pp. 345–405. Anthropological Papers No. 45. Archaeology Southwest, Tucson.

Crown, Patricia L. 1994. *Ceramics and Ideology: Salado Polychrome Pottery*. University of New Mexico Press, Albuquerque.

Dean, Jeffrey S. 1981 [1969]. *Chronological Analysis of Tsegi Phase Sites in Northeastern Arizona*. Papers of the Laboratory of Tree-Ring Research No. 3. Second printing. Laboratory of Tree-Ring Research, University of Arizona, Tucson.

Di Peso, Charles C. 1953. *The Sobaipuri Indians of the Upper San Pedro River Valley, Southeastern Arizona*. Amerind Foundation No. 6. Dragoon, Arizona.

———. 1958. *The Reeve Ruin of Southeastern Arizona: A Study of a Prehistoric Western Pueblo Migration into the Middle San Pedro Valley*. Amerind Foundation No. 8. Dragoon, Arizona.

Dongoske, Kurt, Leigh Jenkins, and T. J. Ferguson. 1993. Understanding the Past Through Hopi Oral History. *Native Peoples* 6(2):24–31.

Dongoske, Kurt E., Michael Yeatts, Roger Anyon, and T. J. Ferguson. 1997. Archaeological Cultures and Cultural Affiliation: Hopi and Zuni Perspectives in the American Southwest. *American Antiquity* 62(4):600–608.

Fenner, Gloria J. 1977. History and Scope of the Amerind Foundation. *The Kiva* 42(3–4):317–329.

Ferg, Alan. 1998. Rare Stone, Fired Clay, Bone, and Shell Artifacts. In *Archaeological Investigations of Early Village Sites in the Middle Santa Cruz Valley: Analyses and Synthesis, Part II*, edited by Jonathan B. Mabry, pp. 545–654. Anthropological Papers No. 19. Center for Desert Archaeology, Tucson, Arizona.

Ferguson, T. J. 2003. Anthropological Archaeology Conducted by Tribes: Traditional Cultural Properties and Cultural Affiliation. In *Archaeology Is Anthropology*, edited by Susan D. Gillespie and Deborah L. Nichols, pp. 137–144. Archaeological Papers of the American Anthropological Association No. 13. American Anthropological Association, Washington, D.C.

Ferguson, T. J., and Chip Colwell-Chanthaphonh. 2006. *History Is in the Land: Multivocal Tribal Traditions in Arizona's San Pedro Valley*. University of Arizona Press, Tucson.

Ferguson, T. J., and Micah Loma'omvaya. 1999. *Hoopoq'yaqam niqw Wukoskavi (Those Who Went to the Northeast and Tonto Basin)*. Hopi Cultural Preservation Office, Kiqötsmovi, Arizona.

Geib, Phil R. 1985. Site Descriptions. In *Archaeological Investigations Near Rainbow City, Navajo Mountain, Utah*, edited by Phil R. Geib, J. Richard Ambler, and Martha M.

Callahan, pp. 69–240. Archaeological Reports No. 576. Northern Arizona University, Flagstaff.

Geib, Phil R., and Jim Collette. 2011. Summary and Interpretation of Puebloan Remains. In *Foragers and Farmers of the Northern Kayenta Region: Excavations Along the Navajo Mountain Road* by Phil R. Geib, pp. 290–373. University of Utah Press, Salt Lake City.

Gerald, Rex E. 1958a. A Pueblo Kiva in Southeastern Arizona. Paper presented at the 23rd Annual Meeting of the Society for American Archaeology, Norman, Oklahoma.

———. 1958b. Davis Ranch Site (Arizona BB:11:7): A Prehistoric Pueblo in Southeastern Arizona. Manuscript on file, Amerind Foundation, Dragoon, Arizona.

———. 1968. *Spanish Presidios of the Late Eighteenth Century in Northern New Spain.* Museum of New Mexico Research Records No. 7. Museum of New Mexico Press, Santa Fe.

———. 1975. *Drought Correlated Changes in Two Prehistoric Pueblo Communities in Southeastern Arizona.* PhD dissertation, Department of Anthropology, University of Chicago, Chicago. ProQuest, Ann Arbor, Michigan.

Harrill, Bruce. 1986. Architecture. In *The Kayenta Anasazi: Archaeological Investigations Along the Black Mesa Railroad Corridor, Vol. 1: Specialists' Reports* by Sara Stebbins, Bruce Harrill, William D. Wade, Marsha V. Gallagher, Hugh Cutler, and Leonard Blake, pp. 71–87. Research Paper No. 30. Museum of Northern Arizona, Flagstaff.

Haury, Emil W. 1950. *The Stratigraphy and Archaeology of Ventana Cave.* University of Arizona Press, Tucson.

———. 1957. An Alluvial Site on the San Carlos Indian Reservation, Arizona. *American Antiquity* 23(1):2–27.

———. 1958. Evidence at Point of Pines for a Prehistoric Migration from Northern Arizona. In *Migrations in New World Culture History*, edited by Raymond H. Thompson, pp. 1–6. University of Arizona Bulletin 29(2). Social Science Bulletin No. 27. University of Arizona Press, Tucson.

Hopi Dictionary Project. 1998. *Hopi Dictionary/Hopìikwa Lavàytutuveni: A Hopi-English Dictionary of the Third Mesa Dialect.* University of Arizona Press, Tucson.

Huckell, Bruce B. 1988. Late Archaic Archaeology of the Tucson Basin: A Status Report. In *Recent Research on Tucson Basin Prehistory*, edited by William H. Doelle and Paul R. Fish, pp. 57–80. Anthropological Papers No. 10. Institute for American Research, Tucson. Arizona.

———. 1995. *Of Marshes and Maize: Preceramic Agricultural Settlements in the Cienega Valley, Southeastern Arizona.* Anthropological Papers of the University of Arizona No. 59. University of Arizona Press, Tucson.

Justice, Noel D. 2002. *Stone Age Spear and Arrow Points of the Southwestern United States.* Indiana University Press, Bloomington.

Kuwanwisiwma, Leigh J., and T. J. Ferguson. 2004. Ang Kuktota: Hopi Ancestral Sites and Cultural Landscapes. *Expedition* 46(2):25–29

————. 2009. *Hopitutskwa* and *Ang Kuktota*: The Role of Archaeological Sites in Defining Hopi Cultural Landscapes. In *The Archaeology of Meaningful Places*, edited by Brenda J. Bowser and María Nieves Zedeño, pp. 90–106. University of Utah Press, Salt Lake City.

Lindsay, Alexander J. 1969. *The Tsegi Phase of the Kayenta Cultural Tradition in Northeastern Arizona*. PhD dissertation, Department of Anthropology, University of Arizona, Tucson.

————. 1987. Anasazi Population Movements to Southeastern Arizona. *American Archaeology* 6(3):190–198.

Lindsay, Alexander J. Jr., J. Richard Ambler, Mary Anne Stein, and Philip M. Hobler. 1968. *Survey and Excavations North and East of Navajo Mountain, Utah, 1959–1962*. Museum of Northern Arizona Bulletin No. 45. Glen Canyon Series No. 8. Northern Arizona Society of Science and Art, Flagstaff.

Lyons, Patrick D. 2003. *Ancestral Hopi Migrations*. Anthropological Papers of the University of Arizona No. 68. University of Arizona Press, Tucson.

————. 2004. Cliff Polychrome. *Kiva* 69(4):361–400.

————. 2012. Ceramic Typology, Chronology, Production, and Circulation. In *Migrants and Mounds: Classic Period Archaeology of the Lower San Pedro Valley*, edited by Jeffery J. Clark and Patrick D. Lyons, pp. 211–308. Anthropological Papers No. 45. Archaeology Southwest, Tucson.

————. 2013. "By Their Fruits Ye Shall Know Them": The Pottery of Kinishba Revisited. In *Kinishba Lost and Found: Mid-Century Excavations and Contemporary Perspectives*, edited by John R. Welch, pp. 145–208. Arizona State Museum Archaeological Series No. 206. University of Arizona, Tucson.

Lyons, Patrick D. (editor). 2017. The Davis Ranch Site: Rex E. Gerald's Excavations at a Kayenta Immigrant Enclave in the Lower San Pedro River Valley, Southeastern Arizona. Submitted to the University of Arizona Press, Tucson.

Lyons, Patrick D., and Jeffery J. Clark. 2012. A Community of Practice in Diaspora: The Rise and Demise of Roosevelt Red Ware. In *Potters and Communities of Practice: Glaze Paint and Polychrome Pottery in the American Southwest A.D. 1250–1700*, edited by Linda S. Cordell and Judith Habicht-Mauche, pp. 19–33. Anthropological Papers of the University of Arizona No. 75. University of Arizona Press, Tucson.

Lyons, Patrick D., J. Brett Hill, and Jeffery J. Clark. 2011. Irrigation Communities and Communities in Diaspora. In *Movement, Connectivity, and Landscape Change in the Ancient Southwest: The 20th Anniversary Southwest Symposium*, edited by Margaret C. Nelson and Colleen Strawhacker, pp. 375–401. University Press of Colorado, Boulder.

Lyons, Patrick D., and Alexander J. Lindsay, Jr. 2006. Perforated Plates and the Salado Phenomenon. *Kiva* 72(1):5–54.

Mabry, Jonathan B. 1998. Architectural Variability and Site Structures. In *Archaeological Investigations of Early Village Sites in the Middle Santa Cruz Valley: Analyses and Synthesis*, edited

by Jonathan Mabry, pp. 209–243. Anthropological Papers No. 19. Center for Desert Archaeology, Tucson.

———. 1999. A Rare Glimpse of the Sobaipuri from Colossal Cave. *Archaeology Southwest*
13(4):11.

Martin, Paul S., John B. Rinaldo, Elaine A. Bluhm, Hugh C. Cutler, and Roger Grange Jr.
1952. *Mogollon Cultural Continuity and Change: The Stratigraphic Analysis of Tularosa and
Cordova Caves*. Fieldiana, Anthropology 40. Chicago Natural History Museum, Chicago.

Masse, W. Bruce. 1980. The Sobaipuri Occupation at Alder Wash Ruin. In *The Peppersauce
Wash Project: Excavations at Three Multicomponent Sites in the Lower San Pedro Valley,
Arizona*, by W. Bruce Masse, edited by Gayle G. Hartmann, pp. 243–264. Arizona State
Museum Contribution to Highway Salvage Archaeology in Arizona No. 53. Manuscript on
file, Arizona State Museum Archives, University of Arizona, Tucson.

———. 1981. A Reappraisal of the Protohistoric Sobaipuri Indians of Southeastern Arizona.
In *The Protohistoric Period in the North American Southwest, A.D. 1450–1700*, edited by
David R. Wilcox and W. Bruce Masse, pp. 28–56. Arizona State University Anthropological
Research Papers No. 24. Arizona State University, Tempe.

Sayles, E. B. 1941. Archaeology of the Cochise Culture. In *The Cochise Culture*, by E. B. Sayles
and Ernst Antevs, pp. 1–30. Medallion Papers No. 29. Gila Pueblo, Globe, Arizona.

———. 1945. *The San Simon Branch, Excavations at Cave Creek and in the San Simon Valley*,
Vol. I: Material Culture. Medallion Papers No. 34. Gila Pueblo, Globe, Arizona.

Schoenwetter, James. 1965. Pollen Studies at Reeve Ruin and the Davis Ranch Site: Preliminary Report. Electronic document, http://hdl.handle.net/2286/qop6qzehopz, accessed
January 10, 2014.

Schroedl, Alan R. (editor). 1989. *Kayenta Anasazi Archaeology and Navajo Ethnohistory on the
Northwest Shonto Plateau: The N-16 Project*. 2 vols. Cultural Resources Report No. 412–01–
8909. P-III Associates, Salt Lake City.

Seymour, Deni J. 1989. The Dynamics of Sobaipuri Settlement in the Eastern Pimería Alta.
Journal of the Southwest 31(2):205–222.

———. 2009. The Canutillo Complex: Evidence of Protohistoric Mobile Occupants in the
Southern Southwest. *Kiva* 74(4):421–446.

———. 2011. *Where the Earth and Sky Are Sewn Together: Sobaipuri-O'odham Contexts of Contact and Colonialism*. University of Utah Press, Salt Lake City.

Sliva, R. Jane. 2005. Developments in Flaked Stone Technology During the Transition to Agri-
culture. In *Material Cultures and Lifeways of Early Agricultural Communities in Southern
Arizona*, edited by R. Jane Sliva, pp. 47–98. Anthropological Papers No. 35. Center for
Desert Archaeology, Tucson.

8

BECOMING HOPI

*Exploring Hopi Ethnogenesis through Architecture,
Pottery, and Cultural Knowledge*

KELLEY HAYS-GILPIN AND DENNIS GILPIN

W E HAVE WORKED with Leigh Kuwanwisiwma and other Hopi cultural experts for more than twenty years on projects ranging from cultural resource management to museum exhibits to repatriation. Our collaborative relationships transformed our archaeological practice and understandings of the past. We find common ground in studying the distributions of pottery and architectural features in the light of traditional Hopi knowledge and clan stories. In this chapter, we will focus on three large pueblos excavated in the late nineteenth and early twentieth centuries: Sikyatki, Awat'ovi, and Kawàyka'a. Taken together, archaeological evidence, traditional knowledge, and clan stories reveal diverse and far-flung geographic and cultural origins of Hopi ancestors. Further, Hopi cultural meanings expressed in historic architecture contribute to deeper levels of knowledge about ancient sites and buildings.

In the late nineteenth century, Smithsonian anthropologist Jesse Walter Fewkes excavated a large pueblo site near First Mesa (Fewkes 1893, 1896, 1898, 1919). He called the site and an associated pottery style Sikyatki (cut canyon). The "cuts" are erosional features in the edge and side of First Mesa, which towers above the ancient village. Like most Southwestern archaeologists, we had read Fewkes's reports and had seen hundreds of examples of Sikyatki Polychrome pottery long before we saw the site itself. One Sunday morning in 1994, Leigh Kuwanwisiwma asked, "Do you want to go to Sikyatki? I have a group visiting from Crow Canyon Archaeology Center and am meeting them in a couple of hours." We eagerly accepted Leigh's invitation and hurried to First Mesa. Touring Sikyatki with Leigh, we gained a perspective that we have tried to incorporate into our collaborative work in archaeology and museology.

We kept collaboration in mind when, more than fifteen years ago, we began work-ing with records and artifacts from another historic archaeological project on Hopi land—the Harvard Peabody Museum's Awat'ovi Expedition of the 1930s (Brew 1937, 1939, 1941, 1942, 1949, 1952, 1971, 1980, 1994). Around 2000, the Harvard Peabody Museum, Museum of Northern Arizona (MNA), and the Hopi Tribe began working on what was meant to be a comprehensive study of kiva mural paintings in the South-west, with a focus on the original mural fragments and field reproductions from the Awat'ovi Expedition that have been shared by the two museums for many decades but rarely studied or displayed.

Leigh and his staff at the Hopi Cultural Preservation Office said that Hopi inter-ests lay in studying cultural affiliation and clan migrations and in finding out more about Hopi collections in non-Hopi museums for the purposes of future repatria-tion. The Peabody was interested in scholarly publications, and the MNA at that time wanted a blockbuster international traveling exhibit. Kelley Hays-Gilpin joined the project to study associated painted ceramics, and Dennis Gilpin joined as an archi-tecture specialist. The museum exhibit never materialized, but mural fragments at the Peabody and the MNA received conservation treatment, several publications were produced (Hays-Gilpin and Schaafsma 2010; Sekaquaptewa and Washburn 2004, 2009), and the project continues as the Hopi Iconography Project. Operating under a memorandum of understanding between the Hopi Tribe and the MNA, the Hopi Iconography Project focuses on research about cultural affiliation and migrations; Hopi ethnogenesis; and explanation of Hopi history, values, and aesthetics to broad audiences through exhibits and popular publications such as *Plateau* (Hays-Gilpin 2006). The Peabody is still pursuing scholarly publications, including Gilpin's (2014) draft monograph on the indigenous architecture of Awat'ovi.

Hopi oral traditions explain how people from different geographic regions, who spoke different languages, came together to become Hopi by submitting to a covenant to live by certain values, including Earth stewardship, hard work, and humility, as explored in detail by Bernardini (2005, 2009). Anthropologists call this process of becoming an ethic group *ethnogenesis*, defined as the way social groups establish dis-tinctiveness (Ferguson et al. 2016:109; Sturtevant 1971). In exploring the relationship between present-day Hopi and the ancient Hohokam of southern Arizona, Ferguson and colleagues show that the Hopi trace their shared identity with all of the archaeo-logical cultures in which their ancestors participated before migrating to Hopi. Thus, the Hopi conform to a reticulated model of ethnogenesis, which they illustrate as a braided stream of development as opposed to a branching development: "In this [reticulated] model, local traditions are linked together by crosscutting ties of contact, diffusion, borrowing, and human movement. In the reticulated model, ethnic groups reorganize themselves so that each new group is rooted in several antecedent societies" (Ferguson et al. 2016:110).

In this chapter we will describe archaeological and historical information about three specific ancestral Hopi sites (figure 8.1) and discuss evidence of Hopi roots in several antecedent cultures including New Mexico Pueblos. We will then explore how some key Hopi values are expressed in architecture and discuss how submitting to a set of common values is key to "becoming Hopi," that is, ethnogenesis.

SIKYATKI

What archaeologists see on approaching Sikyatki is a high rubble mound that appears to have been a multistoried masonry pueblo located on a natural rise, overlooking a broad plaza completely enclosed by continuous room blocks (figure 8.2). Rock alignments in the plaza appear on Fewkes's map (1896:plate 49, 1898:plate 116) as historic garden features. Apparently, nineteenth-century farmers took advantage of moisture retained in the bowl-shaped plaza. In our 1994 inspection of the site, we observed coal-fired yellow ware pottery, including Sikyatki Polychrome, all in a style that dates to the fifteenth century. We did not see any fourteenth-century yellow ware pottery like that we know well from Homol'ovi. We did not see any Mission period (AD 1629–1680) pottery like that we see at Awat'ovi. We did see Little Colorado White Ware sherds, especially Walnut Black-on-white. When Leigh Kuwanwisiwma asked us what we saw, we replied that "the pottery here suggests that people lived here in the late AD 1100s through mid-1200s, and had connections to the south. We do not see any evidence of people living here in the 1300s. Sometime in the 1400s, the big pueblo was built, and probably was occupied only about a century."

Leigh said that our assessment was correct and named the clans who had migrated north from the Hopi Buttes to the Hopi Mesas to settle at Sikyatki, where they lived for a few generations. Then they were admitted to the village of Wàlpi, only a short distance to the south. After moving to Wàlpi, they retained farming and water rights at Sikyatki. After a while, some migrating Kokop and Coyote clan people from somewhere to the east settled at Sikyatki and built the large pueblo. Due to Wàlpi's previous claims on the site, tensions built between Sikyatki and Wàlpi until armed conflict erupted. Wàlpi prevailed and Sikyatki's inhabitants moved on, probably joining other villages.

The Wàlpi people used the plaza for gardens and sometimes as a cemetery. Then Fewkes came along, with permission from the federal government to excavate for pottery and other artifacts to fill the Smithsonian museum. Fewkes recorded some

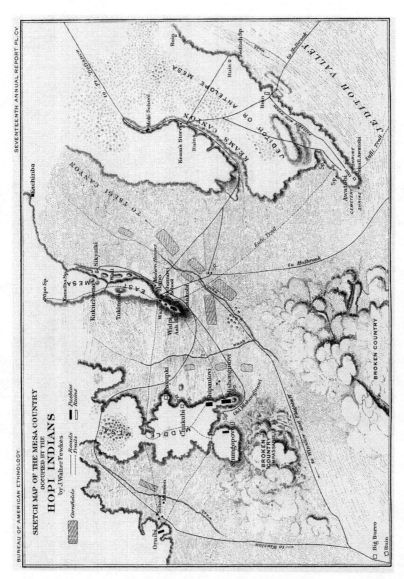

BUREAU OF AMERICAN ETHNOLOGY

SKETCH MAP OF THE MESA COUNTRY
OCCUPIED BY THE
HOPI INDIANS
by J. Walter Fewkes

SEVENTEENTH ANNUAL REPORT PL. CV

FIGURE 8.1 Location of Sikyatki and Awat'ovi (after Fewkes 1898: Plate 105). Kawáyka'a is located 5 km (3 mi.) northeast of Awat'ovi.

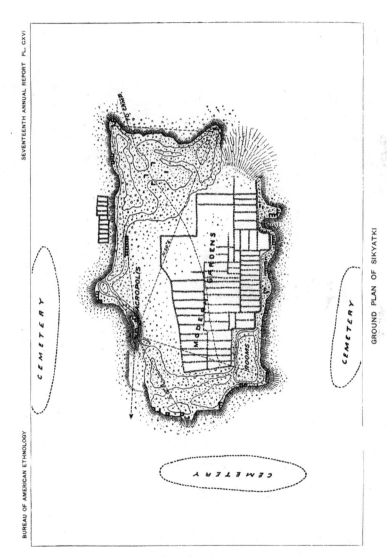

GROUND PLAN OF SIKYATKI

FIGURE 8.2 Plan of Sikyatki (after Fewkes 1898:plate 116).

minimal oral history about the site: "The founders of Sikyatki are said in very cir-cumstantial migration legends, to have belonged to a [Keres?] clan called the Kokop, or Firewood, which previously lived in a pueblo near Jemez, New Mexico" (Fewkes 1919:218; brackets and question mark in the original).

Thus, oral traditions that recount arrival of clans from the Hopi Buttes are mani-fested in the archaeological record by Little Colorado White Ware pottery dating to the late 1100s–1200s. Later occupants came from near Jemez, which archaeologists might take to mean a Towa-speaking group or practitioners of a ceremonial complex with northern Rio Grande origins. Alternately, as Fewkes indicated, these later set-tlers might have been Keresan speakers from the Rio Grande. Sikyatki's mound and enclosed plaza suggest connections to the east as well. Sikyatki-style pottery is dis-tinctive and probably developed locally at Hopi with influences from the upper Little Colorado and possibly Rio Grande areas. Technology is distinctively local (yellow, coal-fired, characteristic shapes; see Hays-Gilpin 2013 for details), but its iconography (imagery) reflects concepts throughout the fifteenth-century Pueblo world—birds, feathers, flowers, clouds, game animals, and *katsinas* (Hays-Gilpin and LeBlanc 2007).

KAWÀYKA'A

Kawàyka'a (a Keresan word meaning lake people) is a large pueblo located on Ante-lope Mesa, on the eastern edge of the Hopi reservation. Its name refers today to Laguna Pueblo, and Hopi oral traditions suggest that Keresan was spoken there. The Harvard Peabody Awatovi Expedition excavated painted kiva murals here, and many Hopi consultants have identified the mural styles as eastern Pueblo. Kawàyka'a has a foundational pottery complex that dates to the AD 1200s. This complex comes from both Kayenta traditions (Tusayan White Ware, Tsegi Orange Ware, and Tusayan Gray Ware) and varieties of White Mountain Red Ware (Kintiel-Klagetoh Polychrome) and Cibola White Ware (Klagetoh Black-on-white) produced in the Ganado area to the southeast in sites such as Wide Ruins (Kintiel). Kawàyka'a was apparently depop-ulated in or before AD 1540 or as a result of conflict with a party of Spaniards from the Coronado expedition (Brew 1949:5–7; Hammond and Rey 1929:footnote 101; Hammond and Rey 1966: footnote 76; Hargrave 1935; Reed 1942).

The earliest building at Kawàyka'a (figure 8.3), in the southern quarter of the site, is a large rectangular building measuring 100 m by 65 m with a completely enclosed plaza, much like Sikyatki as well as earlier sites to the east of the Hopi Mesas such as Bear Springs (Gilpin 1989), Pine Springs Wash (Gilpin 1989), Many Farms (Gilpin 1989), Wide Reed Ruin (Mount et al. 1993), Atsinna (Bradford 2013:figure 39), North Atsinna (Bradford 2013:figure 35), one of the Salina Springs room blocks (Gilpin

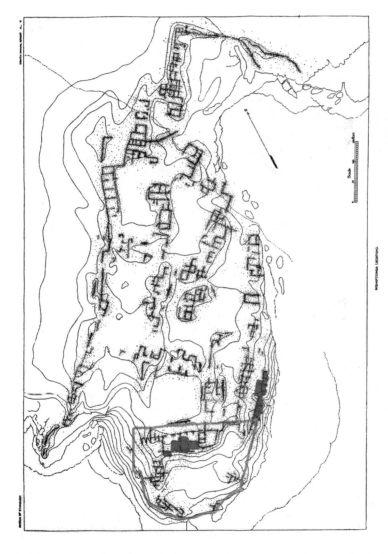

FIGURE 8.3 Plan of Kawàyka'a (after Mindeleff 1891 [1989]:plate 9), with earliest building outlined and excavated kivas highlighted.

1989), and one of the Cornfields room blocks (Gilpin 1989). These earlier sites all have certain architectural attributes that seem to derive from Chacoan architecture. Following the Manuelito Model of post-Chacoan architectural development proposed by Fowler and colleagues (1987; Fowler and Stein 1992) Chacoan great houses were superseded by post-Chacoan buildings with plazas fully enclosed by a row of rooms, which in turn were superseded by pueblos with plazas fully enclosed by room blocks.

Among the Chacoan architectural attributes are the completely enclosed plaza plan, which required planning the building as a whole, and the ladder (or spine) construction of the building. Ladder (or spine) construction entailed building long continuous parallel walls to enclose long corridors that were subdivided into rooms by short walls across the corridors. This type of construction allowed large buildings to be constructed quickly by having large construction teams build the overall outline while smaller groups finished the interior rooms. The kivas were in front of the highest section of the early Kawàyka'a site. Later development of Kawàyka'a was of the accretional type that has been better studied during the excavations of Awat'ovi. The earlier pattern of ladder construction at Kawàyka'a is consistent with an already socially cohesive group migrating and founding a new village, just as the clan migration traditions describe. Later, smaller family groups joined them, and communities grew as new generations were born there.

AWAT'OVI

Awat'ovi lies about 5 km (3 mi.) southwest of Kawàyka'a. It was occupied from about AD 1200 to 1700. It covers about 9.3 hectares (23 acres) and contains an estimated 5,000 ground-floor rooms, although probably no more than 1,500 rooms were in use at any given time. Its most recognizable features (figure 8.4) are the Western Mound in the southwestern quadrant of the site (the earliest part of Awat'ovi), the Eastern Mound in the northeastern quadrant of the site (which was the native village during the Mission period, AD 1629–1680), and the mission complex in the southeastern quadrant of the site.

Awat'ovi was probably established about AD 1200 by people manufacturing black-on-white and corrugated pottery. Several small room blocks were probably built at about that time, but we know little about them because they were deeply buried in the Western Mound and in a room block east of the Western Mound.

Beginning about AD 1275, people of Awat'ovi began constructing buildings on top of the early black-on-white room blocks of the Western Mound (figure 8.5). Between about 1275 and 1300/1325, people arrived who manufactured orange ware pottery and imported or brought with them pottery from both the Kayenta and Ganado

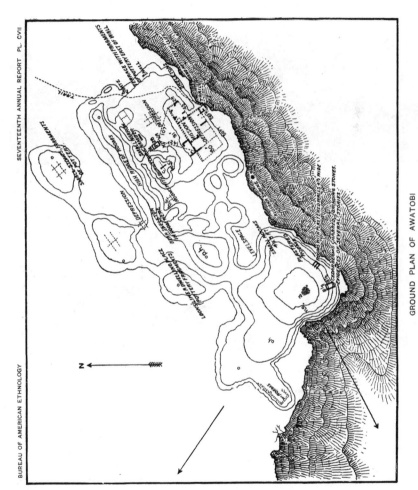

GROUND PLAN OF AWATOBI

FIGURE 8.4 Plan of Awaťovi (after Fewkes 1898:plate 107).

FIGURE 8.5 Photograph of excavations in the Western Mound, with orange ware rooms and two kivas on the right and yellow ware rooms and one kiva on the left. View to the south. © President and Fellows of Harvard University, Peabody Museum of Archaeology and Ethnology. Peabody ID # 2014.1.11.13.1 digital file #99090081.

areas. They constructed a room block approximately 40 m long (east-west) and 10 m wide (north-south) containing approximately 45 rooms with two kivas in front of it. Probably about AD 1300 or 1325, people who manufactured black-on-yellow pottery constructed a room block much like the orange ware room block and immediately to the east of it. The building with the black-on-yellow pottery was approximately 30 m long (east-west) and 20 m wide (north-south) containing approximately 45 rooms with one kiva in front of it. The builders started both of these room blocks by constructing a ladder or spine unit with living rooms in front and storage rooms in back. They then added rooms to the front (south) of the buildings. Both of these buildings looked much like Homol'ovi III in the Little Colorado River valley south of Awat'ovi (Adams 2001; Adams 2002:figure 2.2).

By about AD 1325–1350, construction of additional buildings in the Western Mound resulted in a square building measuring 75 m by 75 m with a small plaza or courtyard in the center. At about that time, the people of Awat'ovi at least partly enclosed a plaza north of the square building by constructing room blocks in an L-shaped or U-shaped configuration. At this point, the Western Mound of Awat'ovi looked much like Homol'ovi I (Adams 2002:figure 2.6) or Four Mile (Plog 1981:figures 31 and 49), and somewhat like Bidahochi (Gilpin 1988; Hays-Gilpin and Gilpin 1998:462; Hough 1903:plate 66) and Chevelon (Adams 2002:186–187), all pueblos to the south of Awat'ovi. A cluster of kivas was east of the Western Mound and another yellow ware room block was east of these kivas.

Between about AD 1350 and 1375, the residents of Awat'ovi vacated the Western Mound and filled it with refuse. At about the same time, coincident with the development of Sikyatki Polychrome (ca. AD 1375), they constructed new buildings to the east and northeast of the Western Mound. Some of these room blocks looked much like those that formed the Western Mound, running east-west with living rooms in the front (southern) row, storage rooms in the back (northern) row, and kivas in front (south) of the room block. Other room blocks constructed at Awat'ovi during the 1400s and 1500s are strikingly different. Perhaps the largest building constructed at Awat'ovi during this period, in what would become the center of the site, was approximately 80 m north-south by 40 m east-west and contained approximately 250 to 350 ground-floor rooms. These rooms were long and narrow with the long axis running north-south, whereas the long axis of earlier rooms ran east-west. Unlike the earlier pattern, in which there was a row of living rooms in front and a row of storerooms in back, few of these rooms contained any floor features. Excavations in the large AD 1350–1375 building identified no kivas

By the time the Spaniards arrived in the AD mid-1500s Awat'ovi was a large square building measuring 130 m east-west by 120 m north-south with a large central plaza. The highest portion of the village was the room block that formed the north side of the plaza (the Eastern Mound). Some kivas were in the plaza, and some were in room blocks. Kiva murals include images of spiritual beings, priests or *katsinas*, flowers, animals, colored corn, prayer feathers, and other images still significant to Hopi and other Pueblo people today. Many Hopis identify these murals as Eastern Pueblo in style, similar to those at Kawàyka'a. Hopi oral traditions say that "many languages were spoken" at Awat'ovi and lots of different ceremonies were performed there. Albert Yava, a Hopi-Tewa, wrote, "Awatovi was originally a Hopi village, according to what the old people told us, but they must have taken in a lot of Kawaikas [Keresans], Payupkis and other Eastern Pueblos, because the ceremonies we inherited from them have a good many songs that are not in the Hopi language" (1978:88).

The Sikyatki period room block that lined the southern side of the plaza was where the Spanish missionaries built their mission complex beginning in AD 1629. What happened then is emotionally fraught for Hopi descendants of those who were abused by the priests, those who took part in the AD 1680 Pueblo Revolt, and those who took part in and were displaced by the conflict of AD 1700 in which Awat'ovi was destroyed and its survivors dispersed to other Hopi villages. Both oral traditions and Spanish records explain conflict and depopulation of Awat'ovi. Many key Hopi ceremonies were carried by survivors from Awat'ovi and "replanted" at Walpi and other Hopi villages. The depopulation of Awat'ovi and redistribution of its survivors thus contributed to the coalescence of the Hopi ceremonial calendar as it was described by observers of European descent in the late nineteenth and early twentieth centuries.

KERESANS AND OTHER IMMIGRANTS

All three sites discussed here became Hopi villages by taking in migrants from other communities to the east and south. Each has a different history. Sikyatki's history is one of sequential occupation. It was initially founded by people from the Hopi Buttes to the south in the AD 1200s; then, following a hiatus, it was refounded by migrants from the east. Its architecture is eastern post-Chacoan, which is consistent with Fewkes's speculation that clans coming from the Rio Grande to settle here might have spoken Keresan. Kawàyka'a's initial construction also conforms to an eastern post-Chacoan pattern. It began as a formal planned unit and then grew by accretion. Oral traditions indicate that villagers spoke Keresan; in fact, the village's name is a Keresan word for the present-day village of Laguna in New Mexico.

Awat'ovi's initial construction (the Western Mound) conforms to a southern pattern of small Pueblo villages aggregating together, side by side. At about the same time as distinctively Hopi yellow ware pottery appeared in the AD 1300s, Awat'ovi's villagers added a plaza to the original buildings. We see the same pattern of constructing a square pyramidal building and then a plaza at other pueblos in the Little Colorado River valley. After about AD 1375, the village grew through construction of new room blocks. A new pottery style, Sikyatki style, appeared along with elaborate kiva murals in the 1400s. Oral traditions indicate that many languages were spoken, including Keresan, and many ceremonies were performed at Awat'ovi. The architectural and oral histories demonstrate that there were multiple ways of becoming Hopi, incorporating the traditions and ceremonies from many contributing Pueblo traditions (and likely non-Pueblo traditions that are not as evident). Hopi values integrated immigrants and their architectural traditions into a functioning whole.

BECOMING HOPI

Becoming Hopi is not only about people with different migration histories joining to build shared communities, learning to speak a common language, or becoming a federally recognized tribe. Many Hopi people say they are still becoming Hopi in the sense that *Hopi* is a set of values to which people aspire: humility, hard work by hand, generosity, living in balance and harmony, and respect for others. Because all humans are flawed and can never fully live up to these high aspirations, one has to work hard to become Hopi. Therefore, in addition to recognizing the multiple origins of Hopi, archaeologists should attend to the common Hopi (and other Pueblo) values and shared material expressions of those values. In several MNA publications, Hopi and non-Hopi authors explain how Hopi values are expressed in mural and pottery painting (Hays-Gilpin 2006; Hays-Gilpin and Schaafsma 2010).

Leigh Kuwanwisiwma has shared with us his insights about the expression of Hopi values in architecture. These enrich archaeologists' understanding of architectural data and contribute to culturally appropriate site management and interpretation. The most important concept for archaeologists to understand is that houses are living beings that nurture Hopi families. In a consultation between Hopi community members and MNA archaeologists working on Puebloan sites in the Grand Canyon, several Hopi consultants asked whether the archaeologists found seeds in the walls of the house structures they had excavated They explained that "a house is alive. You feed it for strength, like you feed yourself. The home itself is a person. That's why they put a box for prayer feathers in each home. They also put prayer feathers in the sheep corral, and in the center of fields." At the eleventh-century site in Furnace Flats, at the bottom of the Canyon, the archaeologists found a slab-lined box with two possible *pahos* (prayer sticks) and a Hopi yellow ware sherd in the upper fill (Neff et al. 2016). This suggested to Hopi consultants that the site was remembered and revisited and given prayer sticks. Their interpretation was much more specific than the usual archaeological practice of simply labeling the feature as an unspecified shrine.

Likewise, knowing that houses are living beings and that plazas are the center places that gather houses into communities helps us to understand Pueblo villages like Sikyatki, Kawàyka'a, and Awat'ovi—what they looked like and what they meant. For Hopis, the home is the caretaker of the family. Children are born there; life begins there. The house is like a womb, nurturing its inhabitants. Historically, home interiors were whitewashed "for purity, for everything good," Leigh told us.

Archaeologists often find grinding stones and bins in ancient pueblo rooms, and they are one of the criteria we use to label a structure as a house. In the Hopi world, the grinding stone (*mata*) and *piki* stone (*tuma*) are seen as female. They go through a birthing ceremony and are secluded like a newborn baby and its mother. "Grinding stones are family members, females," Leigh's mother said, "don't abandon your sisters" (the grinding stones). The term for grinding bin is *mataki'at* (literally, the grinding stone, her home.) Values, kinship, and emotion pervade everything in the Hopi world.

Leigh has observed that modern visitors to Chaco and Wupatki see all masonry with the stones exposed, but it was not like that in the past. Walls were plastered. Plastering was done communally. Men brought the clay and women did the plastering. Hattie Kabotie Lomayesva of Second Mesa told Susan Secakuku that villagers would get ready for the *katsinas* to come by cleaning the yard and plastering the house, and washing and dressing themselves nicely. You want to "be presentable," she said. At the Home Dance, in July, they used to replaster and whitewash the houses and literally "give it a bath." The whitewash means purity. Whitewash is also a prayer for rain. "New plaster dares the cloud people to come and wash away all your hard work," Leigh says. Maintenance is now—and was then—meaningful.

All plazas should have four openings (alleyways) because, when the clans were migrating, they came from all directions and they still maintain connections to ancestral places. The plaza is the center. At dances, the priests leave in four directions. The clans earned the privilege to petition the clouds in all four directions. The plaza is called *kiisonvi* (literally, house-inside). It has a ceremonial name too that refers to dance, song, and happiness. People who attend dances are clouds; they, too, have life, moisture, and breath. Clouds gathering and people gathering are the same. People gather with good thoughts. The whitewashed village looks like a cloud on the mesa top and invites clouds and people to gather.

CONCLUSIONS

What we have learned from Leigh Kuwanwisiwma is that Hopi oral traditions enrich and explain archaeological evidence and that archaeological timeframes and observational data can supplement Hopi histories by adding calendar dates to historical narratives and material confirmation of processes like migration. Dates have not always been important to Hopi people, but they are now, especially for land claims, water rights, and repatriation.

When archaeologists visit contemporary and ancient Hopi villages today, we hope that they can visualize houses as living beings, nurturing families who deliberately came together from many different linguistic and geographic origins to develop the philosophy, history, and aesthetic expressions that are still called Hopi. We can better understand the cycles of movement, construction, renewal, and final repose of houses, plazas, pottery vessels, and painted plaster, as well as people working for a life of balance and reciprocity with generations past and future.

ACKNOWLEDGMENTS

We are grateful to Leigh Kuwanwisiwma, his staff, and the cultural resource advisors, especially Stewart Koyiyumptewa, Susan (Secakuku) Sekaquaptewa, Hattie Kabotie Lomayesva, and others who have shared their knowledge of Hopi history and culture with us for many years. Thanks to T. J. Ferguson for organizing the symposium that began this volume, to Peter Whiteley for help with Hopi place-names and migration histories, and to two anonymous reviewers whose comments helped us to tie it all together. Askwali and Kwakwha!

REFERENCES CITED

Adams, E. Charles. 2002. *Homol'ovi: An Ancient Hopi Settlement Cluster*. University of Arizona Press, Tucson.

Adams, E. Charles (editor). 2001. *Homol'ovi III: A Pueblo Hamlet in the Middle Little Colorado River Valley*. Arizona State Museum Archaeological Series No. 193. Arizona State Museum, University of Arizona, Tucson.

Bernardini, Wesley. 2005. *Hopi Oral Tradition and the Archaeology of Identity*. University of Arizona Press, Tucson.

———. 2009. *Hopi History in Stone: The Tutuveni Petroglyph Site*. Arizona State Museum Archaeological Series 200. Arizona State Museum, University of Arizona, Tucson.

Bradford, James E. 2013. *Without Parallel among Relics: An Archeological History of El Morro National Monument, New Mexico*. Intermountain Cultural Resources Professional Papers No. 71. Archeology Program, Intermountain Region Cultural Resources, National Park Service, Department of the Interior, Santa Fe.

Brew, John Otis. 1937. The First Two Seasons at Awatovi. *American Antiquity* 3(2):122–137.

———. 1939. Preliminary Report of the Peabody Museum Awatovi Expedition of 1937. *American Antiquity* 5(2):103–114.

———. 1941. Preliminary Report of the Peabody Museum Awatovi Expedition of 1939. *Plateau* 13(3):37–48.

———. 1942. Preface. In *The Changing Physical Environment of the Hopi Indians of Arizona*, by John T. Hack, pp. v–x. Papers of the Peabody Museum of American Archaeology and Ethnology Vol. 35, No. 1. Reports of the Awatovi Expedition No. 1. Harvard University, Cambridge, Massachusetts.

———. 1949. Part I: The History of Awatovi. In *Franciscan Awatovi: The Excavation and Conjectural Reconstruction of a 17th-Century Spanish Mission Establishment at a Hopi Indian Town in Northeastern Arizona*, by Ross G. Montgomery, Watson Smith, and John O. Brew, pp. 1–43. Papers of the Peabody Museum of American Archaeology and Ethnology Vol. 36, No. 1. Reports of the Awatovi Expedition No. 3. Harvard University, Cambridge, Massachusetts.

———. 1952. Foreword. In *Kiva Mural Decorations at Awatovi and Kawaika-a, with a Survey of other Wall Paintings in the Pueblo Southwest* by Watson Smith, pp. vii–xii. Papers of the Peabody Museum of American Archaeology and Ethnology, Harvard University, No. 37. Cambridge, Massachusetts.

———. 1971. Foreword. In *Painted Ceramics of the Western Mound at Awatovi*, by Watson Smith, pp. xvii–xviii. Papers of the Peabody Museum of American Archaeology and Ethnology, Harvard University, No. 38. Cambridge, Massachusetts.

———. 1980. The Excavation of Awatovi. In *Camera, Spade and Pen: An Inside View of Southwestern Archaeology*, edited by Marnie Gaede, photographs by Marc Gaede, pp. 103–109. University of Arizona Press, Tucson.

———. 1994. St. Francis at Awatovi. In *Pioneers in Historical Archaeology: Breaking New Ground*, edited by Stanley South, pp. 27–47. Plenum Press, New York.

Ferguson, T. J., Leigh J. Kuwanwisiwma, Micah Loma'omvaya, Patrick Lyons, Gregson Schachner, and Laurie Webster. 2016. Yep Hisat Hoopoq'yaqam Yesiwa [Hopi Ancestors Were Once Here]: Repatriation Research Documenting Hopi Cultural Affiliation with the Ancient Hohokam of Southern Arizona. In *Global Ancestors: Understanding the Shared Humanity of Our Ancestors*, edited by Margaret Clegg, Rebecca Redfern, Jelena Bekvalac, and Heather Bonney, pp. 104–133. Oxbow Books, London.

Fewkes, Jesse Walter. 1893. A-Wa'-To-Bi: An Archeological Verification of a Tusayan Legend. *American Anthropologist* 6(4):363–375.

———. 1896. Preliminary Account of an Expedition to the Cliff Villages of the Red Rock District, and the Tusayan Ruins of Sikyatki and Awatobi, Arizona, in 1895. In *Smithsonian Institution Annual Report for the Year to July, 1895*, pp. 557–588. Washington, DC.

———. 1898. Archaeological Expedition to Arizona in 1895. In *Seventeenth Annual Report of the Bureau of American Ethnology for the Years 1895–1896*, Part 2, pp. 519–742. Washington, D.C.

———. 1919. Designs on Prehistoric Hopi Pottery. In *Thirty-third Annual Report of the Bureau of American Ethnology 1911–1912*, pp. 207–284. Washington, DC.

Fowler, Andrew P., and John R. Stein. 1992. The Anasazi Great House in Space, Time, and Paradigm. In *Anasazi Regional Organization and the Chaco System*, edited by David E. Doyel, pp. 101–122. Anthropological Papers No. 5. Maxwell Museum of Anthropology, University of New Mexico, Albuquerque.

Fowler, Andrew P., John R. Stein, and Roger Anyon. 1987. An Archaeological Reconnaissance of West-Central New Mexico: The Anasazi Monuments Project. Final Draft Report. State of New Mexico, Office of Cultural Affairs, Historic Preservation Division, Santa Fe.

Gilpin, Dennis. 1988. The 1987 Navajo Nation Investigations at Bidahochi Pueblo, A Fourteenth Century Site in the Hopi Buttes, Navajo County, Arizona. Paper presented at the 1988 Pecos Conference, Cortez, Colorado.

———. 1989. Great Houses and Pueblos in Northeastern Arizona. Paper presented at the 1989 Pecos Conference, Bandelier National Monument, Los Alamos, New Mexico.

———. 2014. Building Awatovi: The Architecture of Awatovi Pueblo, Northeastern Arizona, A.D. 1200–1700. Report submitted to the Peabody Museum of American Archaeology and Ethnology, Harvard University, Cambridge, Massachusetts.

Hammond, George P., and Agapito Rey. 1929. *Expedition into New Mexico Made by Antonio de Espejo, Luxán Journal*. Translation. Quivira Society Publication No. 1. Albuquerque.

———. 1966. *The Rediscovery of New Mexico, 1580–1594: The Explorations of Chamuscado, Espejo, Castaño de Sosa, Morlete, and Leyva de Bonilla and Humaña*. Coronado Cuarto Centennial Publications Series No. 3. University of New Mexico Press, Albuquerque.

Hargrave, Lyndon Lane. 1935. The Jeddito Valley and the First Pueblo Towns in Arizona Visited by Europeans. *Museum Notes* 8(4):17–23. Museum of Northern Arizona, Flagstaff.

Hays-Gilpin, Kelley. 2013. Sikyatki Polychrome: Style, Iconography, Cross-Media Comparisons, and Organization of Production. *Kiva* 79(2):175–204.

Hays-Gilpin, Kelley (editor). 2006. Murals and Metaphors, *Plateau* 3(1). Museum of Northern Arizona, Flagstaff.

Hays-Gilpin, Kelley, and Dennis Gilpin. 1998. Little Colorado Branch. In *Archaeology of Prehistoric Native America: An Encyclopedia*, edited by Guy Gibbon, pp. 461–466. Garland Publishing, New York.

Hays-Gilpin, Kelley, and Steven LeBlanc. 2007. Sikyatki Style in Regional Context. In *New Perspectives on Pottery Mound Pueblo*, edited by Polly Schaafsma, pp. 109–135. University of New Mexico Press, Albuquerque.

Hays-Gilpin, Kelley, and Polly Schaafsma (editors). 2010. *Painting the Cosmos: Metaphor and Worldview in Images from the Southwest Pueblos and Mexico*. Museum of Northern Arizona Bulletin No. 67. Flagstaff.

Hough, Walter. 1903. Archeological Field Work in Northeastern Arizona: The Museum-Gates Expedition of 1901. *Report of the United States National Museum for 1901*, pp. 279–358. Government Printing Office, Washington, DC.

Mindeleff, Victor. 1891 [1989]. A Study of Pueblo Architecture: Tusayan and Cibola. In *Eighth Annual Report of the Bureau of Ethnology to the Secretary of the Smithsonian Institution, for the Years 1886–1887*. Government Printing Office, Washington, D.C. 1989 ed. Smithsonian Institution Press, Washington, D.C.

Mount, James E., Stanley J. Olsen, John W. Olsen, George A. Teague, and B. Dean Treadwell. 1993. *Wide Reed Ruin, Hubbell Trading Post National Historic Site*. Professional Papers No. 51. Division of Anthropology, Southwest Cultural Resources Center, Southwest Region, National Park Service, Department of the Interior.

Neff, Ted, Jim H. Collette, Kimberly Spurr, Kirk C. Anderson, Donald R. Keller, and Brian W. Kranzler. 2016. Archaeological Excavations at Nine Sites along the Colorado River in Grand Canyon National Park: The MNA–NPS Grand Canyon River Corridor Archaeological Project. Manuscript on file, Grand Canyon National Park, Arizona.

Plog, Fred. 1981. *Cultural Resources Overview: Little Colorado River Area, Arizona*. Report prepared for Apache-Sitgreaves National Forests and Arizona State Office, Bureau of Land Management, Phoenix.

Reed, Erik K. 1942. Kawaika-a in the Historic Period. *American Antiquity* 8(1):119–120.

Sekaquaptewa, Emory, and Dorothy Washburn. 2004. They Go Along Singing: Reconstructing the Hopi Past from Ritual Metaphors in Song and Image. *American Antiquity* 69(3):457–486.

———. 2009. As a Matter of Practice . . . Hopi Cosmology in Hopi Life: Some Considerations for Theory and Method in Southwestern Archaeology. *Time and Mind* 2(2):195–214.

Sturtevant, William. 1971. Creek into Seminole. In *North American Indians in Historical Perspective*, edited by Eleanor Leacock and Nancy Lurie, pp. 92–128. Random House, New York.

Yava, Albert. 1978. *Big Falling Snow: A Tewa–Hopi Indian's Life and Times and the History and Traditions of His People*. Edited and annotated by Harold Courlander. Crown, New York.

9

PATHWAYS TO HOPI

Cultural Affiliation and the Archaeological Textile Record

LAURIE D. WEBSTER

H OPI TRADITIONAL TEXTILES are the woven expression of Hopi history and an integral part of religious observances, rites of passage, and gift exchange. They incorporate a wide range of styles and weaving technologies whose origins can be traced to different geographical regions and archaeological cultures of the Southwest. During the late pre-Hispanic period, these styles and techniques amalgamated in the Hopi region to create the historic Hopi textile tradition. After European contact, certain Spanish and Euro-American introductions—sheep's wool, new dyes, metal needles, the knitting technique, and probably embroidery—were selectively added to the Hopi textile repertoire. In a very real sense, traditional Hopi textiles are historical archives, their iconographies, garment styles, and weave structures documenting the migrations and cultural interactions of Hopi ancestors (Webster and Loma'omvaya 2004).

In the late 1990s and early 2000s, I was invited to participate in two cultural affiliation studies initiated by Leigh Kuwanwisiwma and organized by T. J. Ferguson to document historical relationships between the Hopi people and the Salado and Hohokam archaeological cultures of southern Arizona. My role was to explore the textile and basketry evidence for these connections (Webster 1999, 2003). In this chapter, I will briefly review some of these findings as well as additional textile data that support the view that Hopi ancestors participated in numerous Southwestern archaeological cultures before coming together at the Hopi Mesas to become the Hopi people. In addition to my own research, I draw from the important contributions of textile scholars Kate Peck Kent (1983a, 1983b) and Lynn Teague (1998), as well as my co-researcher for the Hopi-Salado Project, Micah Loma'omvaya (Webster and Loma'omvaya 2004).

In his early discussions with Euro-American interviewers about Hopi cultural affiliation, Hopi-Tewa elder Albert Yava expressed frustration with the then popular viewpoint that Hopi ancestral connections were primarily confined to archaeological sites in the San Juan or Four Corners region of the Colorado Plateau (Courlander, 1978:36). Citing Hopi oral traditions, Yava underscored the diverse geographical and linguistic origins of the Hopi people, noting for example that the Snake and Horn Clans traced their origins to Toko'navi, the Navajo Mountain area of northern Arizona, whereas the Sand, Water, and Tobacco Clans, among others, traced their roots to Palatkwa or Palatkwapi far to the south. Some clans moved up and down the Colorado and Little Colorado River drainages before settling at Hopi, while others, such as the Coyote Clan, came to Hopi from the east. Similar viewpoints reflecting a reticulated model of Hopi ethnogenesis (Ferguson and Schachner 2003:64–65, figure 19) were recorded more than a century ago by early Euro-American ethnographers such as Fewkes (1900), Mindeleff (1989 [1891]), and Voth (1905), who worked with Hopi consultants, and have been expressed by contemporary Hopi writers (e.g., Nequatewa 1967) and tribal members interviewed for our Salado and Hohokam cultural affiliation studies (Ferguson and Loma'omvaya 1999; Ferguson 2003).

BASKETMAKER AND ANCESTRAL PUEBLO CONNECTIONS TO HISTORIC HOPI TEXTILES

Whereas most archaeologists, museums, and federal land managers readily acknowledge cultural affiliation between the Hopi people and the Ancestral Pueblo archaeological culture of the Colorado Plateau, few are aware of the stylistic and technological continuities that link certain Basketmaker, Ancestral Pueblo, and modern Hopi textiles. Here I will highlight just two Hopi garment styles—the braided sash and the manta with red and blue twill borders—with antecedents in the rich precontact clothing traditions of the Colorado Plateau.

HOPI FRINGED WHITE COTTON BRAIDED SASH

The Hopi flat braided cotton sash (*wuwokwewa*), also known as the rain sash, big sash, or large belt, is a critical component of Hopi ritual regalia (figure 9.1c). It forms an integral part of a Hopi bride's wedding trousseau and is also worn by men and women in various ceremonies, its long flowing fringe evoking falling rain. Fringed flat braided sashes woven in animal or human hair appear in the archaeological record of the northern Southwest during the Basketmaker II period sometime around 200 BC (e.g., Morris and Burgh 1954:67, figures 38 and 100b) and persist through the Basketmaker III and Pueblo I periods. Sometime during this latter period, the southern-introduced fiber of cotton began to replace the animal hair. A directly dated sash (figure 9.1a, top) from Obelisk Cave in northeastern Arizona, half cotton fiber and half dog hair, produced a radiocarbon date that suggests manufacture in the late AD 700s (Freer and Jacobs 2014; Webster 2012:181, figure 9.12d). By the AD 1000s, cotton had effectively replaced animal hair in these sashes, and over time, the fringe became shorter (figure 9.1b). Regardless of the fiber employed, nearly all flat braided bands and sashes on the Colorado Plateau made between about 200 BC and AD 1300 were constructed in a similar manner, incorporating two-ply z-spun S-twist yarns in an over-two, under-two (2/2) braiding rhythm, a period of continuity lasting 1,500 years. Historic Hopi examples differ from their earlier Colorado Plateau counterparts in having a 3/3 braiding rhythm and wrapped cornhusk rings, but the braided garment style has been maintained (figure 9.1c).

HOPI WHITE MANTA WITH RED AND BLUE TWILL BORDERS

The Hopi white manta with red and blue borders (*atö'ö*), the red woven in diagonal twill and the blue in diamond twill, is primarily a woman's shawl that is also worn ceremonially by women and male impersonators of female *katsinas* (figure 9.2c; Kent 1983b:61, plate 11). Colloquially, it is often referred to as a maiden shawl. Its ancestry can be directly traced to the loom-woven cotton white, red, and brown or black banded twill fabrics (figure 9.2b) of the late AD 1000–1300 period (Kent 1983b:61), which were also worked primarily in diagonal twill, sometimes combined with diamond or herringbone twill. As Kent (1983a:178) noted, these Ancestral Pueblo twill fabrics perpetuate the color palette, layout, texture, and self-patterned designs of earlier finger-woven Basketmaker yucca twined bags (figure 9.2a), but in a new fiber type and weave structure. The bags are woven in a compact two-strand weft-twining technique that conveys a diagonal appearance to the weave and are typically decorated with red and brown or black self-patterned designs produced by alternating the colored yarns. Most Pueblo period cotton textiles on the Colorado Plateau incorporate the same mineral pigments, organic dyes, and color palettes as their Basketmaker predecessors (Teague 1998:132–133).

At the Hopi Mesas, the precontact cotton twill tradition persisted into the late twentieth century, with Spanish-introduced wool largely replacing cotton and Spanish-traded indigo dye often replacing the earlier native brown or black elements. The Hopi woman's twill manta with white center and red and blue borders (figure 9.2c), woman's wool manta dress or shawl with black diagonal-twill center

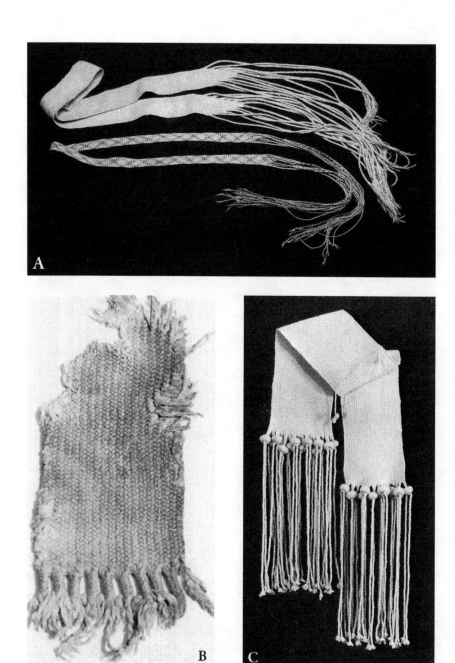

FIGURE 9.1 Braided sashes. (a) 2/2 braided sashes of dog hair and cotton fiber (upper) and dog hair and human hair (lower) from the Prayer Rock District, northeastern Arizona, AD 700–900; (b) cotton 2/2 braided sash from Inscription House in the Kayenta region, ca. AD 1250–1300; (c) modern Hopi 3/3 braided cotton sash.

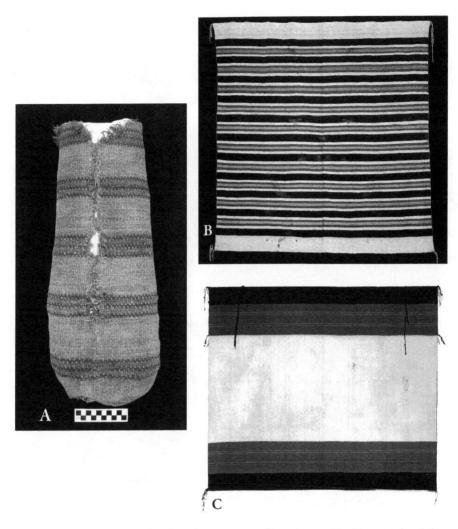

FIGURE 9.2 Comparison of Basketmaker yucca twined bag, Ancestral Pueblo cotton banded twill blanket, and historic Hopi twill manta with red and blue borders. (a) yucca twined bag, southeastern Utah, ca. AD 1–400; (b) cotton banded 2/2 diagonal-twill blanket, southeastern Utah, ca. AD 1250; (c) Hopi woman's manta with white 2/2 diagonal-twill center, red 2/1 diagonal-twill borders, and indigo blue diamond-twill borders, ca.1920s.

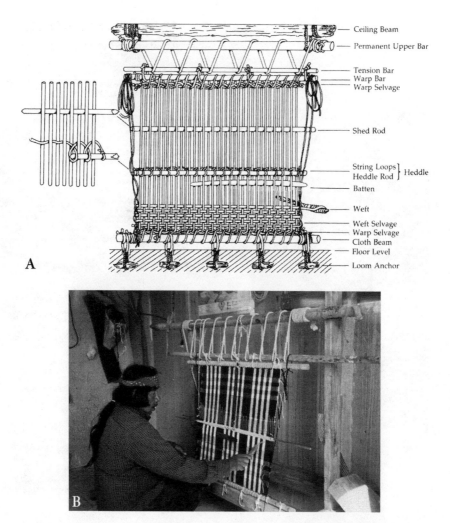

Ceiling Beam
Permanent Upper Bar

Tension Bar
Warp Bar
Warp Selvage

Shed Rod

String Loops ⎤ Heddle
Heddle Rod ⎦
Batten

Weft

Weft Selvage
Warp Selvage
Cloth Beam
Floor Level
Loom Anchor

A

B

FIGURE 9.3 Continuity in use of the Pueblo upright loom. (a) pre-Hispanic upright loom used on the Colorado Plateau; (b) Hopi weaver Harold Polingyumptewa weaving a boy's plaid blanket on an upright loom, Hotvela, 2000.

and blue diamond-twill borders (Kent 1983b:62–65), and man's blue or black wool diagonal-twill shirt (Kent 1983b:71–72, figure 55) all perpetuate Ancestral Pueblo twill weave structures and garment styles.

ADDITIONAL EVIDENCE

In addition to these braided sashes and twill-woven garments, several other Hopi weaving practices represent the continuation of Ancestral Pueblo weaving traditions on the Colorado Plateau. Traditional Hopi weavers still use the same upright loom technology and stick-and-whorl spindle as their ancestors, but with a few modern adaptations (figure 9.3). Kivas were the locus of ceremonial textile production at Hopi well into the twentieth century, just as they were at late pre-Hispanic sites in the Kayenta area and the Little Colorado and Rio Grande drainages, the latter based on archaeological loom-hole evidence. The ubiquitous white cotton blanket found at sites on the Colorado Plateau after AD 1000 continues to play a central role at Hopi as a woman's wedding robe and burial shroud (*oova*), and in its embroidered form, a ceremonial robe (*tuu'ihi*) (Kent 1983b:55–60, 73–75).

SOUTHERN ADDITIONS TO THE HOPI TEXTILE REPERTOIRE

In contrast to those styles that show strong continuity with Basketmaker and Ancestral Pueblo traditions on the Colorado Plateau, other decorative techniques and styles ancestral to the Hopi people—tie-dye, openwork fabrics, warp-faced ties and belts, and plain weaves decorated with supplementary wefts (or embroidery)—spread onto the Colorado Plateau from the south. Examples of these fabrics are found primarily at post AD 1100 Sinagua and Kayenta sites, suggesting an infusion of Hohokam people or influences into the region. Late pre-Hispanic kiva murals from the ancestral Hopi site of Awat'ovi on Jeddito Mesa (Smith 1952) document the presence of most, if not all, of these southern styles and weave structures in the Hopi area by AD 1350–1600 (figure 9.4).

TIE-DYE FABRICS

Tie-dye originated in Mesoamerica or the Andes, probably as a way to decorate cloth with a sacred dot-in-a-square iconography evoking serpent skin and maize (Webster et al. 2006). In the Southwest, tie-dye cotton textiles were present in Chaco Canyon by AD 1100* and were also recovered from twelfth- and thirteenth-century sites in the Verde Valley and Kayenta regions (figure 9.4b). Tie-dye fabrics with the dot-in-a-square motif are not reported from Hohokam sites in southern Arizona, but this could be a function of poor textile preservation in the region. A resist-dye textile with a dot-in-a-circle motif, another important Mesoamerican symbol, was recovered

---

*After the Webster, Hays-Gilpin, and Schaafsma article (2006) was published, I came across two unpublished tie-dye fragments (catalog number H/15752) from Pueblo Bonito in Chaco Canyon at the American Museum of Natural History in New York. Believed to be part of textile H/4189 from Room 32, the fragments probably date to the eleventh century or earlier.

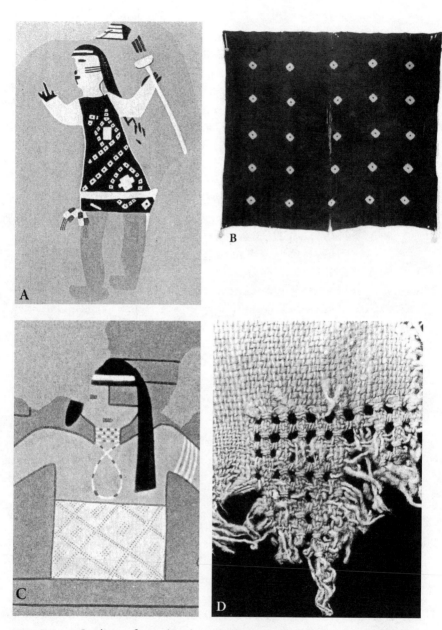

FIGURE 9.4 Southern-influenced tie-dye and openwork in the late pre-Hispanic Awat'ovi kiva murals and textile examples from the Colorado Plateau. (a) tie-dye tunic in an Awat'ovi mural; (b) tie-dye blanket, Lake Canyon, southeastern Utah, ca. AD 1200s; (c) garment probably decorated in weft-wrap openwork in an Awat'ovi mural; (d) cotton fabric decorated in weft-wrap openwork (Inscription House, northeastern Arizona, ca. AD 1200s).

from the late Hohokam site of Casa Grande (Webster et al. 2006:figure 1e). Both the dot-in-a-square (figure 9.4a) and dot-in-a-circle occur on depictions of clothing in the Awat'ovi murals (e.g., Smith 1952:figures 24b, 24c, 24f, 24h, 50c, 51c, 52a, 80b, and 81b), but the tie-dye technique has not been documented in historic Hopi textile collections.

OPENWORK FABRICS

Openwork is another important method of fabric decoration with southern origins. Pre-Hispanic loom-woven weft-wrap openwork and gauze weave were practiced in northern and southern Mexico and Peru (Kent 1983a:153; Teague 1998:78), and both became popular methods of decorating cotton cloth in the Southwest south of the Mogollon Rim. Weft-wrap openwork was present in southern Arizona by AD 900, and gauze weave entered the southern Southwest somewhat later (Kent 1983a:153; Teague 1998:100). The non-loom structure of interlinking, which involves twisting of yarns wrapped around two stationary bars or beams by the sprang or frame-braiding technique, was also used south of the Mogollon Rim to create openwork fabrics, including the well-known Tonto shirt (Kent 1983a:figure 34; Teague 1998:cover image). Despite the strong popularity of openwork fabrics in the southern Southwest, only a few examples are known from the Colorado Plateau prior to AD 1300, primarily in the Kayenta region (figure 9.4d). Openwork shirts and kilts are depicted in the late pre-Hispanic kiva murals from Awat'ovi (figure 9.4c) and Kawàyka'a, indicating their presence in the Hopi region by that time (Smith 1952:figures 66c, 67d, and 86a). Although openwork is rare in historic Hopi textile collections, Fewkes (1903:plate XLI) described the use of a netted shirt by a deer hunter *katsina*, and openwork leggings made by the European-introduced techniques of knitting or crochet are occasionally found. The pre-Hispanic interlinking weave structure and sprang technique persisted in the manufacture of the historic Hopi flat braided sash.

WARP-FACED AND WARP-FLOAT BELTING

Warp-faced and warp-float belting spread from Mesoamerica into southern Arizona and New Mexico after AD 1100 and from there into the northern Southwest. Pre-Hispanic warp-faced belts are common south of the Mogollon Rim (Kent 1983a:140–143, 180–183; Teague 1998:184), but rare in pre AD 1300 assemblages from the Colorado Plateau. An Awat'ovi mural depiction indicates the presence of warp-faced belts in the Hopi area soon after that time (Smith 1952:figure 26u). The remains of several warp-float belts, worked in Spanish-introduced sheep wool, were found at seventeenth-century Awat'ovi and eighteenth-century Wàlpi (Kent 1979:18; Webster

1997:299–301, 2000:table 10.2). Warp-float belts (*kweewa*) are still commonly made and used at Hopi and in many other Pueblo communities.

PLAID FABRICS

Plaid fabrics are another southern style that entered the Hopi textile complex some-time after AD 1300 (Kent 1979:8, 1983a:132). At Hopi, black-and-white plaid blankets are closely associated with males, the man's large plaid twill shoulder blanket (*kwik-wilhoya*) serving as an important article of Hopi male social identity into the late nineteenth century and a smaller plain-weave version (*pösaala, tsirohoya*) still made for young boys (Kent 1983b:50–52) (figure 9.5).

HOPI BRAIDED SASHES

I have already discussed the 2/2 braided sashes found at Basketmaker and Ancestral Pueblo sites on the Colorado Plateau and their stylistic similarity to the Hopi cotton braided sash with its long pendent fringe (*wuwokwewa*) (figure 9.1c). The historic Hopi white cotton braided sash differs from these earlier sashes in several important ways: its 3/3 braided structure, greater width, cornhusk rings on the fringe, and man-ufacture by the sprang or frame-braiding technique rather than simple flat braiding. The 3/3 structure, cornhusk rings, and sprang technique appear to have been intro-duced from the Mogollon region into the upper Little Colorado and Hopi areas after AD 1300 (Kent 1940; 1957:602; 1983a:60, figure 24b; 1983b:82–83, figures 67–69). A 3/3 braided cotton sash from a late pre-Hispanic provenience at Awat'ovi indicates the presence of this fabric structure in the Hopi area by that time (Webster 1997:292, 2000:196). Moreover, the recovery of loom blocks at Awat'ovi (Woodbury 1954:153–157) suggests that these sashes could have been made there by winding the yarns around two beams, as practiced at Hopi today (Kent 1940).

HOPI EMBROIDERED KILTS AND MANTAS

The Hopi embroidered white cotton kilt (*pitkuna*) and manta (*tuu'ihi*) also show strong stylistic connections to pre-Hispanic textile traditions south of the Mogollon Rim. Whereas the large white cotton manta is a northern style, the kilt apparently spread into the southern Southwest from Mexico around AD 1200; kiva mural depic-tions support its presence at Hopi by the AD 1400s (Webster 2007:170–171). The triangle-and-hook and serrated triangle designs used to decorate sixteenth-century Awat'ovi kilts and modern Hopi kilts and mantas (figure 9.6) were prominent fea-tures of Sinagua, Salado, Mogollon, and Hohokam textile design (Kent 1979:9–12,

FIGURE 9.5 Plaid textiles. (a) fragment of plaid fabric, Tonto Cliff Dwellings, ca. AD 1300; (b) Hopi man's plaid blanket, ca.1890–1910; (c) Hopi male infant in plaid blanket, ca.1900.

FIGURE 9.6 Triangle-and-hook and serrated-triangle motifs on sixteenth-century Awat'ovi kilt depictions and modern Hopi kilts and mantas. (a) triangle-and-hook design on an Awat'ovi kilt border; (b) triangle-and-hook design on a Hopi embroidered kilt border, 1890–1920; (c) serrated triangle design on an Awat'ovi kilt border; (d) serrated triangle design on a Hopi embroidered manta, 1920–1940.

1983a:figures 133–134; Smith 1952:figure 25; Webster 2003:184–193; Webster and Loma'omvaya 2004:86–88). In contrast, these designs played only a minor role in the textile design systems of the Ancestral Pueblo of the Colorado Plateau. Hopi cultural advisors interviewed during our studies identified these motifs as symbols for water, clouds, and flowers. Since the early Historic period, most ceremonial kilts and mantas have been embroidered with woolen yarns. The wool and probably also the embroidery technique are Spanish introductions, the latter replacing the precontact decorative technique of plain weave patterned by extra-weft floats (also known as supplementary weft), in which the decorative yarns are added during the weaving process (Kent 1983a:175–178) rather than to the finished cloth, as in embroidery.

CONCLUSIONS

Historic Hopi textiles are an amalgam of weaving techniques and garment styles that originated north and south of the Mogollon Rim. Some garments, such as twill-woven mantas, have their origins in pre AD 1300 Ancestral Pueblo textile traditions of the Colorado Plateau. In historic times, most of these twill-woven garments were made of wool and served primarily as articles of daily dress. The large white cotton plain-weave manta of the Colorado Plateau persists as a woman's wedding robe and burial shroud and also serves as the base fabric for the embroidered ceremonial manta.

The technological and stylistic antecedents of many other historic Hopi ceremonial textiles can be traced to southwestern New Mexico and central and southern Arizona during the period AD 1100–1450. They include the 3/3 braiding structure and yarn-wrapped fiber rings of the historic Hopi wide braided sash belt; the kilt style; and the triangle-and-hook and serrated triangle designs related to clouds, water, and flowers. Important elements of the ancient Mesoamerican Flower World iconographic complex (Hays-Gilpin and Hill 1999), these symbols are used as embroidery motifs on historic Hopi kilts and mantas. All of these garments are closely associated with the *katsina* religion (Webster 1999:288–299). The southern technologies of weft-wrap openwork, gauze, and tie-dye appear not to have survived the early centuries of Spanish contact, but they too are clearly associated with *katsina* ceremonialism in the Awat'ovi murals. Their grid-like dyed and openwork patterns probably served as referents for serpent skin and maize, important symbols in Mesoamerican and Pueblo iconography.

This association of southern textile and iconographic styles with *katsina* religious practices appears to corroborate Hopi oral traditions that identify clans and societies from the southern region of Palatkwapi as the source for the Hopi winter *katsina* ceremonies (Ferguson et al. 2013). These oral traditions also help explain the spread of southern clothing styles onto the Colorado Plateau during late pre-Hispanic times. In addition to these southern textile technologies, the Hopi bundle-foundation coiled plaque of Second Mesa (*poota*) appears to have originated in the south, and the wickerwork plaque of Third Mesa (*yungyapu*) may have a southern origin as well (Teiwes 1996:173–187; Webster and Loma'omvaya 2004:87–88). At historic Hopi, these basket styles are associated with the Lalkont and O'waqölt women's religious societies, which trace their origins to Palatkwapi in the south (Ferguson and Loma'omvaya 2003:111; Parsons 1936:853; Parsons 1939:869–870; Webster and Loma'omvaya 2004:88). Today, these ancient textile and basket styles continue to play a key role in Hopi birth, death, initiation, and marriage ceremonies, evoking and maintaining Hopi clan histories and cultural identity through their use in ritual practice.

REFERENCES CITED

Ferguson, T. J. (compiler). 2003. *Yep Hisat Hoopoq'yaqam Yeesiwa (Hopi Ancestors Were Once Here): Hopi-Hohokam Cultural Affiliation Study*, Hopi Cultural Preservation Office, Kiqötsmovi, Arizona.

Ferguson, T. J., and Micah Loma'omvaya. 2003. Hopi Traditional History Relating to the Hohokam. In *Yep Hisat Hoopoq'yaqam Yeesiwa (Hopi Ancestors Were Once Here): Hopi-Hohokam Cultural Affiliation Study*, compiled by T. J. Ferguson, pp. 69–122. Hopi Cultural Preservation Office, Kiqötsmovi, Arizona.

Ferguson, T. J., and Gregson Schachner. 2003. Social and Geographical Dimensions of the Hohokam as a Past Identifiable Group. In *Yep Hisat Hoopoq'yaqam Yeesiwa (Hopi Ancestors Were Once Here): Hopi-Hohokam Cultural Affiliation Study*, compiled by T. J. Ferguson, pp. 63–68. Hopi Cultural Preservation Office, Kiqötsmovi, Arizona.

Ferguson, T. J., Leigh J. Kuwanwisiwma, Micah Loma'omvaya, Patrick Lyons, Greg Schachner, and Laurie Webster. 2013. *Yep Hisat Hoopoq'yaqam Yeesiwa* (Hopi Ancestors Were Once Here): Repatriation Research Documenting Hopi Cultural Affiliation with the Ancient Hohokam of Southern Arizona. In *Museums, Archaeology and Indigenous Communities*, edited by Margaret Clegg, Rebecca Redfern, Jelena Bekvalac, and Heather Bonney, pp. 104–133. Oxbow Books, Oxford, England.

Fewkes, Jesse Walter. 1900. Tusayan Migration Traditions. *Nineteenth Annual Report of the Bureau of American Ethnology for 1897–1898*, Pt. 2, pp. 957–1011. Smithsonian Institution, Washington, D.C.

———. 1903. Hopi Katsinas Drawn by Native Artists. *Twenty-first Annual Report of the Bureau of American Ethnology*, pp. 15–190. Government Printing Office, Washington, D.C.

Freer, Rachel, and G. Michael Jacobs. 2014. Dog Hair Sashes from Obelisk Cave, Northeastern Arizona. *Kiva* 79(3):300–306.

Hays-Gilpin, Kelley, and Jane H. Hill. 1999. The Flower World in Material Culture: An Icono-graphic Complex in the Southwest and Mesoamerica. *Journal of Anthropological Research* 55(1):1–37.

Kent, Kate Peck. 1940. The Braiding of a Hopi Wedding Sash. *Plateau* 12(3):46–52.

———. 1957. *The Cultivation and Weaving of Cotton in the Prehistoric Southwestern United States.* *Transactions of the American Philosophical Society*, new series, 47(3):457–733, Philadelphia.

———. 1979. *An Analysis of Textile Material from Walpi Pueblo.* Walpi Archaeological Project, Phase II, Vol. 6. Museum of Northern Arizona, Flagstaff, Arizona.

———. 1983a. *Prehistoric Textiles of the Southwest.* School of American Research Press, Santa Fe, New Mexico.

———. 1983b. *Pueblo Indian Textiles.* School of American Research Press, Santa Fe, New Mexico.

Mindeleff, Victor. 1891 [1989]. A Study of Pueblo Architecture: Tusayan and Cibola. In *Eighth Annual Report of the Bureau of Ethnology to the Secretary of the Smithsonian Institution, for the Years 1886–1887.* Government Printing Office, Washington, D.C. 1989 ed. Smithsonian Institution Press, Washington, D.C.

Morris, Earl H., and Robert F. Burgh. 1954. *Basket Maker II Sites Near Durango, Colorado.* Publication 604. Carnegie Institution of Washington, Washington, D.C.

Nequatewa, Edmund. 1967. *Truth of a Hopi: Stories Relating to the Origin, Myths and Clan Histories of the Hopi.* Northland Press and the Museum of Northern Arizona, Flagstaff.

Parsons, Elsie Clews. 1939. *Pueblo Indian Religion.* 2 vols. University of Chicago Press, Chicago.

Parsons, Elsie Clews (editor). 1936. *Hopi Journal of Alexander M. Stephen.* 2 vols. Columbia University Contributions to Anthropology Vol. 23. Columbia University Press, New York.

Smith, Watson. 1952. *Kiva Mural Decorations at Awatovi and Kawaika-a.* Papers of the Peabody Museum of American Archaeology and Ethnology Vol. XXXVII(5). Harvard University, Cambridge, Massachusetts.

Teague, Lynn S. 1998. *Textiles in Southwestern Prehistory.* University of New Mexico Press, Albuquerque.

Teiwes, Helga. 1996. *Hopi Basketry: Artistry in Natural Fibers.* University of Arizona Press, Tucson.

Voth, Heinrich R. 1905. *The Traditions of the Hopi.* Field Columbian Museum Anthropological Series 8. Field Columbian Museum, Chicago.

Webster, Laurie D. 1997. *Effects of European Contact on Textile Production and Exchange in the North American Southwest: A Pueblo Case Study.* PhD dissertation, Department of Anthropology, University of Arizona, Tucson. ProQuest, Ann Arbor, Michigan.

———. 1999. Evidence of Affiliation: Relationships of Historic Hopi and Prehistoric Salado Textiles and Basketry. In *Hoopoq'yaqam Niqw Wukoskyavi (Those Who Went to the Northeast and Tonto Basin): Hopi-Salado Cultural Affiliation Study* by T. J. Ferguson and Micah Loma'omvaya, pp. 261–300. Hopi Cultural Preservation Office, Kiqötsmovi, Arizona.

———. 2000. The Economics of Pueblo Textile Production and Exchange in Colonial New Mexico. In *Beyond Cloth and Cordage: Archaeological Textile Research in the Americas*, edited by Penelope Ballard Drooker and Laurie D. Webster, pp. 179–204. University of Utah Press, Salt Lake City.

———. 2003. Relationships of Hopi and Hohokam Textiles and Basketry. In *Yep Hisat Hoopoq'yaqam Yeesiwa (Hopi Ancestors Were Once Here): Hopi-Hohokam Cultural Affiliation Study*, compiled by T. J. Ferguson, pp. 165–209. Hopi Cultural Preservation Office, Kiqötsmovi, Arizona.

———. 2007. Ritual Costuming at Pottery Mound: The Pottery Mound Textiles in Regional Perspective. In *New Perspectives on Pottery Mound*, edited by Polly Schaafsma, pp. 167–206. University of New Mexico Press, Albuquerque.

———. 2012. The Perishable Side of Early Pueblo Style and Identity: Textiles, Sandals, and Baskets. In *Crucible of Pueblos: The Early Pueblo Period in the Northern Southwest*, edited by Richard H. Wilshusen, Gregson Schachner, and James R. Allison, pp. 159–184. Cotsen Institute of Archaeology Press, Los Angeles.

Webster, Laurie D., Kelley A. Hays-Gilpin, and Polly Schaafsma. 2006. A New Look at Tie-Dye and the Dot-in-a-Square Motif in the Pre-Hispanic Southwest. *Kiva* 71(3):317–348.

Webster, Laurie D., and Micah Loma'omvaya. 2004. Textiles, Baskets, and Hopi Cultural Identity. In *Identity, Feasting, and the Archaeology of the Greater Southwest: Proceedings of the 2002 Southwest Symposium*, edited by Barbara J. Mills, pp. 74–92. University Press of Colorado, Boulder.

Woodbury, Richard. 1954. *Prehistoric Stone Implements of Northeastern Arizona*. Papers of the Peabody Museum of American Anthropology and Ethnology Vol. XXXIV(6). Harvard University, Cambridge, Massachusetts.

Yava, Albert. 1978. *Big Falling Snow, a Tewa-Hopi Indian's Life and Times and the History and Traditions of His People*. Edited and annotated by Harold Courlander. Crown, New York.

10

THE GENETIC DIVERSITY OF HOPI CORN

MARK D. VARIEN, SHIRLEY POWELL, AND LEIGH J. KUWANWISIWMA

O NE ASPECT OF LIFE most important to Hopi people is their relationship to corn (maize) and corn farming (Wall and Masayesva 2004). According to traditional knowledge, this relationship is tied to the origin of Hopi people. When the Hopi emerged into the Fourth World, they approached Màasaw, their guardian spirit, for guidance. Màasaw presented them with a planting stick, a bag of seeds, a gourd of water, and a small ear of blue corn and thereby gave the Hopi the option to pursue this new way of life as farmers. The Hopi accepted this challenge and since then corn has been woven into almost every aspect of Hopi traditional life. In addition to providing sustenance, corn is woven into Hopi life metaphorically (Washburn 2012). It is also an important part of Hopi ceremonial life in which, among other ritual uses, it is integral to rites that mark childbirth and the naming of babies, initiations that signal the transition from childhood to adult life, and the transition that marks the end of life.

Màasaw set the Hopi on a path of life that is not easy: direct precipitation farming in the arid lands of the present day southwestern United States. Perhaps even more important than the agricultural and ceremonial practices, the corn-farming life offered by Màasaw taught Hopi people the values that they refer to as *hopivötskwani*, which loosely translates as "the Hopi way" or "the Hopi path." These values include those that the Hopi hold most dear: hard work, compassion, cooperation, reciprocity, a desire to live in balance and be stewards of the world that sustains all life, and perhaps foremost humility.

Given the importance of corn and corn farming to the Hopi, it is not surprising that the Hopi Cultural Preservation Office (HCPO) encouraged the Crow Canyon Archaeological Center to expand its Goodman Point Archaeological Project

(GPAP) research to include more studies of Ancestral Pueblo agriculture. Crow Canyon archaeologists, along with members of the National Park Service, presented the GPAP research design to the HCPO staff at their offices in Kiqötsmovi, Arizona, in September 2004. At the end of a thorough discussion of the research design, Crow Canyon archaeologists asked if there were research questions not included in the research design that would be of interest to the Hopi. The staff quickly answered that they would like to see additional studies of Ancestral Pueblo agriculture and that they were especially interested in learning whether agricultural practices maintained at Hopi today would work in the Mesa Verde region of southwestern Colorado, which they view as part of their ancestral homeland.

To move forward on the Hopi request, Crow Canyon sought and obtained funding for a meeting to discuss how to best pursue studies of Ancestral Pueblo agricultural practices in the Mesa Verde region (figure 10.1). Held in 2005 at Crow Canyon, this two-day planning meeting was attended by traditional Pueblo farmers from Hopi, Jemez, Ohkay Owingeh, and Tesuque; by anthropologists who study Ancestral Pueblo agriculture and modern Pueblo agriculture; and by Crow Canyon staff. Hopi

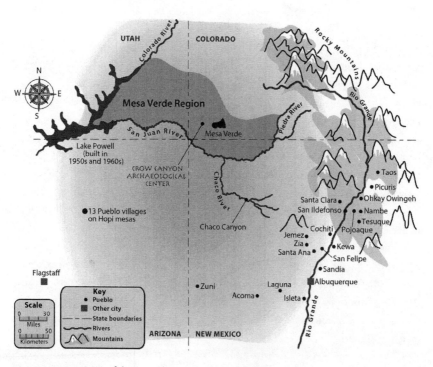

FIGURE 10.1 Map of the central Mesa Verde region and the Crow Canyon Archaeological Center (courtesy Crow Canyon Archaeological Center).

attendees included members of the HCPO staff and the Hopi Cultural Resources Advisory Task Team (CRATT), a group of cultural advisors who represent the diverse villages that comprise the Hopi nation today (figure 10.2).

At the conclusion of our meeting, the group decided to implement an experimental farming program. The group felt it best to focus on direct-precipitation farming, or what is commonly known as *dry farming*, because it is likely that this was the main type of farming practiced by Ancestral Pueblo farmers in the Mesa Verde region. The group agreed that the Hopi would take the lead as the traditional farming experts, since they still practice direct-precipitation farming. The experimental farming program established at this meeting has come to be known as the Pueblo Farming Project (PFP; Bocinsky and Varien 2017b; Varien et al. 2011). The PFP is one of a growing list of experimental studies that examine Indigenous corn in the Southwest and adjacent regions (Adams 2015; Adams et al. 1999, 2006; Bellorado 2010; Bellorado and Anderson 2013; Dominguez and Kolm 2005).

The PFP required funding. In addition to financial support from Crow Canyon, the project has received funding from The Christensen Fund, the History Colorado State Historical Fund, the National Geographic Society Genographic Legacy Fund,

FIGURE 10.2 Attendees of the initial meeting that created the Pueblo Farming Project (courtesy Crow Canyon Archaeological Center).

and the National Science Foundation, for which the PFP was one part of a larger research and education initiative known as the Village Ecodynamics Project (VEP). The PFP began in 2007, when Hopi farmers came to Crow Canyon to select the location for agricultural plots. Our plan was to integrate these gardens into Crow Canyon's education programs; therefore, they needed to be located on the campus of the Crow Canyon Archaeological Center. Hopi farmers used their traditional ecological knowledge to select the locations for agricultural plots, including identifying native plants that indicate good areas for farming and assessing soils, especially in terms of their texture and moisture-holding capacity.

Beginning in 2008, Hopi farmers traveled to Crow Canyon's campus twice a year: once in the spring for a planting meeting and again in the fall for a harvest meeting (figure 10.3). Each meeting includes discussion of the project goals, evaluation of the project's progress, and development of a plan for proceeding with current and future initiatives. Of course, each meeting also includes work in the agricultural plots.

From the beginning, the PFP was designed to create both research and education products. All PFP activities have been documented using numerous techniques—audio and video recording, still photography, written records, and detailed metrics on the plants and their growing environments—producing rich data sets from which several research and educational products have been produced (Bocinsky and Varien 2017a). For example, one of the PFP research goals was to evaluate the effect of annual variation in temperature and precipitation on agricultural yields and to use this knowledge to evaluate the estimates of agricultural yields produced by the VEP computer model (Bocinsky and Varien 2017; Kohler and Varien 2012; Varien et al. 2011). There were also numerous educational goals. Hopi and Crow Canyon educators have worked together to produce lesson plans for fourth and eighth grade students on Hopi lifeways, the importance of corn to Hopi culture and identity, and the ecology and sustainability of Pueblo farming practices. Audio and video recordings have been edited into short film clips highlighting traditional corn roasting and the production of *piiki* bread, as well as a full-length film documenting the PFP from inception to DNA analysis. Finally, a website will document the relationship between the experimental garden yields, weather and soil characteristics, will make our ongoing analyses available to the public, and will provide an exploratory data analysis tool to students and researchers (Bocinsky and Varien 2017b).

HOPI CORN DNA PROJECT HISTORY

Informal and formal discussions leading to the genetics components of the PFP took place at both Crow Canyon and Hopi beginning in 2005. Two initial concerns raised

FIGURE 10.3 Leigh Kuwanwisiwma discussing traditional planting methods during the Pueblo Farming Project (courtesy Crow Canyon Archaeological Center).

by the Hopi farmers were maintaining the purity of the traditional corn varieties and protecting their intellectual property rights. At our meeting that preceded the first planting of the Crow Canyon gardens (May 27, 2008), the archaeologists suggested mixing several varieties of corn in the same garden and holding growing conditions constant to determine if yields varied by variety. The Hopi farmers objected to this strategy, explaining that they separate varieties to maintain their distinctive qualities. They countered with a proposal that only one variety of corn should be planted in each garden—but that the single variety of corn could be planted with cultigens, including beans, squash, and melons, and with wild plants like sunflowers and beeweed, as long as those plants were located far enough from the corn that the plants didn't compete with each other for soil moisture.

While the two alternatives were being considered, the Hopi farmers shared information about their stewardship of the corn—thousands of years of plant husbandry that has produced corn varieties that are morphologically distinct and adapted to very specific (and harsh) conditions. They talked of the many sources of contamination and their concerns that cross-pollination would dilute characteristics of the specific varieties to the point at which they would lose their ability to survive the varied conditions at Hopi. They also noted that modern hybrid corn did not produce viable seed and worried that this characteristic might be transferred to cross-pollinated corn

Additionally, early discussions highlighted the mutual interest in origins that both the Hopi and Crow Canyon Center shared—origins of corn, technology, ritual, and people. In particular, we shared interests in people and corn: When did Ancestral Pueblo people first come to the northern Southwest? What spurred them to come to the northern Southwest? Who, if anyone, was here when they arrived? What happened socially and culturally once they arrived? We all had stories that proposed answers to these questions, but the stories differed and they focused on different agents of causality.

Our years of discussion, during which we bounced archaeological and Indigenous perspectives off of one another, resulted in a shared belief that a project that analyzed the DNA of Hopi corn varieties would provide information useful to both the Hopi Tribe and the Crow Canyon Archaeological Center. We decided to pursue the study in the hope that the DNA analysis might help prevent future contamination of Hopi corn strains, protect Hopi intellectual property rights, help answer questions about early Hopi migrations, and provide evidence for determinations of cultural affiliation between modern Hopi and the Ancestral Pueblo people pursuant to the Native American Graves Protection and Repatriation Act (NAGPRA). The HCPO believed that there was an urgent need to create a DNA baseline of Hopi corn varieties before they became further contaminated with non-Hopi corn and that this same baseline could contribute to answers to the other questions. Thus, the current collaboration was born.

ADDRESSING HOPI CONCERNS

All of our collaborative team, especially the Hopi members, had concerns regarding the DNA analysis of Hopi corn. Frank discussion of these concerns was an important part of designing and implementing this project. Most importantly, the genetic material in Hopi corn has developed as a result of the agricultural practices of Hopi farmers over a period of millennia. Therefore, the Hopi view the information encoded in the DNA of this corn as the intellectual property of all Hopi people—past, present, and future. We realized that analyzing the DNA of Hopi corn implies responsibility for safeguarding this intellectual property and doing right by the ancestors, the Hopi community today, and future generations of Hopi people.

Addressing these concerns remained difficult for our group because none of us— the HCPO staff, the CRATT members, nor the Crow Canyon staff—were experts in the DNA analysis of corn or the laws that govern intellectual property. With regard to the analysis itself, we did not and still do not possess an expert's understanding of the nature of the data produced by these analyses or how those data might be used by others. In addition, there were no lawyers at the table so that we could not obtain expert opinions about the laws that govern the creation and use of the kinds of information that would result from these analyses and whether they could or could not be protected as intellectual property. We moved forward by informing ourselves about these issues as best we could and we used the information we gathered as we designed the project.

We came to believe that a way to address our concerns was to develop a close working relationship with the scientists who would conduct the analysis. To accomplish this goal we contacted Darrell Maddox, who lived in nearby Durango, Colorado, and had developed an interest in Crow Canyon's mission. Darrell had just retired as president of Eurofins STA Laboratories, Inc. (ESTA), an independent laboratory founded in 1987 and located in Longmont, Colorado, that conducts DNA analysis of seeds and plants. He had since formed his own company, Endless Sky Partners, LLC (ELSP), to continue as a consultant in this field. Darrell participated in our corn DNA project in many ways: he came to a meeting at Crow Canyon and explained the basics of the DNA analysis to the HCPO staff, CRATT members, and Crow Canyon staff (and he helped us harvest the 2009 corn crop!). He also established a connection with his former company, ESTA, so that we would have a direct and personal relationship with the company that would conduct the DNA analysis. Darrell directly communicated our concerns about this project to the ESTA scientists and helped to develop the protocols that addressed these concerns.

In the end, we addressed our concerns by developing a written agreement that was signed by ELSP and ESTA and submitted to the Hopi Tribe via the HCPO.

This document was modeled after formal agreements developed by the Hopi Tribe and Crow Canyon when the PFP began. It specified Hopi concerns and defined the working relationship between Hopi and Crow Canyon. The corn DNA agreement that served as the foundation for this analysis acknowledged that ELSP and ESTA recognized the Hopi Tribe's need to protect its corn seed legally and specified that ELSP and ESTA did not have the authority to do any analysis beyond the extraction of DNA. Further, the agreement specified that ELSP and ESTA recognized that the samples, data, and results that were the subject of these analyses were the sole and exclusive property of the Hopi Tribe. Finally, the agreement specified that the genetic material would be properly disposed of or returned to the Hopi at their request and that the results of the analysis would not be revealed to any third party.

GENETIC STUDIES OF MAIZE

The complete genome sequence of *Zea mays* (cv. B73) was first published in 2009 by the Maize Genome Sequencing Project (Schnable et al. 2009) funded by the National Science Foundation. Among the world's major cereals, which include rice (*Oryza sativa*), sorghum (*Sorghum bicolor*), wheat (*Triticum* spp.), and barley (*Hordeum vulgare*), maize has the most thoroughly researched genetic system (Strable and Scanlon 2009) thanks to research that can be traced back to Mendel's 1869 experiments in which he used maize to corroborate his renowned experiments on peas (Coe 2001; Rhoades 1984).

Many characteristics of the plant make it a model species for genetic research that explores a wide range of topics including genome evolution, developmental physiology, epigenetics, pest resistance, heterosis, quantitative inheritance, and comparative genomics (Strable and Scanlon 2009). It is also useful for studies of plant domestication; genetic research has played a pivotal role in understanding the evolution of maize from its wild progenitor, teosinte, and determining that, of the four species of teosinte, *Zea mays* ssp. *parviglumis* is the direct ancestor of maize (Doebley 2004). Genetic research helped to pin down the location of the domestication process to the Rio Balsas region of present-day Mexico (Matsuoka et al. 2002; Piperno and Flannery 2001; Ranere et al. 2009).

Genetic studies of maize have documented its extraordinary level of genotypic diversity. Remarkably, the nucleotide polymorphism observed in the genomes of any two modern maize inbreed lines is equivalent to the sequence diversity between chimpanzees and humans (Buckler et al. 2006). Maize has about two billion bases of DNA, and mapping the maize genome has shown that some 32,000 genes are crammed onto just 10 chromosomes. Compare this to the human genome, which has about 20,000 genes dispersed among 23 chromosomes (Washington University School of Medicine 2009). At 2.3 Gbp, maize is a relatively large plant genome, although it is much smaller than that of plants such as wheat, and its genome is relatively repetitive, with 85 percent of the genome consisting of transposons and repetitive elements (Schnable et al. 2009).

METHODS

The field of maize genetic analysis provides the analytical tools used to analyze the nine Hopi corn varieties examined in this study. The seed from the nine varieties of Hopi corn were submitted to ESTA for analysis by the HCPO. The nine varieties were blue (*sakwapu*), white (*qötsaqa'ö*), red (*pala'qa'ö*), magenta (*wiqw'tö*), yellow (*takuri*), purple (*kokoma*), blue-gray (*masiqa'ö*), speckled (*pintoqa'ö*), and sweet (*tawak'tsi*). The first four were analyzed during a pilot study, and the remaining five were analyzed after this pilot study yielded positive results.

The genetics of these Hopi varieties were compared to those of two modern corn inbreds known to geneticists as B73 and Mo17. Variety B73 is the one analyzed to obtain the complete corn genome (Schnable et al. 2009). The genetic signatures of these modern varieties were compared to those of the Hopi varieties to interpret the results of this analysis.

Between thirty and sixty seeds of each variety were packaged and submitted for analysis. The seeds from each corn variety were planted and allowed to grow at the ESTA laboratory. The leaf material was the source of DNA analysis. Twenty plants of each variety were used for the analysis: plants 1 through 10 were combined for one sample, and plants 11 through 20 were combined for a second sample. Therefore, there were two analyses of each of the nine varieties of Hopi corn submitted for analysis. The analysis was replicated twice for each variety to verify the analytical procedures; drastic differences between replicated samples would indicate a possible mistake in samples processing and analysis. For this study, there was another reason to replicate the analysis of each variety: evaluating twenty seeds in two replications allowed the ESTA scientists to document as many alleles as possible in a given variety. There were slight allelic differences between the replicated samples for each of the nine varieties. However, the differences between replicated samples were so minor that the replication can be seen to demonstrate that there was no error when samples were analyzed and that the two replicated analyses can be interpreted as a single variety that is unique in its own way based on the genetic data.

To evaluate the similarity and difference among the nine varieties and to compare these varieties to the modern controls, ESTA analysts identified eighty microsatellite pairs, also known as simple sequence repeats (SSRs). These SSRs are short sequences of base pairs of DNA repeated many times. The number of the repeating nucleotide sequences varies between members of a species, making SSRs extremely useful in genetic analyses. Although SSRs are good for overall diversity studies, they do not provide enough genomic coverage to map specific traits in outbred landraces (local cultivars improved by traditional agricultural methods) (Barrett and Cardon 2006).

Each of the eighteen samples (two samples for each of the nine varieties of Hopi corn) were screened for these eighty SSRs. Seventy-three of the eighty SSRs were informative for the four samples submitted for the pilot study, and seventy-seven were informative for the five samples submitted for the expanded study. The SSRs that were not informative—seven in the pilot study and three in the subsequent analysis—were *monomorphic*, meaning that these SSRs expressed the same allele/fragment size across all entries. These uninformative SSRs were excluded from the subsequent analyses. More important, in both analyses, allelic differences were detected for almost all SSRs among all entries. These particular SSRs provide excellent coverage of the entire corn genome.

Genotypic data were generated following established protocols using an ABI3730XL capillary sequencer. Included in the documentation provided by ETSA is the list of SSRs along with their respective linkage order by chromosome. Reported values in respective entry marker cells represent DNA fragment sizes in base pairs. When a single value is present, the respective entry is homozygous for the given locus. If separated by a slash (/) the entry is heterozygous. Different fragment sizes or the length polymorphisms among entries for a given marker indicate that those entries are genetically different. Included in the raw data provided by ESTA were diagrams with colored blocks that indicate SSR results for each entry. When two entries have the same color for a given marker, they represent the same alleles.

The values were analyzed using Nei and Li's (1979) dissimilarity genetic distance algorithm, which is a well-accepted method for comparing genetic relationships based on DNA markers. Data were organized into a full-rank matrix where the values in the respective cells represent percent genetic dissimilarity rounded to whole numbers.

RESULTS

The primary goals of this project were to genotype nine varieties of Hopi corn and to determine the genetic relationships among each Hopi variety and the relationship of the Hopi corn to two modern inbred lines (control samples) that commonly serve as baseline standards in corn genotyping. Figure 10.4 presents the results of the DNA analysis as a tree diagram. The numbers at the bottom of the diagram represent percent genetic dissimilarity between entries. Entries that are the most similar are arranged closer together. Not included in this chapter is another figure created as basic documentation for this project. It is a diagram that shows the SSR results for each entry as colored blocks. Entries that have the same color for a given marker represent the same alleles, while entries that have different colors for the same marker represent alleles that produced the dissimilarity between entries.

Two general results are noteworthy. First, the greatest dissimilarity is between the Hopi corn as a group and the modern control samples. On average, the Hopi samples were 65 percent different when compared to the controls, indicating that Hopi corn probably has a distinct genetic background, although comparison to other modern varieties is needed. This is not surprising because B73 and Mo17 are early inbreds developed by Pioneer Hybrid. Both are dent corn that was developed by crossing a Southern Dent, related to maize from southern Mexico, with a Northern Flint, derived from the maize of the Southwest U.S. (Doebley et al. 1986, 1988).

The second important general result is that there is considerable heterogeneity among the Hopi varieties. This heterogeneity can be measured by quantifying the

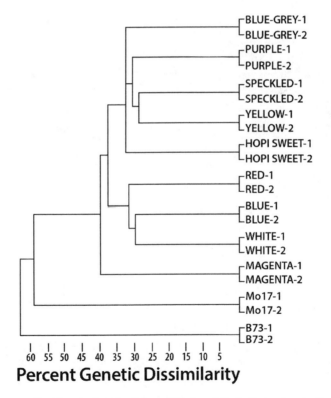

Percent Genetic Dissimilarity

FIGURE 10.4 Tree diagram based on Nei and Li's (1979) dissimilarity-genetic-distance algorithm, illustrating the results of the DNA analysis of Hopi corn (courtesy Crow Canyon Archaeological Center).

percentage of heterozygous loci for each entry when compared to all other entries. Among the eighteen entries for the nine varieties, heterozygous loci ranged from a low of 50 percent for Magenta-1 to a high of 68.8 percent for Speckled-1. To put this considerable heterogeneity into perspective, the heterozygous loci for the two modern controls were 2.5 percent for B73 and 3.75 percent for M017. One might think that the color differences among the Hopi corn varieties are just morphological, but this analysis dispels that notion. Instead, it shows that the different Hopi corn varieties, visually distinguished by color variations that are sometimes obvious and sometimes quite subtle, are in fact genetically distinct. This result supports the Hopi view and the view of other Pueblo groups that varieties of Hopi (and Pueblo) corn, distinguished by color, have distinct characteristics that were important to the survival of Pueblo people (Ford 1980). Each Hopi variety can be characterized as heterozygous when compared to the other varieties but homogenous in terms of the phenotypic similarity within each variety. This contrasts with the modern inbred lines that companies have developed to produce commercial hybrids; heterozygous loci on these inbred lines are so few (two of eighty for M017) that these hybrids could almost be characterized as homozygous.

Figure 10.4 shows that the Hopi varieties form two general groups. In one, blue and white corn are the most similar. The next variety to join this group is red. In the other group, speckled and yellow are the most similar. The next variety to join this group is purple, followed by blue-gray and then by Hopi sweet. The two groups come together at that point, and then magenta (colloquially known in Hopi as "greasy head"), which is the genetically most dissimilar, joins the remaining eight varieties. Blue and white are the two varieties that are most similar: 30 percent of their genetic makeup is dissimilar. Speckled and magenta are the most different: 50 percent of their genetic makeup is dissimilar.

Scientists at ESTA concluded that the Hopi corn varieties are maintained by open-pollination and that they are grown in areas that are physically isolated from one another. This conforms to Hopi agricultural practices. The DNA analysis of Hopi corn demonstrated the uniqueness of the nine Hopi varieties. Clearly, thousands of years of Hopi plant husbandry have created and preserved morphologically and genetically distinct corn varieties that are uniquely suited to the highly variable environmental conditions of the northern Southwest.

DISCUSSION

The DNA analysis demonstrated that all nine varieties sampled in this study were genetically distinct and concluded that this was a result of Hopi farmers planting only one variety of corn in a field so that the distinctive characteristics of each variety were not mixed by cross-pollination. As Hopi and Crow Canyon team members discussed the analysis they realized that this result created a new question for consideration: if Hopi agricultural practices are designed to perpetuate the distinctiveness of each variety, how did new varieties come into existence?

We have discussed three hypotheses that address this question. The first is that new varieties developed in different locations and were then brought to Hopi through clan migrations. The second was that new varieties were created at Hopi through Hopi cultural and agricultural practices. The third was that new varieties came to Hopi through exchange with other Pueblo groups.

In discussing clan migrations, we realized that archaeologists and Hopi both have stories about how the origins of corn farming were related to migrations. These stories overlap in some respects but also diverge in important ways. Very simply stated, the archaeological story focuses on the Archaic, Basketmaker II, and Basketmaker III periods. Archaeologists have traced people and corn as they moved north out of Mexico into southern Arizona (figure 10.5) and eventually onto the Colorado Plateau. Once on the Colorado Plateau (figure 10.6), the corn-bearing immigrants, who have become known to archaeologists as Western Basketmaker II people, encountered Indigenous populations that by most archaeological reckonings were hunter-gatherers who did not have corn but adopted corn farming after it was introduced. This second group likely included at least two groups: hunter-gatherers who lived in the Western Basketmaker II area in northeastern Arizona and southeastern Utah and a different group of hunter-gatherers who lived in northeastern New Mexico and southwestern Colorado. The New Mexico-Colorado hunter-gatherers who adopted corn farming after it was introduced have become known to archaeologists as the Eastern Basketmaker II people. Western and Eastern Basketmaker II people eventually coalesced into a more homogenous group during the period archaeologists call Basketmaker III (figure 10.7), and in many ways this marks the beginning of a Pueblo tradition that spans the entire Ancestral Pueblo world, a tradition that integrates Pueblo people who have different histories and languages, one that has continued to the present.

The Hopi story starts with Hopi clans and their emergence into this, the Fourth World. It features the Motisinom—the "first people," who originated in the north—people who inhabited what is North America today. A distinct group, the Nutungqwsinom, arrived later, migrating from the south and moving into the vast area occupied by the Motisinom. Clans from both of these groups eventually made their way to the Hopi Mesas, the center place known as Tuuwanasavi (figure 10.8), where they combined to form a single group that today are called Hopisinom (Bernardini 2011; Judge et al. 1991; Kuwanwisiwma 2004). At first glance, the Hopi and archaeological stories

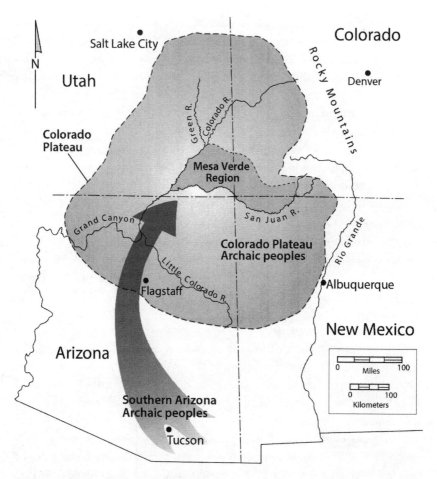

FIGURE 10.5 Southern Arizona Archaic peoples move north onto the Colorado Plateau and encounter an Indigenous Archaic population (courtesy Crow Canyon Archaeological Center).

converge, with one population indigenous to the Colorado Plateau (and perhaps the Great Basin) and the second population of later immigrants from points south.

Unlike the archaeological story, however, the Hopi story says that both the Motisinom and the Nutungqwsinom had corn. The Motisinom had blue corn that was well adapted to the cold arid conditions of the Colorado Plateau, while southern immigrants brought with them red corn that originated in the warmer and wetter climes to the south.

These two versions of Hopi migration were shared during many discussions over several years. As we accumulated a larger picture, we came to wonder whether the stories were variations on the same theme. In particular, Leigh Kuwanwisiwma noted

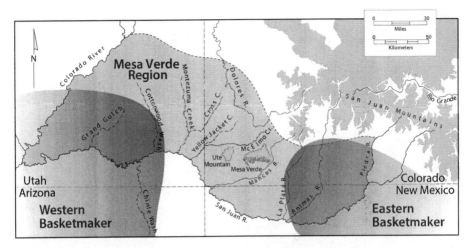

FIGURE 10.6 Western and Eastern Basketmakers (courtesy Crow Canyon Archaeological Center).

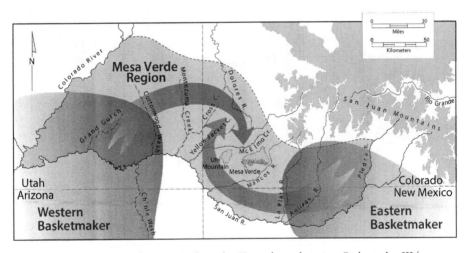

FIGURE 10.7 Western and Eastern Basketmaker II peoples coalesce into Basketmaker III (courtesy Crow Canyon Archaeological Center).

that the blue and red corn varieties associated with the Motisinom and the Nutungq-wsinom corresponded to the colors associated with the different directions recognized by the Hopi, blue with the northwest and red with the southeast. He suggested that the corn could be used as a surrogate for the people themselves: blue corn for the Motisinom and red corn for the Nutungqwsinom. We reasoned that, if this were true, we could use the corn genetics and the distributions of blue and red corn over time to reconstruct the migrations of the Motisinom and the Nutungqwsinom. Further,

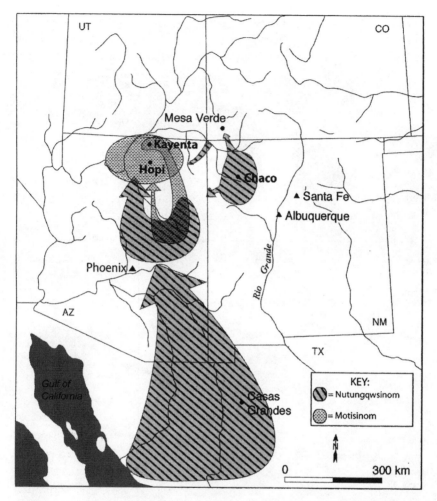

FIGURE 10.8 The migrations of the Nutungqwsinom (people from the south [directional color red, bearers of red corn]) and Motisinom (people from the north [directional color blue, bearers of blue corn]) (Bernardini 2011:figure 10.1; courtesy Crow Canyon Archaeological Center).

this has led us to wonder to what degree clan migrations were a means by which other varieties of corn were first introduced to the Hopisinom. We hope to examine this question in our future collaborative research.

In our collective discussions we also speculated on whether other Hopi cultural practices—cultural dynamics that were internal to Hopi society—could have resulted in the development of new varieties of corn. As an example, the HCPO staff and CRATT members shared how at certain times Hopi *katsinam* distribute bags of seeds to Hopi people; these bags include seeds from many different varieties of corn and from other cultigens. These seeds are planted in a single hole. Of course, this is the opposite of typical Hopi corn farming practices because different varieties of corn grow together in a single clump. The different varieties of corn cross-pollinate and produce multicolored ears of corn known to Hopi people as Kachina corn. It is possible that Hopi farmers in the distant past selected the new and unusually colored seed from these ears of Kachina corn and propagated them, eventually producing new and distinct varieties of corn.

Finally, the Hopi and the other Pueblo groups in the Southwest have detailed accounts of interacting over a period that probably spans millennia. It is entirely possible, even likely, that this interaction included the exchange of different varieties of corn. Distinct varieties of corn may have arrived at Hopi through exchanges in the distant past and may have been planted again and again in Hopi fields. Gradually, this corn would have become increasingly adapted to the local conditions of the Hopi area until it became thought of today as distinct varieties of Hopi corn. One possibility for future studies would be to compare the genetics of Hopi varieties in use today with the varieties in use at other Pueblos.

CONCLUSIONS

The staff at Crow Canyon conducts research and education programs about the lives of Ancestral Pueblo people and seeks to connect the distant past to the lives of Pueblo people living today. We know from a variety of studies that Ancestral Pueblo people derived the majority of their calories from corn, and we know that this crop was the centerpiece of their agricultural efforts (Coltrain et al. 2006; Matson 1991, 2016; Matson and Chisholm 1991). Although we were well aware of the importance of corn and corn farming to Ancestral Pueblo subsistence, the Crow Canyon staff had almost no practical knowledge of how farming was conducted in the past.

Thanks to the Pueblo Farming Project and the knowledge shared by the Hopi farmers, we now have a much better practical understanding of how direct-precipitation corn farming was accomplished. Perhaps more importantly, we learned that corn farming is much more than an activity that provides food and that instead corn and corn farming are central to how Hopi and other Pueblo people think of themselves as people and how they view their place in the world. We have also learned how collaborative research like the Pueblo Farming Project can lead to new research like the corn DNA project.

The Hopi perspective on the corn DNA project goes back to the mission of the HCPO, which has a constitutional and legal mandate to protect Hopi culture for

the future. The HCPO initiated the corn DNA project because, after careful delib-
eration, Hopi staff decided that analyzing the DNA of Hopi corn was vital to that
cultural preservation effort. The Hopi also have a perspective on this project as collaborative research: they view the corn DNA study as an educational project in which
Hopi and Crow Canyon learn from each other.

Although the Hopi viewed this project as a pioneering and innovative study, they
entered into it not merely for the sake of using science to create new knowledge.
Instead, they wanted to create knowledge that was consistent with their mandate
of protecting Hopi culture for the future. The use of modern science to document
the genetic distinctiveness of Hopi corn is seen as a progressive endeavor that is not
entirely free from risk, but in the words of one CRATT member, "The DNA is information that the corn has to give to us, and we have to trust the corn. Corn has always
taken care of us, and it will help us save our culture into the future." In the end, the
DNA analyses were scientific methods that were seen as justified because they could
help the Hopi to achieve their larger goals. The baseline genetic data gathered by
this project are seen as information gathered in order to benefit future generations
of Hopi people.

This study also lays the groundwork for future collaborative research. First, we
hope to expand the DNA analysis of modern Hopi corn to include all extant Hopi
varieties and to sample varieties being used by different farmers whose fields are
located throughout Hopi lands. Second, we hope to compare the DNA of Hopi corn
with that of other Pueblo varieties and with that of corn grown by other Indigenous
groups in the Southwest and adjacent areas. Third, we hope to conduct DNA analyses
of ancient Pueblo corn recovered from Ancestral Pueblo archaeological sites and to
compare this DNA to the DNA from modern Hopi corn. These future studies will
require ongoing collaboration among Crow Canyon, the HCPO, other Indigenous
groups, the institutions where samples are curated, and the scientists who conduct
the DNA analysis. We look forward to working together to achieve our shared goals.

ACKNOWLEDGMENTS

Components of the Pueblo Farming Project have been funded by the Christensen
Fund, the History Colorado State Historical Fund, the National Geographic Society
Genographic Legacy Fund, the National Science Foundation, and the Qwest Foun-
dation. The corn DNA analysis was funded by the History Colorado State Historical
Fund. We are grateful to collaborators in this research, Darrell Maddox of Endless
Skies Partners, LLC, and the scientists at Eurofins-STA Laboratories, who patiently
answered the authors' many technical questions about the analysis, helping us to

clarify the results presented in this chapter. We are grateful for the comments provided by the volume editors and two anonymous reviewers. We are especially grateful to Kelly Swarts, who reviewed and commented on an early draft of this chapter, providing many insights into the interpretation of these data. Finally, we want to thank the Hopi Cultural Preservation Office staff and the Hopi Cultural Resource Task Team members who worked with us on the Pueblo Farming Project and the corn DNA analysis.

REFERENCES CITED

Adams, Karen R. 2015. The Archaeology and Agronomy of Ancient Maize (*Zea mays L.*). In *Traditional Arid Land Agriculture: Understanding the Past for the Future*, edited by S. Ingram and R. Hunt, pp. 15–53. University of Arizona Press, Tucson.

Adams, Karen R., Cathryn M. Meegan, Scott G. Ortman, R. Emerson Howell, Lindsay C. Werth, Deborah A. Muenchrath, Michael K. O'Neill, and Candice A. C. Gardner. 2006. *MAÍS (Maize of American Indigenous Societies) Southwest: Ear Descriptions and Traits That Distinguish 27 Morphologically Distinct Groups of 123 Historic USDA Maize (Zea mays L. ssp. mays) Accessions, and Data Relevant to Archaeological Subsistence Models.* Unpublished report submitted to the James S. McDonnell Foundation 21st Century Research Award/ Studying Complex Systems, JSMF Grant No. 21002035.

Adams, Karen R., Deborah A. Muenchrath, and Dylan M. Schwindt. 1999. Moisture Effects on the Morphology of Ears, Cobs and Kernels of a South-Western U.S. Maize (*Zea Mays L.*) Cultivar, and Implications for the Interpretation of Archaeological Maize. *Journal of Archaeological Science* 26:483–496.

Bellorado, Ben A. 2010. Reconstruction of Prehistoric Subsistence Agriculture in Ridges Basin. In *Animas-La Plata Project*, Vol. XIII: Special Studies, edited by J. M. Potter, pp. 215–233. University of Arizona Press, Tucson.

Bellorado, Ben A., and Kirk C. Anderson. 2013. Early Pueblo Responses to Climate Variability: Farming Traditions, Land Tenure, and Social Power in the Eastern Mesa Verde Region. *Kiva* 78(4):377–417.

Bernardini, Wesley. 2011. North, South, and Center: An Outline of Hopi Ethnogenesis. In *Religious Transformation in the late Pre-Hispanic Pueblo World*, edited by Donna M. Glowacki and Scott Van Keuren, pp. 196–220. University of Arizona Press, Tucson.

Bocinsky, R. Kyle, and Mark D. Varien. 2017a. Calibrating Maize Paleoproductivity Models Using Experimental Data. *Journal of Ethnobiology* 37(2):282–307.

Bocinsky, R. K., and M. D. Varien. 2017b. *The Pueblo Farming Project: A Collaboration Between Hopi Farmers and the Crow Canyon Archaeological Center*. Electronic document, http:// shiny.crowcanyon.org/pfp, accessed February 5, 2017.

Buckler, Edward S., Brandon S. Gault, and Michael D. McMullen. 2006. Molecular and Functional Diversity of Maize. *Current Opinion in Plant Biology* 9:172–176.

Coe, E. H. Jr. 2001. The Origins of Maize Genetics. *National Review of Genetics*, 2:898–905.

Coltrain, Joan Brenner, Joel C. Janetski, and Shawn W. Carlyle. 2006. The Stable and Radio-Isotopic Chemistry of Eastern Basketmaker and Pueblo Groups in the Four Corners Region of the American Southwest. In *Histories of Maize: Multidisciplinary Approaches to Prehistory, Linguistics, Biogeography, Domestication, and Evolution of Maize*, edited by J. Staller, R. Tykot, and B. Benz, pp. 275–287. Lesevier, Amsterdam.

Doebley, John. 2004. The Genetics of Maize Evolution. *Annual Review of Genetics* 38:37–59.

Dominguez, Steven, and Ken E. Kolm. 2005. Beyond Water Harvesting: A Soil Hydrology Perspective on Traditional Southwestern Agricultural Technology. *American Antiquity* 70(4):732–765.

Ford, Richard I. 1980. The Color of Survival. *Discovery, 1980*, pp. 17–30. School of American Research, Weatherhead Foundation, Santa Fe, New Mexico.

Judge, James, David Breternitz, Linda Cordell, George Gumerman, Leigh Jenkins, Edmund Ladd, and William Lipe. 1991. *The Anasazi. Why Did They Leave? Where Did They Go? An Informal Discussion.* Southwest Natural and Cultural Heritage Association, Albuquerque, New Mexico.

Kohler, Timothy A. and Mark D. Varien (editors). 2012. *Emergence and Collapse of Early Villages: Models of Central Mesa Verde Region Archaeology.* Origins of Human Behavior and Culture No. 6. University of California Press, Berkeley.

Kuwanwisiwma, Leigh J. 2004. *Yupkövi*: The Hopi Story of Chaco Canyon. In *In Search of Chaco: New Approaches to an Archaeological Enigma*, edited by David Grant Noble, pp. 41–47. SAR Press, Santa Fe.

Matson, R. G. 1991. *The Origins of Southwestern Agriculture.* University of Arizona Press, Tucson.

———. 2016. The Nutritional Context of the Pueblo III Depopulation of the Northern San Juan: Too Much Maize? *Journal of Archaeological Science: Reports* 5:622–631.

Matson, R. G., and Brian Chisolm. 1991. Basketmaker II Subsistence: Carbon Isotopes and Other Dietary Indicators from Cedar Mesa, Utah. *American Antiquity*, 56(3):444–459.

Matsuoka, Yoshihiro, Yves Vigouroux, Major M. Goodman, Jesus G. Sanchez, Edward Buckler, and John Doebley. 2002. A Single Domestication for Maize Shown by Multilocus Microsatellite Genotyping. *Proceedings of the National Academy of Sciences* 99:6080–6084.

Nei, M., and W. H. Li. 1979. Mathematical Model for Studying Genetic Variation in Terms of Restriction Endonucleases. *Proceedings of the National Academy of Sciences* 76:5269–5273.

Piperno, Dolores R., and Kent V. Flannery. 2001. The Earliest Archaeological Maize (*Zea mays L.*) from Highland Mexico: New Accelerator Mass Spectrometry Dates and Their Implications. *Proceedings of the National Academy of Sciences* 98:2101–2103.

Ranere, Anthony J., Dolores R. Piperno, Irene Holst, Ruth Dickau, and José Iriarte. 2009. The Cultural and Chronological Context of Early Holocene Maize and Squash Domestication in the Central Balsas River Valley, Mexico. *Proceedings of the National Academy of Sciences,* 106:5014–5018.

Rhoades, M. M. 1984. The Early Years of Maize Genetics. *Annual Review of Genetics* 18:1–29.

Schnable, Patrick S., Doreen Ware, Robert S. Fulton, Joshua C. Stein, Fusheng Wei, Shiran Pasternak, and Chengzhi Liang. 2009. The B73 Maize Genome: Complexity, Diversity, and Dynamics. *Science* 326(5956):1112–1115.

Strable, Josh, and Michael J. Scanlon. 2009. Maize (*Zea mays*): A Model Organism for Basic and Applied Research in Plant Biology. *Cold Spring Harbor Protocols* 4(10). doi: 10.1101/pdb.emo132.

Varien, Mark D., Scott G. Ortman, Paul Ermigiotti, Timothy A. Kohler, and Leigh Kuwanwisiwma. 2011. Modeling Agricultural Potential in the Mesa Verde Region: Combining Computer Simulation with Experimental Gardening. Paper presented at the Annual Meeting of the Society for American Archaeology, Sacramento, California.

Wall, Dennis, and Virgil Masayesva. 2004. People of the Corn: Teachings in Hopi Traditional Agriculture, Spirituality, and Sustainability. *American Indian Quarterly* 28(3-4):435–453.

Washburn, Dorothy K. 2012. Shared Image Metaphors of the Corn Lifeway in Mesoamerica and the American Southwest. *Journal of Anthropological Research* 68(4):473–502.

Washington University School of Medicine. 2009. Amaizing: Corn genome decoded. *Science Daily.* 21 November. Electronic document, https://www.sciencedaily.com/releases/2009/11/091119193636.htm, accessed October 26, 2017.

11

HOPI FOOTPRINTS

What Really Matters in Cultural Preservation

JOËLLE CLARK AND GEORGE GUMERMAN IV

Our ancestors are here still in the water, in the land, in spirit. We're all here together being happy. That's something real precious. . . . It's what we live for. Back then they were living real hard. We're living easy lives, but we come back and recognize what they have done.

(A. S., HOPI YOUTH IN HOPI FOOTPRINTS PROGRAM 2009)

A S ARCHAEOLOGISTS, WE FREQUENTLY speak about cultural preservation. Traditionally, archaeologists refer to preservation in terms of artifacts and sites. Are we fully preserving culture when we curate artifacts and our field notes and nominate a site to the National Register? We believe it is important to define cultural preservation in a broader sense—to encompass current and future language, beliefs, traditions, and practices. We therefore applaud the expanded definition of cultural preservation that includes intangible heritage (United Nations Educational, Scientific and Cultural Organization [UNESCO] 2003). We might, however, ask what is meant by "intangible" and to whom. We realize that "intangible" refers to nonmaterial rather than to immaterial, imperceptible, insubstantial, ethereal, vague, immeasurable, or intrinsic culture. As such, intangible cultural heritage includes cultural practices, beliefs, language, and knowledge (e.g., Alivizatou 2012; Shepherd 2009; UNESCO 2003). By broadening cultural preservation to include intangible heritage we have come a long way; however, we believe that this has the potential to set up divisive

This chapter uses the *Hopi Dictionary/Hopìikwa Lavàytutuveni: A Hopi-English Dictionary of the Third Mesa Dialect* (Hopi Dictionary Project 1998). While we recognize that there are different dialect variations, as non-native Hopi speakers, we opted to use the Third Mesa dialect presented in the dictionary. The quotes provided by Hopi youth do not include their full names. We decided to use initials instead of full names to protect their identities as minors. Permissions to use quotes, photos, and video were obtained by signed parental permission when the youth joined the program.

dichotomies—archaeologists and descendant communities, artifacts and beliefs, sites and sense of place, for instance. How then do we operationalize cultural preservation holistically (e.g., Alivizatou 2012) and in what contexts can this be applied? We believe that the answer lies not only in participating in collaborative research as illustrated by other chapters in this volume, but more importantly for educational efforts, in facilitating broader efforts of the people whose culture is being preserved while also looking ahead toward the future.

If, as archaeologists, we emphasize the *culture* in cultural preservation, we begin to focus on people—viewing cultural preservation "in relation to its producers and practitioners" (Alivizatou 2012:35)—rather than as researchers. It is not about us as archaeologists, but about the people who live the culture and depend on their past to seek a better future (see Balenquah 2012). As Shepherd (2009:57) asks, "whose heritage is being preserved and managed, by whom, for what purposes?" By incorporating multiple stakeholder values and realizing that various reasons for cultural preservation exist, we also delve into the realm of differing values and ethics (see Colwell-Chanthaphonh and Ferguson 2006; Smith et al. 2010).

We follow Colwell-Chanthaphonh and Ferguson (2006:150) in viewing the role of archaeologists as anthropologists, not just understanding the past "but how people use the past to make meaning in their lives today." Cultural preservation is thus more about sustaining and engaging the present and future through the past (Alivizatou 2012:192; Bauer 2009:87). Intangible heritage is not about "a set of preciously safeguarded and unchanging traditions, but [about] . . . knowledge and practice inherited from the past and revived in the present . . . [led by] active and ongoing engagement of practitioners" (Alivizatou 2012:190). New traditions build upon the past and are "recreated and reinterpreted through practice" (Bauer 2009:87). Lyle Balenquah (2012:14), Native Hopi archaeologist, confirms the power of the past to influence the everyday lives of present-day Hopi by arguing that "the meaning of the past is what it contributes to life in the present. This understanding provides a continual connection between modern Hopi people and their predecessors. I believe this connection is the bond that Hopi people share in the way they know and feel about their ancestors." As such, the Hopi use the past to inform the present; but importantly also to shape the future.

Our twelve-year collaboration with the Hopi Tribe shifted our cultural preservation lens to focus on the future for Hopi youth by grounding students in the past and the present. Leigh Kuwanwisiwma, director of the Hopi Cultural Preservation Office (HCPO), along with his staff, elders, and youth, pushed us to use archaeology to appropriately connect Hopi youth and elders with their ancestral past. At Leigh's request, the Hopi Footprints program developed as a collaboration between the HCPO and Northern Arizona University (NAU).

rints program is an intergenerational partnership that connects
lers, cultural specialists, archaeologists, and educators on expe-
ative trips to Hopitutskwa (Hopi land), the Hopi cultural land-
includes Hisatsinom sites (Hopi ancestral places) and the stories,
songs, and deep meanings that surround them (Gumerman et al. 2012). Referred to
as ancestral "footprints," these places provide a profound context for engaged cultural
preservation (figure 11.1). The Hopi believe that the ancestors did not abandon these
archaeological sites. Instead, these sites provide physical evidence that both verifies
Hopi clan histories and religious beliefs (Bernardini 2005; Kuwanwisiwma 2002) and
communicates strong emotional messages that are relevant for Hopi people today
(Balenquah 2008, 2012). Embodied in these messages are instructions for how to live
the Hopi way. When the Hopi Footprints program participants visit ancestral sites,
the elders instruct them to respect the presence of the Hisatsinom or Motisinom and
to ask for permission to visit and learn what they have to communicate. In a way, the
footprints of the ancestors have provided the path for modern Hopi cultural preservation efforts.

Many Hopi argue that the survival of Hopi culture and tradition depends on teaching the younger generations to speak and preserve the Hopi language, to maintain
traditional values and beliefs, and to continue to be caretakers of the land, including
respecting ancestral sites. Visiting these ancestral places provides opportunities for

FIGURE 11.1 Hopi Footprints program group photo at Mesa Verde National Park.

mutual sharing of knowledge about Hopi traditions, culture, language, and history, as well as a living context for Hopi cultural preservation into the future. To us, this relationship among past, present, and future generations is the essence of cultural preservation.

Our program is not what one thinks of as traditional archaeological research. Our approach even differs from what is thought of as applied archaeology—using archaeological knowledge and methods to help solve broader societal concerns (Downum and Price 1999). Although the Hopi Footprints program does address societal needs, it was Leigh Kuwanwisiwma and his team of HCPO staff and Cultural Resource Advisory Task Team (CRATT) elders who taught us a deeper set of cultural preservation values and goals. Indeed, this work changed our understanding of what archaeology should be about—honoring and respecting the knowledge ancestors left for future generations along with scientific evidence from the past while also giving back to living communities in culturally appropriate ways. We learned that archaeology is not just about research, cultural history, or processual explanations—what one thinks of as the typical goals of archaeology. To the Hopi, archaeology is so much more. The elders and youth with whom we work are interested in cultural historical information. They wonder about what the Hisatsinom ate and how they lived, what roles men and women played, and how Hopi life from the past has changed yet remained the same. As archaeologists we share these questions—standard cultural historical types of questions. However, the elders and youth are not usually interested in the other goals of our discipline, at least not in terms of the usual interpretations provided by archaeologists. They have their own explanations and cultural meanings about the past. They are interested in what archaeologists find out, but the most relevant evidence is not buried in the ground or in archives; it is found within the specific songs, stories, and clan histories of the Hopi. Applying cultural preservation then is about making meaning of archaeological knowledge along with cultural knowledge to understand the past, be grounded in the present, and inform the future.

HOPI CULTURAL PRESERVATION THROUGH EDUCATION

Our revised ideas about cultural preservation grew as the Hopi Footprints program evolved. The program began in 2002 during a collaborative planning session about archaeology education among the HCPO, the Anthropology Department, and the Center for Science Teaching and Learning at NAU. The HCPO is often approached by non-Hopi people to conduct research on and about Hopi that they want to share in various public venues and publications. Leigh Kuwanwisiwma, director of the

HCPO, wanted to change the fundamental approach of archaeological education *about* the past to cultural education *for* Hopi people. Our shift in focus enabled Hopi teachers and elders to design culturally relevant education for Hopi youth about what it means to be Hopi and about Hopi history through learning from the Hisatsinom. This type of educational approach in which Indigenous youth incorporate the study of ancestral sites and artifacts with their native language and traditions supports their mental, spiritual, and physical health and provides them with a stronger self-identity, which in turn empowers them to learn and live successfully in both Native and Western worlds (Demmert and Towner 2003).

Hopi blue corn provides a powerful analogy for the culturally relevant educational efforts of our Hopi Footprints program (figure 11.2). Traditionally, the Hopi are and have always been farmers. Upon emergence into this Fourth World, the Hopi chose the short blue ear of corn that grows in the high desert. These plants thrive only with careful attention, respect, and nurturing. Indeed, corn is raised and cared for like children. Much like the seeds of the blue corn, the seeds of the program are derived from the need to increase the use of Hopi language and understand Hopi traditions. In the words of Anita Poleahla, President and Founder, Mesa Media, Inc.,

> "*Hopilavayi* ([Hopi] language) is rooted in our culture as a people, if we lose our language, there will no longer be Hopisinom ([Hopi] people). Our language defines who we are spiritually," Poleahla said. "If we no longer are able to speak *Hopilavayi* then we will never really understand the full meaning of what our Hopi ceremonies mean, even if we participate. The depth of *Hopilavayi* cannot be expressed in English; our language is unique to our worldview. We hold great responsibility as stewards of this land we live on and have yet to fulfill our covenant to Maasawu [Màasaw]. This transfer of knowledge is usually done through our language and understanding how our cultural reinforces these responsibilities. *Hopilavayi* is just not a language; it is a teaching tool of life, it is our life." (*Navajo-Hopi Observer* 2013; italics original)

Sadly, there is a growing crisis of language and culture loss among Hopi youth. Most Hopi youth are not learning the Hopi language, and elders are finding it increasingly difficult to pass on their traditional cultural knowledge. The Hopi Language Assessment Project, conducted in 1997, analyzed fluency and practice of the Hopi language in Hopi villages and homes. The survey found that 100 percent of Hopi elders (sixty years or older), 84 percent of adults (forty to fifty-nine years old), 50 percent of young adults (twenty to thirty-nine), and only 5 percent children (age two to nineteen) speak and understand the Hopi language (Poleahla 2014). In response, the HCPO began the Hopilavayi Project, a tribal initiative to revitalize Hopi culture and language in Hopi school communities (HCPO 2009).

FIGURE 11.2 Hopi summer cornfield in Orayvi Wash, August 1, 2005 (photograph by T. J. Ferguson).

Concurrently with the Hopilavayi project, the Hopi Footprints program evolved to create a complementary culturally relevant curriculum for Hopi teachers that focused on Hopi cultural history and preservation. Using initial seed money from the Society for American Archaeology's Public Education Committee and funding from Arizona's Improving Teacher Quality program, we created "Hopi Footprints: Building Better Teachers with a Community-Based Culture Curriculum" for Hopi youth in grades K-6. The curriculum was developed through collaborative efforts of Hopi teachers, elders, archaeologists, anthropologists, technology specialists, and tribal professionals.

As part of our curriculum development process, we traveled to Hisatsinom sites across the Southwest, sharing meals, stories, laughter, and cultural information. We videotaped elder oral history, archaeologists' interpretations, and conversations between members of the group that would later be edited and shared in a CD resource as part of the written curriculum. We gathered for numerous hours in teachers' classrooms at Moencopi Day School to discuss critical ideas for what a curriculum for Hopi youth should or should not include. The HCPO professionals and elders selected from CRATT were instrumental in ensuring that our materials were culturally and age appropriate. The final curriculum materials were provided to teachers in Hopi schools and are currently being distributed by the HCPO.

Following the dissemination of the curriculum, we saw a need to work directly with Hopi youth. The Hopi Footprints grew, much like the blue corn, into a continued partnership that would enact the enduring understandings of the curriculum (e.g., Wiggins and McTighe 2005). The foundation of the program is built upon what it means to be Hopi by learning about Hopi culture and history. We explored key questions for Hopi youth such as who am I, what is my role in Hopi society, where do I come from, and where am I going? Hopi elders and youth thus engage in and develop their own meanings about the connections among past, present, and future Hopi life.

The goal of the growing youth program is to promote Hopi cultural preservation by collaboratively tracing these footprints of Hopi ancestors, participating in community service projects, and expressing the impact of learning through educational products such as digital media and a museum exhibit. The current Hopi Footprints program includes a summer-camp-style component along with weekend youth workshops throughout the school year. We recruit youth from all Hopi communities. The summer camps involve multiple-day journeys to visit Hisatsinom or archaeological sites. At the sites, elders share their knowledge about the importance of the place to Hopi history, often in the Hopi language, and impress upon the youth that the ancestors are speaking to them. The Hisatsinom left intentional messages to inform them what it means to be Hopi and how to live a Hopi life. The youth, then, are reminded of their responsibility to future Hopi generations and to Hopi cultural preservation. They will be the keepers of language, traditions, prayers, songs, roles, and practices.

Although many of the youth do not fully understand all the information that is shared, the elders strongly insist on using Hopilavayi so that nuances of cultural traditions and language are interwoven. Often, an elder serves as translator to help all youth connect to the crux of what is being taught. If Hopi youth are not fluent, they miss some of what the elders are trying to convey. At the same time, archaeologists on the summer trips share information about the sites from a Western scientific perspective. The students are encouraged to make connections between the two ways of thinking, relating that knowledge to their own lives. To support these efforts, the program provides additional activities that emphasize themes such as health, food, ethnobotany, community, sustainability, Hopi language, and environment. The youth often focus their attention on a comparison of Hopi life and culture then and now. The follow-up workshops offered during the school year are designed to help youth learn skills to create digital media using their own voices and images to share what they have learned about the Hisatsinom.

To express their learning, Hopi youth in collaboration with elders created four films, a museum exhibit, and several digital stories about their journeys to ancestral

places. The Hopi Footprints program visited Homol'ovi alon[g]
River in Arizona; Kawestima (Navajo National Monument);
ture National Historic Park); Mesa Verde National Park, w[ith]
affiliations to places like Salapa (Spruce Tree House); and the San Juan ι..
eastern Utah, where the elders and youth have adopted and now care for the spring at
River House (figure 11.3)

The creation of the museum exhibit provided an opportunity for the youth to
express their emerging views about the connections among the past, present, and
future—what we think of as Hopi cultural preservation. In 2009, the Hopi Footprints youth, elders, archaeologists, and educators traveled to Washington, D.C., to
gather ideas and learn how to develop a museum exhibit. The Smithsonian's National
Museum of the American Indian and Natural History Museum hosted workshops
about exhibit creation and changes in how Native peoples are portrayed in museums.
Participants also toured the collection center to view Hopi artifacts. Throughout the
following year, the Hopi youth gathered once a month to design and create their own
exhibit, which was on display from July through December 2010 at the Museum of
Northern Arizona (figure 11.4). The museum exhibit focused on the core values of
Hopi culture as told through the voices of Hopi youth. The text and images were all
conceived, written, and produced by the youth. Throughout the exhibit, Hopi youth
used personal narratives to communicate their ideas, realities, and hopes for the future
(Gumerman et al. 2012).

The summer component of the program now provides an annual journey along
the San Juan River in southeastern Utah with elders, youth, and archaeologists. The
Hisatsinom footprints along the river include petroglyphs and dwellings where youth
learn about Hopi farming and lifeways. The youth and elders have also adopted and
are caring for a spring near one of the ancestral sites. Together, they actively practice
cultural preservation through sharing language, knowledge, and physical work toward
honoring the past and sustaining the future. The subsequent workshops involve
youth and elders creating and narrating digital stories about various Hopi cultural
topics discussed on the trip. These short films reflect the importance of learning the
Hopi language, how the Hopi idea of *kyaptsi* (respect) is involved in every aspect of
Hopi life, the significance and use of native plants for Hopi cooking and medicines,
what petroglyphs symbolize for Hopi, and why learning about one's clan's history is
important.

It is critical to note that not all that transpires among the Hopi Footprints participants, especially among the youth and elders, is meant to be published—either in print
or on film. We listen to and respect the elders and HCPO staff when we are asked
not to share information or to delete a video recording or to turn off the camera. Yet
there are also times when the elders tell us to "grab the camera and get this on film"

FIGURE 11.3 Shadow of Hopi youth visiting the Hisatsinom at Chaco Culture National Historic Park.

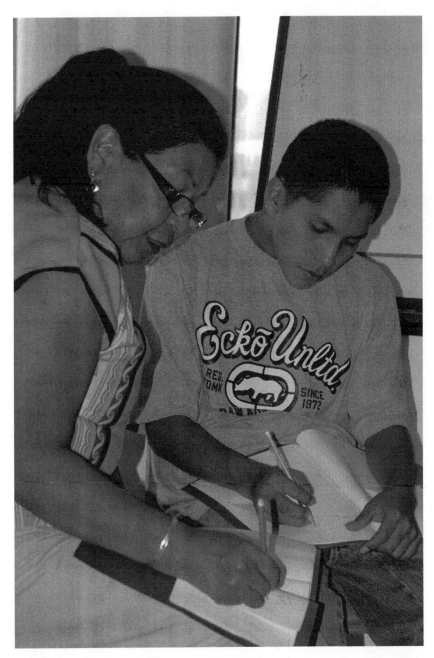

FIGURE 11.4 Collaboration in preparing the Hopi Footprints Youth Exhibit, Museum of Northern Arizona, July–December 2010.

FIGURE 11.5 Hopi youth filming elders speaking at Mesa Verde National Park.

(figure 11.5). They want to relate different pieces of culture connecting a place with language and meaning for Hopi life. As facilitators of the program, we accommodate these requests and take responsibility to help bring people together, garner funding, and structure the project. As proponents of Hopi cultural preservation, we recognize that the information and experiences generated by the program are really meant for Hopisinom—not Pahaana (Anglo-American people).

Like the nurturing of blue corn, the Hopi Footprints program has grown and developed in specific stages with changing emphases and unwavering philosophical ideals. From seeds of language to written formal lessons, journeys across the southwestern landscape. and development of digital media and a museum exhibit, the program is based on the following Hopi core values of *kyaptsi*:

- *Naminangwa* is the respect found in taking care of one's self and helping others without being asked. This type of respect demands accountability for one's own actions and inactions. During the summer programs, the Hopi youth are taught to rise in the early morning so as not to burden the sun on its journey across the sky each day. They eat well and take care of their bodies. They listen to and learn from the elders as they visit the Hisatsinom at ancestral places. They treat each other with compassion and humor.
- *Pasinangwa* is the respect garnered through interactions with others and involves treating people as one would want to be treated. It involves being both intentional and cautious about what one does. The youth in the program learn to actively listen to the elders. They are encouraged to speak Hopi and to ask questions. They do not gossip or harmfully tease one another.
- *Suminangwa* is respect that comes from helping one another for the good of all the community. This type of respect promotes interdependence and a spirit of community helpfulness. The youth and elders become like a family, helping one another with camp duties and sharing in the digital media creations. The following quote from one of the participants illustrates this *kyaptsi* value:

I'd like to thank all the adults for having all of us here, having a good time on the river, making jokes. It feels like one big family. It feels real good, it feels so good in the heart making new friends. (I. B., Hopi youth in Hopi Footprints program 2009)

The corn growing in the field does not stand alone. It is part of a larger field planted from seeds born of those who came before. To date, more than 150 Hopi participants (including youth, elders, and educators) contributed to this program (figure 11.6). The program continues without its original grant funding and through continued support from the HCPO and NAU. It is currently managed "by Hopi for Hopi" (Lyle J.

FIGURE 11.6 Hopi youth mural created for the Hopi Footprints Youth Exhibit, Museum of Northern Arizona, July–December 2010.

Balenquah, personal communication, 2014). Our goal each year is to raise funds to connect Hopi youth with elders and their ancestral heritage in meaningful ways.

IMPACT ON YOUTH AND FAMILIES

We know that this project has deeply affected Hopi youth, their families, and communities. Many youth come on the trips not understanding the depth of the Hopi cultural learning involved in the program. All are affected by the generosity of the elders and are grateful for the language and knowledge that are shared. Not all youth express their emotions verbally. They are encouraged to sing Hopi songs or to write their thoughts. The following quotes provide differing examples of how Hopi youth have expressed their learning and experiences. The first quote expresses a simple yet heartfelt gratitude: "I would like to thank the elders for giving us advice, seeing who we truly are" (S. H., Hopi youth in Hopi Footprints program 2009).

It is often challenging for youth to fully convey what being on the trips and interacting closely with elders means to them. The following reflection speaks to a participant's budding recognition of the importance of learning about her ancestral traditions.

> Well, all the trips I've been on have been very interesting for me to see all the plazas and houses of our ancestors. When you get there you are the same person but when you stay for about a week, and then ready to go home you seem like you're taking a part of your ancestors with you and you have more respect for other people and yourself. Also, you meet a lot of different people. The first time I went, I really liked it. It was so peaceful and I felt like I was back in time and saw all the people who were there a long time ago. There were a lot of animals, grass, and clear water that came down the waterfall. That's what I experienced when I went on my first trip. When I kept on going it felt like I was getting stronger and stronger. I felt I was understanding why our people were here. The reason why they are here is for respect, happiness, health, and prayers. (K. H., Hopi youth in Hopi Footprints program 2009)

For many youth, these experiences embody what it means to be Hopi, what the ancestors' messages are, and how to live a good life:

> *Water is tied to life. Water is alive*
> *I pray for water*
> *I ask the spirits for water*
> *to feel sorry for me*
> *I do good things and try*

to be a good person
I try to do it with heart
I have always watching
Even when you're all by yourself
Working, there watching
Water is a message
From the spirits
They tell us how they
Feel about us
They always test us
Through rain
We have to live Hopi
which is hard
Water is life
Water is strong
It can be mean
It can be nice
That's why it should be respected
In a storm in the ocean
In the desert, everywhere
You have to respect or die
(R. L., Hopi youth in Hopi Footprints program 2010)

Parents of participating youth also express how important it is to have these types of cultural learning opportunities with elders. They often emphasize how the program has helped their children to resist temptations, such as drugs and alcohol. Several parents have shared how they think the summer journeys to their ancestral sites have changed their sons' and daughters' lives. In addition, these gatherings provide an important social opportunity. The youth and elders truly love getting together and reconnecting not only with the past but also with each other.

WHAT ABOUT FOOTPRINTS OF THE FUTURE?

Leigh Kuwanwisiwma's leadership and his insistence that elders be involved helped make the Hopi Footprints program a success for Hopi cultural preservation. The program works because it is about Hopi cultural legacy, language, and heritage in a nonlinear path. The past, present, and future affect Hopi people and require an expanded vision of cultural preservation and archaeology that promotes Hopi language and traditions.

The future of the Hopi depends on their youth. It is imperative that the youth carry on the material and nonmaterial messages from the footprints of their ancestors by learning their cultural traditions and speaking the Hopi language. Hopi youth preserve their culture by connecting to the past and their elders while expressing their deepened knowledge in modern ways (i.e., digital media). In essence, the youth are planting the seeds for their own futures and those of the next generations.

In reality, today's Hopi youth face many challenges. They must balance living in a globalized world with being traditional Hopi (figure 11.7). On a daily basis, they confront increasing pressures on multiple fronts, including gangs, violence, substance abuse, media, school, jobs, and changes in subsistence—all with burdens that are often incompatible with traditional Hopi lifeways (Oetting and Beauvais 1990–1991). The design of the program provides a forum for youth to express and explore these challenges. One youth spoke of living in two worlds:

> We all live normal teenage American lives, so we have to try to balance that with being Hopi. It's pretty stressful, because if there's something going on in our Hopi life, which there always is, we have to bake or cook. If not, we're helping with cleaning. There's a lot of times when we won't go to sleep until 1 in the morning. Then the following day we have to wake up and go to school. At school we learn like everyone else in America, it's tough there too. Usually, we come home at 4:30 in the afternoon unless we're in sports; then we won't get home until it's really late. Balancing Hopi and Pahaana or non-native life is very different and hard. (J. A., Hopi youth in Hopi Footprints program 2010)

CONCLUSION

The elders speak about the tradition of Hopi people not choosing an easy path because, upon emergence into this world, they took the short blue ear of corn. In this way, Hopi life has always been difficult and resilient. Hopi cultural preservation is equally complex. We believe that Hopi cultural preservation depends on a holistic approach in which elders, youth, archaeologists, and others learn from the ancestors within cultural contexts of the present and future. It is vital to involve elders and youth in a continuing dialogue about cultural heritage: what it means to them, the vital role that language plays in preservation, the importance of visiting and respecting ancestral places, what can be learned from scientific approaches to studying the past and how that relates to ancestral knowledge, and what lessons must be carried forth for future generations. Much of this work happens beyond the scope of any individual youth, elder, or archaeologist. Programs like Hopi Footprints can provide only initial

FIGURE 11.7 Hopi youth image of living in two worlds.

opportunities for these interactions to occur. Ultimately, it is up to Hopi youth to honor and build upon the knowledge of their ancestors as they grow, eventually perpetuating the cycle by becoming elders themselves and interacting with future youth.

Our intent for this chapter was to illustrate that the Hopi Footprints program is one small piece of a bigger picture for Hopi cultural preservation. Preserving and sustaining Hopi cultural heritage—both the tangible and intangible—depend on nurturing youth as cultural stewards in a manner that supports the dualities of living in a modern society while thriving in Hopi traditions. The youths' connections to the elders and their teachings at ancestral sites, along with language, songs, and stories, are all elements of cultural footprints that matter in cultural preservation. It is thus most appropriate to conclude with the following quote from a Hopi Footprints' youth participant, written for their museum exhibit in 2010 about the role of Hopi youth in cultural preservation:

> Today's generation may be the last hope of saving our Hopi culture, language, and spiritual beliefs. We find our strength in prayer, kyaptsi, running, singing (especially to our plants) and the happiness that comes from being with our families. (R. L., Hopi youth in Hopi Footprints program 2010)

ACKNOWLEDGMENTS

We are humble in presenting this work as it reflects collaboration among many people involved in the Hopi Footprints program. We thank Leigh Kuwanwisiwma, the HCPO staff, and the dedicated Hopi elders, especially Gilbert Naseyowma, E. J. Satala, and Ruby Chimerica, for the opportunity to be a part of this cultural preservation effort. We are grateful to the youth who share their laughter, ideas, concerns, and hearts with each other and with us. We look forward to more years of interacting with Hopi youth, elders, and educators. Our collaborative efforts have been the most rewarding part of our archaeological careers.

The project was made possible through grants from the following generous funders: National Endowment for the Humanities; Arizona Humanities Council; Western National Parks Association; John and Sophie Ottens Foundation; Christensen Fund; National Park Foundation through Mesa Verde National Park; the Hopi Cultural Preservation Office; Grand Canyon Youth; Northern Arizona University: Anthropology Department, Honors Program; Center for Science Teaching and Learning, and Technology & Research Initiative Fund (TRIF); and individual donors.

Asquali—Kwakwah.

REFERENCES CITED

Alivizatou, Marilena. 2012. *Intangible Heritage and the Museum New Perspectives on Cultural Preservation*. Left Coast Press, Walnut Creek, California.

Balenquah, Lyle J. 2008. A Hopi Perspective on the Preservation of Ruins (and Culture). *Heritage Management* 1(2):145–162.

Balenquah, Lyle J. 2012. They Are Still Here: Wupatki Pueblo and the Meaning of Place. In *Hisat'sinom: Ancient Peoples in a Land Without Water*, edited by C. E. Downum, pp. 11–16. School for Advanced Research, Santa Fe, New Mexico.

Bauer, Alexander. 2009. The *Terroir* of Culture: Long-Term History, Heritage Preservation, and the Specificities of Place. *Heritage Management* 2(1):81–104.

Bernardini, Wesley. 2005. *Hopi Oral Tradition and the Archaeology of Identity*. University of Arizona, Tucson.

Colwell-Chanthaphonh, Chip, and T. J. Ferguson. 2006. Memory Pieces and Footprints: Multivocality and the Means of Ancient Times and Ancestral Places Among the Zuni and Hopi. *American Anthropologist* 108(1):148–162.

Demmert, William G., and John C. Towner. 2003. *A Review of the Research Literature on the Influences of Culturally Based Education on the Academic Performance of Native American Students*. Northwest Regional Educational Laboratory, Portland, Oregon.

Downum, Christian E., and Laurie J. Price. 1999. Applied Archaeology. *Human Organization* 58(3):226–229

Gumerman, George, Joëlle Clark, Elmer J. Satala, and Ruby Chimerica. 2012. Footprints of the Ancestors: Reengaging Hopi Youth with Their Culture. *Museums & Social Issues* 7(2):149–166

Hopi Cultural Preservation Office. 2014. Hopilavayi Project. *Hopi Cultural Preservation Office Past Projects*. Electronic document, http://www8.nau.edu/hcpo-p/Hopilavayi.html, accessed February 5, 2017.

Hopi Dictionary Project. 1998. *Hopi Dictionary/Hopìikwa Lavàytutuveni: A Hopi-English Dictionary of the Third Mesa Dialect*. University of Arizona Press, Tucson.

Kuwanwisiwma, Leigh J. 2002. *Hopi Navotiat*, Hopi Knowledge of History: Hopi Presence on Black Mesa. In *Prehistoric Culture Change on the Colorado Plateau: Ten Thousand Years on Black Mesa*, edited by Shirley Powell and Francis E. Smiley, pp. 161–163. University of Arizona Press, Tucson.

Navajo-Hopi Observer. 2013. Keeping the Hopi Language Alive, First Things First and Hopi Language Specialists to Develop New Program Aimed at Connecting Young Hopi Children to Native Language in Critical Early Years. 22 October. Electronic document, http://www.nhonews.com/news/2013/oct/22/keeping-the-hopi-language-alive, accessed February 5, 2017.

Oetting, Eugene R., and Fred Beauvais. 1990–1991. Orthogonal Cultural Identification Theory: The Cultural Identification of Minority Adolescents. *International Journal of the Addictions* 25(5A-6A):655–685.

Poleahla, Anita. 2014. Status of Hopi language. *Hopilavayi Pavan Öqawi'yta, Keeping Hopi Language Vibrant*. Mesa Media, Inc. Electronic document, http://www.mesamedia.org /Status_of_Hopi_language.html, accessed February 5, 2017.

Shepherd, Robert. 2009. Cultural Heritage, UNESCO, and the Chinese State. *Heritage Management* 2(1):55–79.

Smith, George S., Phyllis M. Messenger, and Hilard A. Soderland (editors). 2010. *Heritage Values in Contemporary Society*. Left Coast Press, Walnut Creek, California.

United Nations Educational, Scientific and Cultural Organization. 2003. *Text of the Convention for the Safeguarding of Intangible Cultural Heritage*. Electronic document, https://ich .unesco.org/en/convention, accessed October 27, 2017.

Wiggins, Grant, and Jay McTighe. 2005. *Understanding by Design*. 2nd ed. Association for Supervision and Curriculum Development, Alexandria, Virginia.

12

ORAL TRADITIONS AND THE TYRANNY OF THE DOCUMENTARY RECORD

The Moquis and Kastiilam Hopi History Project

THOMAS E. SHERIDAN

PROLOGUE: COMCAAC (SERI) ORAL TRADITIONS

The Moquis and Kastiilam Hopi History Project began soon after I finished editing *Empire of Sand: The Seri Indians and the Struggle for Spanish Sonora, 1645–1803* (Sheridan 1999). That documentary history chronicled the failure of the Society of Jesus to missionize the small independent bands of Comcaac (Seri Indians) who inhabited the bone-dry Sonoran coast and Tiburón and San Esteban islands in the Gulf of California. Their failure culminated in a policy of cultural genocide as Spanish officials, with the support of the Jesuits, attempted to kill or deport the Seris to *las islas ultra-marinas* (the outlying islands) of the Caribbean. This "final solution" transformed petty raiders into guerrilla fighters who, in concert with their Lower and Upper Pima allies, wreaked havoc on the mines and ranches of central Sonora from 1748 to the 1770s. It took the largest military expedition in Sonoran colonial history to battle the Comcaac to a bloody standoff, and Seris continued to conduct sporadic raids until the late nineteenth century (McGee 1971 [1898]).

When I finally held the volume in my hands, however, I had one major regret: that I never investigated whether the Comcaac today have any oral traditions of those struggles. After reading thousands of pages of handwritten Spanish colonial letters, *informes, relaciones, diarios,* and *autos,* I was painfully aware of how biased and distorted the documentary record was. Convinced of their cultural and religious superiority, Spaniards and Jesuit missionaries dismissed Native spirituality as superstition or the work of the devil.* They rarely probed the complexities of either Native ritual

---

*Many of the Jesuit missionaries came from other areas of Europe and were not native Spaniards.

or Native political organization. And they rarely bothered to describe Native society in any detail, at least not until the late eighteenth century, when Enlightenment currents influenced some attempts at systematic empirical observation.* Silences as well as ethnocentric misrepresentations haunt the Spanish written record.

Luckily, one of my students—Natalia Martínez Tagüeña—has begun collecting Comcaac narratives about the Spaniards, whom the Seris call Cazoopin.† When the Spanish empire began intruding on their territory in the late 1600s, the Comcaac were living in small family groups organized into a number of bands with distinct but permeable territories (Martínez Tagüeña 2015; Rentería Valencia 2015; Sheridan 1982). At least one band—Heeno Comcaac—lived on Tiburón Island. As conflict with the Spanish empire and the Mexican Republic intensified, band organization broke down as Seri territory shrank and Seri population declined. The population reached its nadir of about 130 individuals in the 1920s, when many observers felt that the Seris would soon disappear as a people (Felger and Moser 1985). By the 1940s, the Comcaac had aggregated themselves into three groups: the largest at Haxöl Iihom ("where there are multicolored clams"; Desemboque de los Seris) on the Sonoran coast, another at Hajhax ("many waters"; Tecomate) around a major spring on the north end of Tahejcö (Tiburón Island), and a third at Zoozni Cmiipla near Punta San Miguel on the mainland. Nonetheless, many Seris remember their former band identities even though most no longer live in their former homelands (Martínez Tagüeña and Torres Cubillas, in Martínez Tagüeña 2015).

According to Martínez Tagüeña and her Seri colleagues, Comcaac oral traditions follow the three-part temporal framework first proposed by anthropologist Jan Vansina, a pioneer in the study of oral traditions. The oldest focuses on a time when giants occupied Seri territory, a time Vansina would call "traditions of origin and genesis" or a "timeless past" and other scholars would label *myth* (Vansina 1985:21–23). The most recent is linear time, composed of personal accounts and group traditions that relate events and the actions of individuals—what Western scholars would classify as *history*. In between is Vansina's famous "floating gap," a period of indeterminate length between myth and history: "The gap is best explained by reference to the capacity of different social structures to reckon time. Beyond a certain time depth, which differs for each type of social structure because time is reckoned by reference to generations or other social institutions, chronology can no longer be kept." He continued, "Historical consciousness works on only two registers: time of origin and recent times.

---

*Perhaps the best examples of this Enlightenment empiricism are the famous *relaciones* written in response to Charles III's demand for a geographical survey of New Spain (West 1972; Sheridan and Naylor 1979). See, for example, Padre Fray Joseph Agustín Falcón Mariano's remarkably detailed 1777 *relación* of the Franciscan mission of Guaguachique (Sheridan and Naylor 1979:102–117).
†Probably from the Spanish *gachupín*, which means "Spaniard" or "Spanish-born settler in the Americas."

Because the limit one reaches in time reckoning moves with the passage of generations, I have called the gap a floating gap" (Vansina 1985:24).

The problem for ethnohistorians is to determine how far back "recent times"
go. While previous scholars thought that Comcaac historical memory extends
only into the 1800s, Martínez Tagüeña and her colleagues argued that it stretches
back to 1750 or earlier (Martínez Tagüeña et al. 2015:126). Several oral traditions
narrated by Lorenzo Herrera Casanova from the Comcaac settlement of Socaiix
(Punta Chueca) may even chronicle events in the 1600s. Those narratives refer to
brief and peaceful encounters with Spanish ships by Seris living on Tiburón Island.
The Spaniards on these vessels may have been unregistered pearl hunters; at present
it is not possible to correlate Comcaac accounts with Spanish records of specific
voyages.

At least two oral traditions correspond to major events noted by the Spaniards,
however. The first concerns Governor Diego Ortiz Parrilla's invasion of Tiburón
Island in 1750. In late summer, the only time when monsoon storms would have provided enough water to sustain a major campaign, Ortiz Parrilla ferried 720 presidial
soldiers, civilian militia, and O'odham (Upper Pima) allies across the Canal de Infi-
ernillo. They landed in a place the Comcaac call Hataamt Ihoozla (where the sandals
come off). Seris had poisoned springs and seasonal water holes in the area, and after
two weeks of inconclusive skirmishes, Ortiz Parrilla and his chronicler, Jesuit chaplain
Padre Francisco Pimentel, declared the expedition a grand success and returned to the
mainland. But only a handful of Comcaac had been captured or killed, and the Seris
soon became the greatest threat to Spanish Sonora other than the Apaches. A year
later, Luis Oacpicagigua, captain general of the O'odham who saved Ortiz Parrilla
from a mutiny by his heat-crazed soldiers, led his own rebellion across the Pimería
Alta (Sheridan 1979, 1999).

Herrera heard a Comcaac account of the invasion from Porfirio Díaz, a blind relative of his father, in 1951. Díaz was the last survivor of the Xiica Hast Ano Coii, the Seri
band living on San Esteban Island southwest of Tiburón. According to his version,
it took the Spaniards three days to shuttle their horses from the mainland. Watching
from Hast Moozaaxo, a hill on Tiburón where Seri warriors had gathered, the Comcaac saw a group of Spaniards prepare their horses with "riding chairs" and head off to
meet them. Enraged by this invasion of their homeland, an older Seri warrior named
Haliit Cmotiisi Quiiho (the one who could see a hair from a far distance) "attacked,
shooting like crazy, letting loose his anger against the soldiers. They left only one sol-
dier alive and they let him go." When the survivor alerted the rest of the expedition,
"all the soldiers mobilized towards Hast Moozaaxo but no one was there anymore. The
Comcaac had left; only the dead bodies of the soldiers remained" (Martínez Tagüeña
et al. 2015:146).

Martínez Tagüeña and her colleagues collected other narratives of Spanish hostilities as well: "They all have in common the Spaniards' betrayal, exemplified by armed assaults to drastic measures like forcing the Comcaac to eat the flesh of their own murdered people. The commonality clearly indicates the high degree of outrage committed and felt, which led to strong feelings of resentment and anger" (2015:147). They also pointed out "the importance of Comcaac historical figures like the just mentioned, Haliit Cmotiisi Quiiho, who had the power to see hair from a far distance. His vision and aiming was enhanced; he simply would not miss his target. It was through such extraordinary men that the Comcaac were able to defend themselves from Spanish attacks." In a mobile and fluid hunting and gathering society like the Seris, individual initiative and individual leadership were highly prized: "Leaders were not established through lineage or inheritance but through merit in war and hunting . . . and through spiritually enhanced power" (Martínez Tagüeña et al. 2015:147).

A second set of oral traditions describes the murder of a missionary at Hax Caail (Pozo Carrizal) northeast of modern Bahia de Kino. In all probability, these narratives describe the killing of Franciscan Padre Fray Crisóstomo Gil de Bernabé in 1773. Gil was attempting to establish a mission at Carrizal even though he himself acknowledged that the site was "completely useless for any kind of farming" (Sheridan 1999:405). Instead, he envisioned the mission Seris supporting themselves by fishing and gathering salt. According to one Comcaac account, narrated by Herrera, "the Father had punished and killed a child for killing one of his pigeons and thus deserved to die in the same manner, with his mouth filled with salt" (Martínez Tagüeña et al. 2015:147–148).

These Comcaac narratives do not, on their own, provide information about events that can be anchored to a specific time in the Western historical record. In that sense, they require Spanish accounts to complement them. What they do provide, however, are windows into Seri values and beliefs in ways that Spanish narratives often ignore or misrepresent. "The invasion of Spaniards at Tiburón island, the Comcaac refuge, was considered an unforgettable outrage," Martínez Tagüeña and her colleagues observed (2015:153). Comcaac accounts also can be quite specific about individual Seris endowed with extraordinary—what Western observers would call supernatural—powers. As we pointed out in volume I of *Moquis and Kastiilam: Hopis, Spaniards, and the Trauma of History*, Spanish documents "present the 'who,' 'where,' 'when,' and 'what' enshrined in Western narrative tradition, at least when those factual touchstones involved prominent Spaniards" (Sheridan et al. 2015:10). But they rarely express the "why" of Native actions. Nor do they present cause and effect from a Native point of view. When ethnohistorians rely entirely on the documentary record, their interpretations remain imprisoned by the limitations of their documents. The documents can be complemented and supplemented by archaeological evidence, climatic reconstructions, and other Western records of the past. But those tools, indispensable though they are, will not allow us to comprehend the values, beliefs, and often radically different epistemologies of the so-called "people without history" (Wolf 1982).

THE HOPI HISTORY PROJECT

In order to move beyond what I only half ironically call the tyranny of the documentary record, I decided that the next project of the Office of Ethnohistorical Research (OER), which I directed at the time, would gather and analyze Native oral traditions as well as Spanish documents. Noted Hopi scholar Emory Sekaquaptewa, a member of the Eagle Clan and an appellate court judge of the Hopi court system, was working at the Bureau of Applied Research in Anthropology at the University of Arizona. He and his colleagues had recently completed the monumental *Hopi Dictionary/Hopìikwa Lavàytutuveni* (Hopi Dictionary Project 1998), a major step in Emory's goal of making Hopis literate in their own language. Another Hopi scholar—Hartman Lomawaima, a member of the Bear Clan and Wuwtsim Kiva—was associate director of the Arizona State Museum, where the OER is located. With their support, I approached Leigh Kuwanwisiwma, a member of the Greasewood Clan from Paaqavi and director of the Hopi Cultural Preservation Office, who agreed to collaborate with us. Leigh assigned Stewart B. Koyiyumptewa, a member of the Badger Clan from Hotvela who had just been hired as tribal archivist, to interview Hopi elders for the project. With the formal approval of the Hopi Tribal Council, we began Moquis and Kastiilam: The Hopi History Project in 2000 with the first of five grants from the National Historic Preservation and Records Commission (NHPRC). We later received a National Endowment for the Humanities We the People grant beginning in 2008.

In his magisterial *Cycles of Conquest: The Impact of Spain, Mexico, and the United States on the Indians of the Southwest, 1533–1960*, anthropologist and ethnohistorian Edward Spicer wrote:

> The expansion of Spain in the New World, like the expansion of other European nations in the Americas, Africa, and Asia, is a series of events the record of which will remain forever incomplete. . . . It is not that there was any lack of European commentators— there were many. But the natives of the invaded regions were not literate people, and therefore what they thought and said about what was happening to them was never adequately recorded. (Spicer 1962:21)

Even though we are always "looking through a glass darkly," there are methods to see beyond at least some of the documentary record's biases, distortions, and silences.

Researchers, including the OER, have long consulted ethnographies of Native American societies written by trained anthropologists. This technique, known as *upstreaming*, has inherent limitations; nineteenth- and twentieth-century peoples may have been living very different lives from their sixteenth-, seventeenth-, and eighteenth-century ancestors (Sheridan 1988). Nonetheless, the ethnographic record brings a much more detailed and sophisticated understanding of Native societies to bear on historical encounters between their ancestors and the Europeans and Euroamericans who sought to conquer them. But what neither the OER nor many other documentary researchers had done—at least not in a comprehensive fashion—was to draw upon the insights and oral traditions of tribal elders and tribal scholars. Archaeologists of the Southwest now regularly consult with Native experts in interpreting their findings, yet few scholars have employed this methodology for understanding written texts. One exception is Dennis Tedlock's discussion with a Mayan spiritual leader as he read the *Popol Vuh*; the Maya consultant found humor in sections of the myth that scholars had assumed were ponderous (Tedlock 1983:312–320). Moquis and Kastiilam: The Hopi History Project expanded this approach by collaborating with Hopi consultants in the annotation of documents and the production of commentary.

This is a critical step and one that must be taken if we are ever going to do anything more than peer through that dark glass at the interactions of Native peoples with imperial Europe. In 1977, David Laird published a bibliography on Hopi history and culture consisting of nearly 3,000 items (Laird 1977). That number has grown by leaps and bounds since then. Hopis authored a few of the sources, but ever since Coronado's soldiers first encountered the people they called Moquis in 1540, non-Hopis have dominated both the published and archival record. Only a handful, including activist Harry James (1974), anthropologist Peter Whiteley (1988, 1998), and archaeologists Wesley Bernardini (2005, 2008) and T. J. Ferguson (Ferguson 1998, Ferguson and Colwell-Chanthaphonh 2006; Ferguson and Lomaomvaya 1999), have tried to understand Hopi history from Hopi points of view. Hopi scholar Lomayumtewa Ishii of First Mesa called this neglect *historicide*—"the mass execution of Hopi intellect, agency, and epistemology" (2001:3). He believes that this extensive "cultural archive" alienates Hopis from their past by interpreting it in terms of Western concepts rather than Hopi themes of cyclical "destruction and renewal" (2001:20).

Despite such historicide, however, Hopis remain far more conscious of their pasts than most Western peoples. But their archives are neither paper archives nor codified collections of oral traditions like the Bible. Instead, Hopi "texts" include features of the landscape, kiva murals, ritual songs, clan migration narratives, former village sites, architectural features, and rock art as well as stories: *itaakuku* (footprints) left behind as small groups of matrilineal kin honored their original covenant with Màasaw, lord of the Fourth World, by setting off on journeys from their place of emergence (Hopi Dictionary Project 1998:219). Those migrations eventually led them to Tuuwanasavi, the Earth Center, on the Hopi Mesas (Ferguson and Colwell-Chanthaphonh 2006). According to Ferguson and Lomaomvaya (1999:76),

> The Hopi have always considered themselves to be one people. In the ancient past, this people separated and traveled widely to discover the world. During these travels, they were led by spiritual forces to the promised land of the Hopi Mesas. Hopi traditions account for the various peoples who experienced different ecological zones on their migrations, and who brought the knowledge they gained to Hopi. Each clan has its own history of migration that relates to the places where they traveled, settled, and left for various reasons.

Ferguson and Colwell-Chanthaphonh observed that, because of these travels, Hopi clan migration stories are complex and diverse: "Families, portions of clans, entire clans, and groups of clans related in phratries are all variously referred to as migrating groups in Hopi traditions" (2006:101). Later in their analysis, they stated, "Accounts of Hopi migration that attempt to synthesize or homogenize Hopi history in simplified linear narratives rather than embrace their marvelous variation fail to grasp the subtle but important differences in the routes and past experiences of different migrating groups" (2006:103).

Similar diversity distinguishes other Hopi historical narratives as well. Oral traditions are transmitted from one generation to another in numerous settings. In a meeting of the Hopi History Project in Kiqötsmovi in 2008, Donald Dawahongnewa, a member of the Water Clan from Sòongopavi, noted that the right time to tell stories was in December:

> In our Hopi culture, the earth is busy all year, taking care of everybody, growing everything and all that, and then in December, the earth rests. So that's when everybody keeps still to give the earth time to rest. That one whole moon, the whole month. That's when everybody stays put and learns about their history and all that, and that's when all these stories are told.*

Different types of stories are also told in different places. "In the houses and villages, there's kid's stories and those stories," Dawahongnewa continued. "But in the kiva there's more deeper stories that are told. In the kivas. That's how we maintain

*Hopi History Project meeting, Hopi Cultural Preservation Office (HCPO), Kiqötsmovi, Arizona, September 18, 2008: 1:35. Digital recording on file with the HCPO.

our knowledge of the place histories and all that."* Only initiated members of ritual societies can listen to some of those tales, just as only clan members—and sometimes only clan leaders—can hear the full versions of their migration stories. Knowledge is power in Hopi culture, and only those who have been trained to handle that power responsibly are supposed to have access to certain domains.

Knowledge is also proprietary. When new groups of people petitioned to be allowed to live in Tuuwanasavi as the clans were gathering, they had to prove that they possessed a special talent or ceremony that would enhance *hopivötskwani*, "the Hopi way of life." The first time the Honanngyam (Badger Clan) requested to settle at Orayvi, they were turned down. So they planted corn below Third Mesa, and the corn sprouted and matured overnight. That so impressed the leaders of Orayvi that they invited the Badger Clan to share their Powamuya ceremony with the rest of the Hopis. The Badger Clan owns the ritual, an elaborate event in February that culminates with the Bean Dance, which is primarily "a ritual to promote fertility and germination" (Titiev 1992 [1944]:120).

The Badger Clan also selects the head of the Powamu society, who supervises the sprouting of bean plants in all the kivas and the initiation ceremonies into both the *katsina* religion in general and the Powamu society in particular. Initiation into the Powamu society begins in the Powamu kiva. At least in the past, *katsinam* lashed initiates of both sexes with yucca whips, and the Powamu chief admonished them to never share the secrets that had been revealed to them there, not even with their mothers and fathers. Once initiated, boys can participate in *katsina* dances and eventually become 'fathers,' who lead the *katsinam* into the plazas and sprinkle them with corn meal. The Powamu initiation also dramatizes the Badger Clan's ownership of the ceremony, its control over the first half of the *katsina* ritual cycle, which lasts roughly from the winter to the summer solstice, and its admission into Orayvi. At the same time, it reinforces the traditional leadership of Hopi communities such as the *kikmongwi* (village chief), who comes from the Bear Clan (Titiev 1992 [1944]).

Powamuya is just one example of how crosscutting ties of clan and ritual society not only establish the primary social networks of Hopi children but also determine what types of knowledge they acquire. In order to evaluate the authority of Hopi knowledge, including knowledge about the past, we first have to understand where an individual fits into this complex web of kinship ties and ritual training. Such positionality influences what narratives the individual is privy to and likely to hear.

Anthropologist Jan Vansina devoted much of his career to exploring oral traditions and their genres, especially in Africa. "The truly distinctive characteristic of oral tradition is its transmission by word of mouth over a period longer than the contemporary

*Hopi History Project meeting. Hopi Cultural Preservation Office, September 18, 2008, 1:35.

generation," he observed. "This means that a tradition should be seen as a series of successive historical documents all lost except for the last one and usually interpreted by every link in the chain of transmission" (1985:29).

Like all records of the past, oral traditions are both selective and interpretive. "Selectivity occurs mainly for social reasons," Vansina explained. "Some topics are worthwhile, others are not. Certain individuals or groups of people are interesting, others are not. The effects are loss of information and the creation of a profile of past history which is the historical consciousness of the *present*" (1985:190; italics original). But the same could be said of the documentary record. Even if the original author was an eyewitness, he or she emphasized certain details and ignored others. And each generation of readers brings its own preoccupations to the scrutiny of written documents. History is an interpretive discipline, even when carried out by specialists.

Generations of anthropologists from Robert Lowie (1915, 1917) to Fred Eggan (1967), T. O. Beidelman (1970), and Ronald Mason (2002) have relegated oral traditions to the realm of myth. They argue that, because such traditions have been transmuted by cultural conventions or contemporary concerns, they are not valid records of the past. "Selectivity implies discarding certain information one has about the past and from that pool of information keeping only what is still significant in the present," Vansina conceded. Nonetheless, he pointed out that "the information that is retained still comes from the past. Interpretation means to alter information from the past to give it new meaning and as interpretation is more creative than selection it is also more dangerous, but not to the point that all is to be rejected. This is rather like the cleric in the seventeenth century who held that there never had been a Roman Empire at all, since none of the manuscripts about it were contemporary with the supposed Empire" (Vansina 1985:191). Scholars who refuse to consider oral traditions as historical would have to argue that "in every generation people invent a brand new past for themselves and believe it to be the past" (Vansina 1985:190–191).

Anthropologist Arjun Appadurai argued that all societies, literate and nonliterate, have rules about the "debatability of the past." He criticized widespread assumptions that "the past is a limitless and plastic symbolic resource, infinitely susceptible to the whims of contemporary interest and the distortions of contemporary ideology" (1981:201). Appadurai acknowledged that societies have different kinds of pasts with different durations, including ritual and mundane, similar to Vansina's "time of origin" and "recent times." He also recognized that "such pasts are subject to disagreement and debate," that "collectively held, publicly expressed and ideologically charged versions of the past . . . are likely to vary within the groups that form a society." He proposed that "there is, however, a third kind of past whose essential purpose is to *debate* other pasts. It generally partakes of both ritual and everyday kinds of discourse and indeed makes it possible for people to pass from one to another" (1981:202; italics original). More to the point, Appadurai insisted that there is a "definable *cultural framework* with which such debates concerning meaning [about the past] must take place" (1981:203; italics original).

In Appadurai's opinion, there is "a minimal set of *formal* constraints on *all* such sets of norms" (1981:203; italics original): *authority*, "some cultural consensus as to the kinds of source, origin or guarantor of 'pasts' which are required for their credibility"; *continuity*, "some cultural consensus as to the nature of the linkage with the source of authority which is required for the minimal credibility of a 'past'"; *depth*, "cultural consensus as to the relative values of different time-depths in the mutual evaluations of 'pasts'"; and *interdependence*, "the necessity of some convention about how closely any past must be interdependent with other 'pasts' to ensure minimal credibility." As anthropologist Michel-Rolph Trouillot (1995:8) noted, "nowhere is history infinitely susceptible to invention."

Unfortunately, Native North American oral traditions, when they have been collected at all, have rarely been analyzed with the rigorous scrutiny they deserve. For example, Harry James's *Pages from Hopi History* (1974) contains four chapters about Hopis and Spaniards, the same time period covered by the Hopi history project. But James never identified when or where he heard Hopi narratives or who told them to him. He justified this omission in his acknowledgments by stating, "It was nearly always the desire of these Hopi friends that their names should not be used if I ever wrote and published the things they told me. To be singled out from the Hopi community is contrary to the Hopi way of life. With reluctance I have deferred to their wishes, but I am deeply indebted to all of them" (James 1974:vii). James's respect for his consultants is admirable, but the lack of basic information prevents us from evaluating their positionality within the nexus of clan and ritual society described above. Positionality is one of the primary characteristics establishing and legitimizing authority in Hopi culture.

Moquis and Kastiilam, in contrast, provides that information as long as consultants agree to be identified. At the beginning of the project, however, Stewart Koyiyumptewa encountered considerable resistance among many Hopis. "Why are you trying to bring up those painful periods in our past?" they asked him. Some Hopi elders refused to talk with him.

As word of the project got around, however, other elders consented to be interviewed, usually in Hopi. In October 2008, the project held a three-day workshop on the reservation with the Hopi Tribe's Cultural Resources Advisory Technical Team (CRATT), which includes representatives from all Hopi communities there. After that, Stewart and I were invited to give presentations on the project at numerous Hopi villages. Those presentations often developed into passionate conversations among the audience about whether or not sensitive topics like missionary abuses, the Pueblo

Revolt of 1680, or the destruction of Awat'ovi in 1700 should be confronted. As we borrowed a quote from William Faulkner in the introduction to Volume I of *Moquis and Kastiilam: Hopis, Spaniards, and the Trauma of History*, the Hopi past "is never dead. It's not even past" (Sheridan et al. 2015:15). Instead, parts of that past remain open wounds more than three centuries after they occurred.

None of the oral traditions gathered by the Hopi History Project fall into Vansina's "timeless past." All are clearly based on recent or linear time (i.e., historical narratives passed down over four or five centuries). In some cases, such as the destruction of a Hopi village on Antelope Mesa by Coronado's soldiers, we have not only published Clark Tenakhongva's interview with Stewart B. Koyiyumptewa in 2002, but we have also analyzed other narratives of the event (Sheridan et al. 2013, 2015). Those narratives evince at least two of the four characteristics outlined by Apparadurai: continuity and depth. Chroniclers of both the Francisco de Ibarra expedition in the 1560s and the Antonio de Espejo expedition in the 1580s recorded versions of the assault. The story continued to be told to both Harry James and Harold Courlander in the twentieth century (James 1974; Courlander 1971) and to Stewart in 2002, a time span of nearly four and a half centuries.

And even though earlier accounts do not always give the names or clan and ritual society affiliations of Hopis relating the stories, our research does. Clark Tenakhongva comes from Hotvela on Third Mesa and is a member of the Rabbit and Tobacco Clan. The Rabbit and Tobacco Clan originally settled at Awat'ovi on Antelope Mesa. Stories about a Spanish attack on an Antelope Mesa community, perhaps Kawayka'a, would more likely have been shared among clans relocated to Wàlpi and Orayvi after Awat'ovi was destroyed. Moreover, Clark Tenakhongva based his narrative on stories he heard from his grandfather, George Sakhongva, who was more than one hundred years old when he died. George Sakhongva belonged to the Badger Clan, which in Orayvi comes from Awat'ovi. Badger Clan members also maintain close relationships with and often marry Rabbit and Tobacco Clan members (Whiteley 2002:154). Finally, George Sakhongva "held many of the religious priesthoods both in Orayvi and Hotvela," according to his grandson. By clan and ritual society membership, he was positioned to hear stories about Awat'ovi and other Antelope Mesa communities like Kawayka'a. Hence, both he and Clark Tenakhongva should be considered authorities about what happened when Hopis and Spaniards met (Sheridan et al 2015:49).

At present, we have only one version of Leigh Kuwanwisiwma's narration of the torture and death of Sitkoyoma for hosting a Niman ceremony (Home dance) at Tip-kya, a natural amphitheater in the Katsina Buttes south of Orayvi, also published in volume I of *Moquis and Kastiilam: Hopis, Spaniards, and the Trauma of History*. But all the narratives are undoubtedly amalgams of accounts that have been communicated from one generation to the next over centuries. Some are what Vansina calls group accounts: "oral memories of groups such as villages, chiefdoms, associations, and various kinship groups." In his words, they "embody something which expresses the identity of the group in which they are told or substantiate rights over land, resources, women, office, and herds" (Vansina 1985:19). Hopi clan migration traditions are group accounts not only because they are specific to particular clans but also because "they are often the property of a group" (Vansina 1985:19).

Other historical narratives, in contrast, cut across clans and communities and appear to be collective social memories. Two common examples from the Spanish colonial period are accounts of missionary abuses of Hopi women and the forced labor of Hopi men, especially hauling beams for mission churches from faraway mountains like the San Francisco Peaks. During the three-day workshop with CRATT, representatives from both Second and Third Mesas talked about how missionaries would send men off to get water from distant springs so they could take advantage of their wives. When asked if similar stories were told on First Mesa, Elmer Satala Sr. replied, "They don't talk to us about that. They [the missionaries] weren't really there [at First Mesa]. They don't talk about—[the Spaniards] were mainly at Awat'ovi. So the story they talk about are from Awat'ovi, people talking to them" (Sheridan et al. 2015:189).

These narratives do not refer to missionaries by name, and they may reflect a general portrait of Franciscan sexual abuse. During a discussion at the CRATT workshop, however, Marlene Sekaquaptewa of Paaqavi on Third Mesa said, "there was always one individual that wanted this service." The discussion continued:

ANTON DAUGHTERS (UNIVERSITY OF ARIZONA): One particular priest?

MARLENE: One particular person. And they called him Tota'tsi.

ANTON: What was his name again?

MARLENE: Tota'tsi. Because he wanted everything just so. So that's the Hopi word for someone who is so particular now [laughs]. We refer to them as *tota'tsi* because he wanted certain special things for himself. (Sheridan et al. 2015:191)

As noted earlier, Hopi history consists of different genres. Some belong to clans or even clan segments. Some narratives are told only to those initiated into religious societies. There are oral traditions about the past that may never be shared, even with other Hopis, and there are traditions that are context dependent, requiring an investigator to be in the right place at the right time. As I noted in our introduction to volume I, "Even after more than a decade of work on this project, we believe that the Hopi traditions recorded here are nothing more than waves on a vast ocean of knowledge about the past passed down through many different lines of transmission from one Hopi generation to another" (Sheridan et al. 2015:12).

Nonetheless, we hope the Moquis and Kastiilam Project will stimulate other scholars, especially Hopi scholars, to collect such oral traditions in a rigorous and systematic fashion. Otherwise, they may be lost forever as those elders with the positionality and authority to relate them die. The tragedy of Hopi historicide—a century of dismissal and neglect by anthropologists and historians—is that so much knowledge about the past has already been forgotten. A uniquely Hopi historical archive needs to be created so that future generations of Hopis can learn about the enormous sacrifices their ancestors made to preserve the Hopi way of life. And that archive needs to be interrogated so that the narratives within it can be evaluated according to criteria pertinent to oral traditions themselves.

Some of those major criteria are as follows:

Who related the narrative and what was his or her positionality and authority?

What was the time and place of the telling, and was the telling restricted to certain times and places?

Who was the intended audience? Clan members? Initiates? Hopis in general or the general public?

Are there variations of the same narrative, and can those variations be explained? Do they vary through time? According to clan, village, or mesa? Can the cultural or political motives for the variations be identified?

Over time, are the narratives being transmuted from historical accounts to accounts belonging to a "timeless past?"

These are but some of the relevant questions that must be asked to determine the authority, positionality, continuity, depth, and interdependence of Hopi oral traditions. But the same criteria apply to the documentary record as well. As ethnohistorian Bernard Fontana observed,

What we call "history" is a recitation of events selected from the past, which in its most literal sense is all that has preceded the present: a rock that fell, a dog that barked, an infant who cried, a woman who coughed, a prince who was enthroned king. All historians—and on occasion each of us is a historian—select from this infinity of events those we deem worth telling. The basis of that selection provides the built-in bias of history. History, more than being a debate about the past, is an argument about the present and future. It often tells us less about what was and more about who we are. It is a tool used by all of us either to justify or to condemn the status quo. It is a statement of the world either as we now perceive it to be or as we think it ought to be. The past is immutable, but history, a battleground for the public mind, is ever changing. (Fontana 1994:xi)

REFERENCES CITED

Appadurai, Arjun. 1981. The Past as a Scarce Resource. *Man* 16:201–219.

Beidelman, T. O. 1970. Myth, Legend, and Oral History: A Kaguru Traditional Text. *Anthropos* 65:74–97.

Bernardini, Wesley. 2005. *Hopi Oral Tradition and the Archaeology of Identity*. University of Arizona Press, Tucson.

———. 2008. Identity as History: Hopi Clans and the Curation of Oral Tradition. *Journal of Anthropological Research* 64(4):483–509.

Courlander, Harold. 1971. *The Fourth World of the Hopis: The Epic Story of the Hopi Indians as Preserved in Their Legends and Traditions*. Crown, New York.

Eggan, Fred. 1967. From History to Myth: A Hopi Example. In *Studies in Southwestern Ethnolinguistics*, edited by Dell Hymes and William E. Bittle, pp. 33–53. Mouton, The Hague.

Felger, Richard S., and Becky M. Moser. 1985. *People of the Desert and Sea: Ethnobotany of the Seri Indians*. University of Arizona Press, Tucson.

Ferguson, T. J. 1998. *Öngtupqa Niqw Pisisvayu (Salt Canyon and the Colorado River): The Hopi People and the Grand Canyon*. Manuscript on file at the Hopi Cultural Preservation Office, Kiqötsmovi, Arizona

Ferguson, T. J., and Chip Colwell-Chanthaphonh. 2006. *History Is in the Land: Multivocal Tribal Traditions in Arizona's San Pedro Valley*. University of Arizona Press, Tucson.

Ferguson, T. J., and Micah Lomaomvaya. 1999. *Hoopoq'yaqam niqw Wukoskyavi (Those Who Went to the Northeast and Tonto Basin): Hopi-Salado Cultural Affiliation Study*. Hopi Cultural Preservation Office, Kiqötsmovi, Arizona.

Fontana, Bernard L. 1994. *Entrada: The Legacy of Spain & Mexico in the United States*. Southwest Parks and Monuments Association, Tucson, Arizona.

Hopi Dictionary Project. 1998. *Hopìikwa Lavàytutuveni/Hopi Dictionary: A Hopi-English Dictionary of the Third Mesa Dialect*. University of Arizona Press, Tucson.

Ishii, Lomayumtewa Curtis. 2001. *Voices from Our Ancestors: Hopi Resistance to Scientific Historicide*. PhD dissertation, Department of History, Northern Arizona University, Flagstaff.

James, Harry. 1974. *Pages from Hopi History*. University of Arizona Press, Tucson.

Laird, W. David. 1977. *Hopi Bibliography*. University of Arizona Press, Tucson.

Lowie, Robert. 1915. Oral Traditions and History. *American Anthropologist* 17:597–599.

———. 1917. Oral Tradition and History. *Journal of American Folklore* 30(116):161–167.

Martínez Tagüeña, Natalia. 2015. *And the Giants Keep Singing: Comcaac Anthropology of Meaningful Places*. PhD dissertation, School of Anthropology, University of Arizona, Tucson.

Martínez Tagüeña, Natalia, Lorenzo Herrera Casanova, and Luz Alicia Torres Cubillas. 2015. Blood and Pearls: *Cazoopin* (Colonial Spaniards) in the Comcaac Region. In *And the Giants Keep Singing: Comcaac Anthropology of Meaningful Places*, by Natalia Martínez Tagüeña, pp. 120–163. PhD dissertation, School of Anthropology, University of Arizona, Tucson.

Martínez Tagüeña, Natalia, and Luz Alicia Torres Cubillas. 2015. Walking the Desert, Paddling the Sea: Comcaac Mobility in Time. In *And the Giants Keep Singing: Comcaac Anthropology of Meaningful Places*, by Natalia Martínez Tagüeña, pp. 83–119. PhD dissertation, School of Anthropology, University of Arizona, Tucson.

Mason, Ronald. 2002. Archaeology and Native American Oral Traditions. *American Antiquity* 65(2):239–266.

McGee, W. J. 1971 [1898]. *The Seri Indians of Bahia Kino and Sonora, Mexico.* Annual Report of the Bureau of American Ethnology of the Smithsonian Institution, Vol. 17, 1895–1896. 1971 facsimile ed. with Introduction by Bernard Fontana, Rio Grande Press, Glorieta, New Mexico.

Rentería Valencia, Rodrigo. 2015. *Hunting Cartographies: Neoliberal Conservation among the Comcaac.* PhD dissertation, School of Anthropology, University of Arizona, Tucson.

Sheridan, Thomas E. 1979. Cross or Arrow? The Breakdown in Spanish-Seri Relations, 1729–1750. *Arizona and the West* 21(4):317–334.

———. 1982. Seri Bands in Cross Cultural Perspective. *The Kiva* 47(4):185–213.

———. 1988. How to Tell the Story of the "People without History": Narrative vs. Ethnohistorical Approaches to the Study of the Yaqui Indians through Time. *Journal of the Southwest* 30(2):168–89.

———. 1999. *Empire of Sand: The Seri Indians and the Struggle for Spanish Sonora, 1645–1803.* University of Arizona Press, Tucson.

Sheridan, Thomas E., Stewart B. Koyiyumptewa, Anton Daughters, Dale S. Brenneman, T. J. Ferguson, Leigh Kuwanwisiwma, and Lee Wayne Lomayestewa. 2015. *Moquis and Kastiilam: Hopis, Spaniards, and the Trauma of History.* Vol. I, 1540–1679. University of Arizona Press, Tucson.

Sheridan, Thomas E., Stewart B. Koyiyumptewa, Anton T. Daughters, T. J. Ferguson, Leigh Kuwanwisiwma, Dale S. Brenneman, and Lee Wayne Lomayestewa. 2013. Moquis and Kastiilam: Coronado and the Hopis. *Journal of the Southwest* 55(4):377–434.

Sheridan, Thomas E., and Thomas H. Naylor (editors). 1979. *Rarámuri: A Tarahumara Colonial Chronicle, 1607–1791.* Northland Press, Flagstaff, Arizona.

Spicer, Edward H. 1962. *Cycles of Conquest: The Impact of Spain, Mexico, and the United States on the Indians of the Southwest.* University of Arizona Press, Tucson.

Tedlock, Dennis. 1983. *The Spoken Word and the Work of Interpretation.* University of Pennsylvania Press, Philadelphia.

Titiev, Mischa. 1992 [1944]. *Old Oraibi: A Study of the Hopi Indians of Third Mesa.* Papers of the Peabody Museum of American Archaeology and Ethnology Vol. XXII(1). Harvard University, Cambridge. 1992 reprint by University of New Mexico Press, Albuquerque.

Trouillot, Michel-Rolph. 1995. *Silencing the Past: Power and the Production of History.* Beacon Press, Boston.

Vansina, Jan. 1985. *Oral Tradition as History.* University of Wisconsin Press, Madison.

West, Robert C. 1972. The Relaciones Geográficas of Mexico and Central America, 1740–1792. In *Handbook of Middle American Indians*, Vol. 12, Robert Wauchope, series editor and Howard F. Cline, volume editor, pp. 396–449. University of Texas Press, Austin.

Whiteley, Peter M. 1988. *Deliberate Acts: Changing Hopi Culture through the Oraibi Split*. University of Arizona Press, Tucson.

———. 1998. *Rethinking Hopi Ethnography*. Smithsonian Institution, Washington, D.C.

———. 2002. Re-Imagining Awat'ovi. In *Archaeologies of the Pueblo Revolt: Identity, Meaning, and Renewal in the Pueblo World*, edited by Robert Preucel, pp. 147–66. University of New Mexico Press, Albuquerque.

Wolf, Eric. 1982. *Europe and the People without History*. University of California Press, Berkeley.

13

FORGING NEW INTELLECTUAL GENEALOGIES IN SOUTHWEST ARCHAEOLOGY

GREGSON SCHACHNER

O VER THE LAST FEW DECADES, the increasing involvement of American Indian archaeologists, elders, and cultural preservation specialists in Southwest archaeology has changed the practice and content of that endeavor. Although these changes may not be as far-reaching as some have hoped, they mark a significant shift in the field, often influencing the formulation of research questions, field methodologies, and interactions with the wider public in both obvious and unacknowledged ways. One of the most important changes has involved the training of students as undergraduate and graduate students increasingly enroll in courses addressing archaeological ethics and cultural resource law. Many students now experience direct interaction with American Indian colleagues during their training and early on in their careers. These experiences often play a crucial role in shaping both how these individuals practice archaeology and the types of questions they explore in their research.

A number of other authors have pointed out the challenges and benefits of increasing American Indian involvement in archaeology in the Southwest and elsewhere in North America (e.g, Colwell-Chanthaphonh 2010; Ferguson 1996; Ferguson and Colwell-Chanthaphonh 2006; Kristensen and Davis 2015; Liebmann 2012; McGuire 1992; Watkins 2003; Whiteley 2002; Wilcox 2009; see also Murray 2011 and Nicholas 2010 for discussions of Indigenous involvement beyond North America). In this chapter, I hope to add to that discussion by examining the changing intellectual genealogies of Southwest archaeologists and how that affects the discipline today and going forward. Although often characterized as consultants or collaborators, many of our American Indian colleagues are increasingly teachers, formally and informally shaping how Southwest archaeologists study the ancient and recent past of the region. I will explore these developments, briefly tracing how American Indian people have long influenced Southwest archaeologists (also see Whiteley, this volume) before turning to a more personal exploration of how my own work with members of the Hopi Tribe has shaped my intellectual development and research trajectory.

Southwest archaeologists, now and in the future, must more explicitly acknowledge how Native Americans have shaped current practice and research efforts in order to fully understand the current state of Southwest archaeology and its likely trajectory going forward. More direct acknowledgment of these links provides a more accurate depiction of the connections between American Indian people and the archaeology of their ancestors, the complicated partnership of American Indians and the archaeological community as advocates of the ancient past, and a more complete understanding of how archaeological scholarship is shaped by wider sociopolitical concerns.

INTELLECTUAL GENEALOGIES

Philosophers of science and others interested in the historical development of scholarly disciplines have proposed that tracing intellectual genealogies—the educational and social ties rather than epistemological and theoretical allegiances—among groups of researchers is a more effective way to understand the actual practice and development of science than explorations of changes in high-level paradigms. In anthropology, this approach has been pursued by Regna Darnell (2001) in *Invisible Genealogies*, a history of Americanist cultural anthropology. More relevant to archaeology, *Archaeology as Process* (2005), by Michael O'Brien, Lee Lyman, and Michael Schiffer, provides a history of the development of American archaeology, and in particular, processual archaeology, from roughly World War II to the early 2000s. Although one may disagree with some of the authors' interpretations, this volume demonstrates how the successes and content of certain schools of thought in archaeology are as much a product of the formation of strong social and educational cohorts as the supposed superior explanatory power of particular theories.

As scholars, what we study is shaped by who we know in the field, in the classroom, and in the hallway at conferences. This is not a particularly novel idea in that these are precisely the types of interactions that social scientists study to understand nearly any phenomena, but it does emphasize that the content of scholarship is not determined by ideas alone. As American Indians assume more central and varied positions in the field, they are more directly influencing the research and practice of archaeology, particularly in the Southwest. While this influence is in some cases informal, it has also expanded as more tribal governments formulate cultural resource policies and support personnel and government entities to carry out those policies. Thus, individuals working in many of these formal contexts, such as the Hopi Cultural Preservation Office (HCPO), are exerting increased influence over both the content and practice of scholarship aimed at exploring the history of the ancient Southwest and have become key figures in the intellectual development and genealogies of archaeologists working today.

It is not surprising that an anthropologist may find it useful to think about disciplinary history in terms of genealogies, as this is a social construction that is understood by a discipline at least traditionally interested in kinship. It also lends itself to an inherently personal view of disciplinary history, and here I will, despite the conceit of doing so, use my own history to illustrate the effects of these ties, in particular through my work with Leigh Kuwanwisiwma, the staff of the HCPO, and other members of the Hopi Tribe. While in graduate school, I had the opportunity to work on a multiyear project documenting cultural affiliation between the modern Hopi and the Hohokam archaeological culture (Ferguson 2003; Ferguson et al. 2013), and subsequently I have collaborated with Wesley Bernardini of the University of Redlands and HCPO staff on field projects conducted on the reservation (see Bernardini, this volume).

Many aspects of my scholarly work, as well as many of my goals in the training of students, have been strongly shaped by my work at Hopi. Importantly, however, this work, and in particular the role of Leigh and other individuals, would be underrepresented in traditional tracings of my intellectual genealogy, which would likely focus on facts more obvious in the documentary record, such as my dissertation advisors, the universities I have attended, or supervisors and members of the field projects in which I have participated. The influence of any of these individuals and institutions on my intellectual development, including the research topics I have chosen to pursue and the frameworks within which I have tried to explain past phenomena, would be fairly obvious to most scholars of the last few decades of archaeological and anthropological thought. Although the impact of my work with Hopi may be less obvious, I would argue that this work has been more influential in shaping how I have approached my archaeological research and teaching over the last fifteen years. The influence of Leigh and other Hopi individuals on all of the authors in this volume is far-reaching yet may still be underplayed unless we make a concerted effort to recognize those intellectual ties and to illustrate their importance in our work. The potential for these ties to be masked is all too obvious in the histories of archaeology written so far. While the structural influences of the Native American Graves Protection and Repatriation Act (NAGPRA) and consultation requirements enshrined in other U.S. cultural resource laws are important, the personal ties and experiences of individuals working over the last few decades with American Indian peoples are no less significant in tracing long-term shifts in archaeological theory and practice.

TRACING AMERICAN INDIAN
INFLUENCE IN THE DEVELOPMENT
OF SOUTHWESTERN ARCHAEOLOGY

Recent histories of Southwest archaeology often focus on major figures and projects—Kidder, Hewett, and Haury; Pecos, Pueblo Bonito, and Awat'ovi—but one criticism that could be leveled is that a history of the interactions among the largely Anglo archaeologists and Native peoples of the Southwest can often only be dimly discerned by reading between the lines. Native Americans appear as occasional minor characters, nameless crew members completing much of the actual physical labor on early projects, or sometimes relatively well-known figures such as Nampeyo, but the intellectual debt of our archaeologist forebears to these individuals is not always clear. Now this criticism is not necessarily fair because the primary sources from the era are often equally silent and many of the participants in these early projects, both Anglo and Native, have long passed on, but it nonetheless stands as an allegory for the engagement between American Indians and Southwest archaeologists over much of the last century. The lack of this history is especially sad since it is clear that Native people were often the primary sources of the foundational interpretations of the archaeological record of the Southwest during its earlier development, as is made perfectly clear, for example, by occasional snippets from Bandelier (1890–1892) in the Rio Grande, Fewkes (1898, 1900) in Hopi country, Hodge at Hawikku (Smith et al. 1966), or later McGregor (1943) at Ridge Ruin. When discussing the distinctive character of Southwest archaeology with students, I point out that it is not just the preservation of a desert environment and dendrochronology that make working in the Southwest so thought provoking, but also the fact that many early archaeological studies were endeavors of interpretation involving descendant peoples, whether those participants were willing, interested, or given their own voice or credit. Imagine, if you will, the development of Southwest archaeology and where our current interpretations would be without these Native insights, which ranged from fairly direct interpretations of individual artifacts, to multifaceted interpretations of complex archaeological contexts (e.g., McGregor 1943), and to discussions of long-term patterns of the history and movement of American Indian people across the Southwest (see Kristensen and Davis 2015 for a thought-provoking comparison of archaeology in different parts of Canada with varying input from First Nations groups).

Chip Colwell-Chanthaphonh (2010) has attempted to remedy the one-sided historiography of Southwest archaeology in his excellent *Living Histories* book, but given the paucity of the documentary record of relationships between archaeologists and American Indians over much of the twentieth century, that history can only reach so far. Further exploring the Native perspective on the early development of Southwest archaeology would be useful but difficult given the lack of voices from that era. Perhaps a project of this sort is still worth pursuing, however, and if so, it will require close collaboration with our Native colleagues to engage the oral and tribal histories of this earlier work.

What I found most striking about Colwell-Chanthaphonh's book is that his history of American Indian involvement in Southwest archaeology starts out relatively richly during the late 1800s and early 1900s, continuing that way up to the use of archaeology as a line of evidence for cases brought before the Indian Claims Commission beginning in the 1950s; then the history goes largely silent, picking up again in our modern post-NAGPRA era. Interaction between archaeologists and Native peoples of the Southwest was not absent during the 1960s, 1970s, and 1980s, however. Major projects, such as the Grasshopper and Point of Pines field schools and the Black Mesa Archaeological Project, occurred on modern reservations. The first tribal archaeology programs were also initiated during this period. However, with regard to the disciplinary concerns of that era, it is significant to note that, in the move toward a more scientific archaeology, the archaeological record was primarily seen as data relevant to the study of general cultural processes rather than connected to living traditions and histories (McGuire 1992). This era may be more accessible in a still to be written history of Southwest archaeology as many participants are still with us. What exactly were the interactions between American Indians and archaeologists of this era? Were relationships between archaeologists and Native people as rare as the written histories suggest? Or is this a case in which the silence of our received histories is more about recent rhetoric and perspectives than about the lived realities of the time? In some ways we may be overplaying the novelty of the decades after NAGPRA, but it seems fair to suggest that the perspectives of American Indian people, if not their personal ties with archaeologists of the era, were minimally represented in the scholarship of much of the mid-1900s.

AMERICAN INDIAN INFLUENCE ON THE CONTENT AND PRACTICE OF CURRENT SOUTHWESTERN ARCHAEOLOGY

As with a growing number of archaeologists, albeit often trained and led by individuals both Native and non-Native whose experience spans that temporal and practical divide, my experience in archaeology is exclusively in a post-NAGPRA world. It is probably too simple to use NAGPRA as the marker for a change in attitudes because cultural preservation offices and tribal cultural resource management organizations have a longer history in the Southwest going back to the 1970s (Anyon and Ferguson

1995; Anyon et al. 2000; Ferguson 1996). However, the effects of NAGPRA and the interaction that it mandates are increasingly becoming apparent in the research and practice of Southwest archaeology. In this section, I will discuss what I see as some of the major trends in Southwest archaeological research that have been strongly shaped by the engagement between Native peoples and archaeologists, who are sometimes now one and the same, and then turn to changes in training, which I think will move those interactions and influence even further.

It would be fair to say that mobility, particularly migration, and the study of ancient landscapes have been among the dominant subjects of archaeological research in the Southwest since the 1990s (e.g., Bernardini 2005; Clark 2001; Cameron 2013; Duwe and Anschuetz 2013; Gilman and Whalen 2011; Lyons 2003; Ortman 2012; Schachner 2012). Southwest archaeology is rife with studies that have transformed our understanding of the scale of ancient migrations and their social effects, as well as myriad new studies that have moved beyond simply documenting settlement patterns and their changes to interpreting the meaning of natural places and cultural geographies created through movement in the ancient past (Bernardini et al. 2013; Fowles 2010; Snead 2008; Van Dyke 2007). In the study of both migration and landscapes, the impacts of Leigh Kuwanwisiwma's publications and teaching and that of many other Native colleagues are readily apparent. Although some of this impact is apparent in academic literature (e.g., Ferguson, et al. 2009; Kuwanwisiwma 2002; Kuwanwisiwma and Ferguson 2009; Naranjo 1995, 2008), much of this influence also derives from the numerous instances of participation in consultation related to NAGPRA, the National Historic Preservation Act of 1966, and their state equivalents. A view of this era solely through the published record probably underrepresents the extent to which American Indian perspectives have shaped scholarly inquiry, as many of these interactions are more likely to be unrecorded or found in the often confidential products of the cultural resource process.

Unsurprisingly, both migrations and Native cultural geographies were last of major interest when Southwest scholars were working closely with Native peoples in the late nineteenth and early twentieth century (e.g., Fewkes 1900); these topics then fell out of favor for many years. Now some might contend that these types of studies never disappeared. For example, migration has always been a major theme in University of Arizona research along the Mogollon Rim (Graves et al. 1982; Reid and Whittlesey 2007) and is simply an unavoidable fact when examining the depopulation of many regions, such as Mesa Verde (Cordell 1995; Glowacki 2015). In addition, the study of migrations and landscapes have seen resurgence in archaeology in general, irrespective of region, time period, or involvement of descendant populations (Kintigh et al. 2014). However, I think one can make the case that, with the creation of NAGPRA and the social and intellectual ties that it has facilitated, the recent move toward these subjects in the Southwest would have occurred regardless of wider disciplinary trends. Rather than putting an end to the field as some archaeologists feared, NAGPRA and the larger push for reevaluation of the ethics and practices of archaeology have sent the discipline in many directions different from those that may have been anticipated when the law was being debated in the 1980s.

James Snead (2008) and Severin Fowles (2010) have made similar arguments, noting that research in the Southwest has given rise to a distinctive Southwest School of Landscape Archaeology that seriously considers the insights of our Native collaborators in thinking about the construction of meaning and place-making in the past. As noted by Fowles (2010), studies of Southwest landscapes informed by American Indian perspectives provide a foil that can be compared to the phenomenological approaches to ancient landscapes common in the archaeology of many other parts of the world that have been the subject of much disciplinary hand-wringing (e.g., Barrett and Ko 2009).

I clearly see the effects of shifting disciplinary interests and the influence of working with American Indian colleagues in my own research trajectory over the last two decades. My archaeological research began with an interest in social organization and its inference from the archaeological record, as well as a deep skepticism of religious belief as anything other than a sociopolitical process ripe for manipulation by aspiring elites (e.g., Schachner 2001). My interests began to change as I worked closely with Leigh, HCPO staff, and Hopi elders on the Hopi-Hohokam cultural affiliation project in the early 2000s. An interest in mobility and how it shapes social organization both as practiced and in its ideological underpinnings began to appear in my work (Schachner 2008, 2012). And then I began to write about journeys to natural places and the role of those travels in shaping the social networks that would have enabled migrations and the experience of Pueblo religion (Schachner 2011). My prior understandings of social organization were oversimplified, seeing social organization as the nesting and competition of largely faceless groups, but over time I began to see the importance of the movement of actual people across landscapes of various scales as being key to the process through which social groups formed, were defined, and eventually transformed. This perspective is more closely grounded in the content of the archaeological record, as well as more complete in its explanation of cultural process.

More recently I see the echoes of working in Leigh's cornfields and hearing him and other Hopi elders discuss the centrality of farming in Hopi life. I have begun to think more critically about the role of farming in shaping the cultural processes (social organization, leadership, and mobility) studied by my anthropological forebears, but often without the strength of lived insights that provided a richer illustration of how farming was implicated in individual lives, longer term histories, and the organization of society. Thus, much to the consternation of my students, in recent surveys in the

Petrified Forest we have paid particularly close attention to ephemeral distributions of sherds and stone slabs that provide at least some evidence for thinking about how farming shaped ancient people's travels on the landscape.

Much like farming on the Hopi mesas (Hack 1942), dune farming must have been a central facet of agricultural systems in the windswept Petrified Forest region, providing one of the stronger influences on patterns of local mobility that influenced regional settlement. Although rarely studied by Southwest archaeologists, dune farming is one of the few types of Pueblo agriculture that may leave common physical traces accessible to surface survey, as stone windbreaks would have been needed to protect young plants and inhibit erosion (Hack 1942:33, 70–71). Although windbreaks could be constructed of brush or other perishable material, in the vegetation-poor Petrified Forest, stone and sherds would have been less costly resources. Thus, detailed recording of the locations of sandstone slabs, which derive from spottily distributed outcrops, as well as sherds, which have the added benefit of providing some semblance of temporal control, enable the delineation of fields on the landscape.

Figure 13.1 illustrates AZ Q:2:176 (ASM), a sizeable dune field a few hundred meters south of the Pueblo IV period village of Stone Axe (AZ Q:2:22 [ASM]), most likely the last Ancestral Pueblo village occupied in the Petrified Forest prior to migrations to Hopi, Zuni, and elsewhere further afield ca. AD 1400. Modern surface remains consist primarily of broken sandstone slabs and groundstone implements, along with numerous (unmapped) large sherds, dating to the Pueblo IV period, that represent the remains of features necessary for the success of agriculture in this challenging environment. Future research in the region employing detailed non-site-based surface recording has the potential to yield unprecedented views of the distribution and extent of ancient agricultural systems in the Petrified Forest, even though they have been heavily influenced by the impacts of centuries of erosion. Although archaeologists are increasingly able to employ high-tech methods to assess the locations of ancient fields, such as geographic information system reconstructions of agricultural potential, direct evidence of fields is often rare, providing us an incomplete view of this central activity.

Prior to my experiences at Hopi, I had often viewed studies of ancient agricultural systems as peripheral to my own interests in social organization and change, but I now realize that understanding these systems and the social and economic networks created through farming is vital to approaching a myriad of questions, including Ancestral Pueblo migration and identity. Farming brought people out onto the landscape. Additionally, the variation in the range of farming strategies within communities and across the Southwest may have been an important facet of ancient identities, just as it is in many modern ethnographic contexts. Again, the firsthand experience of farming and its centrality in Hopi life and identity had a far more powerful and direct impact on my

FIGURE 13.1 AZ Q:2:176 (ASM), a probable Pueblo IV period dune field near Stone Axe Pueblo (AZ Q:2:22 [ASM]), Petrified Forest, Arizona.

own interests than more than a decade of academic training, even though many of my advisors studied and continue to study Ancestral Pueblo farming. Importantly, experience of Hopi farming also encouraged me to see agriculture as more than just subsistence and to consider its effects on society and ideology (also see Wolverton et al. 2016).

CHANGING HOW WE TRAIN ARCHAEOLOGY STUDENTS

My experiences working with Hopi people have also shaped my teaching endeavors, both in the classroom and beyond. Some of my students have been fortunate enough to work on projects at Hopi (figure 13.2), enabling them to see firsthand how Native

FIGURE 13.2 Lee Wayne Lomayestewa (HCPO staff) and Reilly Murphy (undergraduate at the University of California, Los Angeles [UCLA]), recording a historic period site on the Hopi reservation, 2011. Photo by A. J. White, UCLA undergraduate.

people experience and think about archaeology in differing and intellectually challenging ways. A number of field projects that incorporate the training of students in the Southwest now provide opportunities for close collaboration with Native peoples, enabling students to grapple with many of the ethical challenges of archaeology early in their careers (Mills et al. 2008). These experiences require them to confront important questions about how and why they conduct archaeological research: How do I navigate a research career that may conflict with the values and traditions of descendant people? How do I create an archaeology that may be meaningful beyond the narrow confines of my discipline? These are particularly difficult questions that most of us still struggle with, at least if we allow ourselves to think about them. Early struggles with these questions prepare students for the realities of an archaeological career and will enable them to develop an archaeology that is meaningful and responsive to different audiences.

My work with Hopi people has also led me to regularly teach an undergraduate course on archaeological ethics, as well as to incorporate at least one lecture on the political and social contexts of archaeological research in every course I teach (see Kuwanwisiwma 2008). When I first envisioned an archaeological career, I never thought that I would be teaching a class in archaeological ethics and helping students navigate the challenges of studying a record that many believe to be simply of the past, but that all of us who practice archaeology also know is clearly of the present. I and others who teach these types of classes find them to be among the most rewarding of our careers, often captivating students who thought archaeology had little importance in the modern world. In fact, many of the most positive course evaluations I have received for these courses come from students interested in cultural anthropology, who had long avoided archaeology classes as being irrelevant to their own interests and providing little insight into the modern sociopolitical conflicts and cultural endeavors that brought them to anthropology. Although some may fear the ever-growing influence (or some might say domination) of modern heritage concerns on archaeological research, understanding the modern sociopolitical context of archaeology is one of the few ways in which anthropological archaeology can productively reach out to its most estranged fellow subdiscipline.

I have witnessed the results of these teaching efforts firsthand as some of my students become involved with and think deeply about the intersection of scientific and cultural interests in the past, not only as students, but as professional archaeologists. The vast majority of the students in these courses will never pursue archaeology as a career, but hopefully realizing that the archaeological record is of interest to modern people other than archaeologists and that it is subject to public control and influence of various sorts will encourage them to be better "archaeological citizens," a necessity for a profession so dependent on the financial support and good will of a wider public. The creation of our intellectual genealogies through links of co-authorship and citation, fellow department members, and formal academic advisors will miss the influence of our American Indian colleagues on our increasingly crucial teaching and public outreach efforts. The Native influence on modern archaeology reaches well beyond the acknowledgement of "separate, but equal" intellectual and practical interests in the archaeological record to an intertwined development of how archaeology is practiced and taught. The recent controversies over the creation of Bears Ears National Monument and the development of the Dakota Access Pipeline further illustrate the increasing importance of Native voices in shaping the public and governmental view of archaeology as well.

CONCLUSION

What I hope is that this chapter will inspire archaeologists to think deeply about what we would like future histories of archaeology, some of which our productive colleagues are already writing and others that remain to be written, to incorporate as the major factors shaping our discipline. Many of us have important teachers among

American Indian communities who are less visible in the fairly rigid confines of academia and professional life, but these men and women are no less important in shaping how we think about the past or the conduct of our work in the present than those who may be more obviously part of our traditional intellectual genealogies. We should acknowledge that debt and ensure that it is no longer lost in our own traditions going forward. This acknowledgment is not a matter of simply paying our debts, but rather a key part of the reshaping of our discipline in the present as we respond to the interests of scholars and the multiple publics that have an interest in the archaeology.

ACKNOWLEDGMENTS

I would like to thank T. J. Ferguson for inviting me to participate in the Society for American Archaeology session where this book originated, as well as for taking me on as a young graduate student during his work at Hopi. Wesley Bernardini has also included me in a number of recent projects at Hopi during which I have been able to renew many friendships. Finally, I would like to acknowledge Joel Nicholas, Lee Wayne Lomayestewa, Stewart Koyiyumptewa, and especially Leigh Kuwanwisiwma of the Hopi Cultural Preservation Office, as well as many Hopi elders, for their invaluable knowledge and perspectives on the practice of archaeology, the ancient past, and modern Hopi life.

REFERENCES CITED

Anyon, Roger, and T. J. Ferguson. 1995. Cultural Resources Management at the Pueblo of Zuni, New Mexico, USA. *Antiquity* 69:913–930.

Anyon, Roger, T. J. Ferguson, and John R. Welch. 2000. Heritage Management by American Indian Tribes in the Southwestern United States. In *Cultural Resource Management in Contemporary Society: Perspectives on Managing and Presenting the Past*, edited by Francis P. McManamon and Alf Hatton, pp. 120–141. Routledge, London.

Bandelier, Adolph F. 1890–1892. *Final Report of Investigations Among the Indians of the Southwestern United States, Carried on Mainly in the Years from 1880 to 1885*, Parts I and II. Papers of the Archaeological Institute of America, American Series III and IV. Archaeological Institute of America, Cambridge, Massachusetts.

Barrett, John C., and Ilhong Ko. 2009. A Phenomenology of Landscape: A Crisis in British Landscape Archaeology? *Journal of Social Archaeology* 9:275–294.

Bernardini, Wesley. 2005. *Hopi Oral Tradition and the Archaeology of Identity*. University of Arizona Press, Tucson.

Bernardini, Wesley, Alicia Barnash, Mark Kumler, and Martin Wong. 2013. Quantifying Visual Prominence in Social Landscapes. *Journal of Archaeological Science* 40:3946–3954.

Cameron, Catherine M. 2013. How People Moved Among Ancient Societies: Broadening the View. *American Anthropologist* 115:218–231.

Clark, Jeffery J. 2001. *Tracking Prehistoric Migrations: Pueblo Settlers Among the Tonto Basin Hohokam.* Anthropological Papers 65. University of Arizona Press, Tucson.

Colwell-Chanthaphonh, Chip. 2010. *Living Histories: Native Americans and Southwestern Archaeology.* AltaMira Press, Lanham, Maryland.

Cordell, Linda S. 1995. Migration and the Movement of Southwestern Peoples. *Journal of Anthropological Archaeology* 14:104–124.

Darnell, Regna. 2001. *Invisible Genealogies: A History of Americanist Anthropology.* University of Nebraska Press, Lincoln.

Duwe, Samuel, and Kurt F. Anschuetz. 2013. Ecological Uncertainty and Organizational Flexibility on the Prehispanic Tewa Landscape: Notes from the Northern Frontier. In *Mountain and Valley: Understanding Past Land Use in the Northern Rio Grande Valley, New Mexico*, edited by Bradley J. Vierra, pp. 95–112. University of Utah Press, Salt Lake City.

Ferguson, T. J. 1996. Native Americans and the Practice of Archaeology. *Annual Review of Anthropology* 25:63–79.

Ferguson, T. J. (compiler). 2003. *Yep Hisat Hoopq'yaqam Yeese (Hopi Ancestors Were Once Here): Hopi-Hohokam Cultural Affiliation Study.* Hopi Cultural Preservation Office, Kiqötsmovi, Arizona.

Ferguson, T. J., G. Lennis Berlin, and Leigh J. Kuwanwisiwma. 2009. *Kukehpya*: Searching for Hopi Trails. In *Landscapes of Movement: Trails, Paths, and Roads in Anthropological Perspectives*, edited by James E. Snead, Clark L. Erickson, and J. Andrew Darling, pp. 20–41. University of Pennsylvania Press, Philadelphia

Ferguson, T. J., and Chip Colwell-Chanthaphonh. 2006. *History Is in the Land: Multivocal Tribal Traditions in Arizona's San Pedro Valley.* University of Arizona Press, Tucson.

Ferguson, T. J., Leigh Kuwanwisiwma, Micah Loma'omvaya, Patrick Lyons, Gregson Schachner, and Laurie Webster. 2013. *Yep Hisat Hoopoq'yaqam Yeesiwa* (Hopi Ancestors Were Once Here): Repatriation Research Documenting Hopi Cultural Affiliation with the Ancient Hohokam of Southern Arizona. In *Global Ancestors: Understanding the Shared Humanity of our Ancestors*, edited by Margaret Clegg, Rebecca Redfern, Jelena Bekvalac, and Heather Bonney, pp. 104–133. Oxbow Books, Oxford, England.

Fewkes, Jesse W. 1898. *Archaeological Expedition to Arizona in 1895.* Seventeenth Annual Report of the Bureau of American Ethnology, pp. 519–744. Government Printing Office, Washington, D.C.

———. 1900. Tusayan Migration Traditions. *Nineteenth Annual Report of the Bureau of American Ethnology for the Years 1897–1898*, Pt. 2, pp. 573–634. Government Printing Office, Washington, D.C.

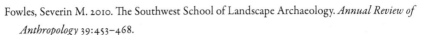

Fowles, Severin M. 2010. The Southwest School of Landscape Archaeology. *Annual Review of Anthropology* 39:453–468.

Gilman, Patricia A., and Michael E. Whalen. 2011. Moving on the Landscape: Mobility and Migration. In *Movement, Connectivity, and Landscape Change in the Ancient Southwest* edited by Margaret C. Nelson and Colleen Strawhacker, pp. 45–56. University Press of Colorado, Boulder.

Glowacki, Donna M. 2015. *Living and Leaving: A Social History of Regional Depopulation in Thirteenth-Century Mesa Verde*. University of Arizona Press, Tucson.

Graves, Michael W., Sally J. Holbrook, and William A. Longacre. 1982. Aggregation and Abandonment at Grasshopper Pueblo: Evolutionary Trends in the Late Prehistory of East-Central Arizona. In *Multidisciplinary Research at Grasshopper Pueblo, Arizona*, edited by William A. Longacre, Sally J. Holbrook, and Michael W. Graves, pp. 110–121. Anthropological Papers No. 40. University of Arizona Press, Tucson.

Hack, John T. 1942. *The Changing Physical Environment of the Hopi Indians of Arizona*. Papers of the Peabody Museum of American Archaeology and Ethnography Vol. XXXV(1). Cambridge, Massachusetts.

Kintigh, Keith W., Jeffrey H. Altschul, Mary C. Beaudry, Robert D. Drennan, Ann P. Kinzig, Timothy A. Kohler, W. Frederick Limp, Herbert D. G. Maschner, William K. Michener, Timothy R. Pauketat, Peter Peregrine, Jeremy A. Sabloff, Tony J. Wilkinson, Henry T. Wright, and Melinda A. Zeder. 2014. Grand Challenges for Archaeology. *American Antiquity* 79:3–24

Kristensen, Todd J., and Reade Davis. 2013. The Legacies of Indigenous History in Archaeological Thought. *Journal of Archaeological Method and Theory* 22:512–542.

Kuwanwisiwma, Leigh. J. 2002. *Hopi Navotiat*, Hopi Knowledge of History. In *Prehistoric Culture Change on the Colorado Plateau, Ten Thousand Years on Black Mesa*, edited by Shirley Powell and Francis E. Smiley, pp. 161–163. University of Arizona Press, Tucson.

———. 2008. Collaboration Means Equality, Respect, and Reciprocity: A Conversation About Archaeology and the Hopi Tribe. In *Collaboration in Archaeological Practice: Engaging Descendant Communities*, edited by Chip Colwell-Chanthaphonh and T. J. Ferguson, pp. 151–169. AltaMira Press, Lanham, Maryland.

Kuwanwisiwma, Leigh J., and T. J. Ferguson. 2009. *Hopitutskwa* and *Ang Kuktota*: The Role of Archaeological Sites in Defining Hopi Cultural Landscapes. In *The Archaeology of Meaningful Places*, edited by Brenda J. Bowser and Maria Nieves Zedeño, pp. 90–106. University of Utah Press, Salt Lake City.

Liebmann, Matthew. 2012. *Revolt: An Archaeological History of Pueblo Resistance and Revitalization in 17th Century New Mexico*. University of Arizona Press, Tucson.

Lyons, Patrick. 2003. *Ancestral Hopi Migrations*. Anthropological Papers No. 68. University of Arizona Press, Tucson.

McGregor, John C. 1943. Burial of an Early American Magician. *Proceedings of the American Philosophical Society* 86:270–298.

McGuire, Randall H. 1992. Archeology and the First Americans. *American Anthropologist* 94:816–836.

Mills, Barbara J., Mark Altaha, John Welch, and T. J. Ferguson. 2008. Archaeology Without Trowels: Teaching Archaeology and Heritage Preservation in Collaborative Contexts. In *Collaborating at the Trowel's Edge: Teaching and Learning in Indigenous Archaeology*, edited by Stephen W. Silliman, pp. 25–49. University of Arizona Press, Tucson.

Murray, Tim. 2011. Archaeologists and Indigenous People: A Maturing Relationship. *Annual Review of Anthropology* 40:363–378.

Naranjo, Tessie. 1995. Thoughts on Migration by Santa Clara Pueblo. *Journal of Anthropological Archaeology* 14:247–250.

———. 2008. Life as Movement: A Tewa View of Community and Identity. In *The Social Construction of Communities*, edited by Mark D. Varien and James M. Potter, pp. 251–262. AltaMira Press, Lanham, Maryland.

Nicholas, George P. (editor). 2010. *Being and Becoming Indigenous Archaeologists*. Left Coast Press, Walnut Creek, California.

O'Brien, Michael J., R. Lee Lyman, and Michael B. Schiffer. 2007. *Archaeology as Process: Processualism and Its Progeny*. University of Utah Press, Salt Lake City.

Ortman, Scott G. 2012. *Winds from the North: Tewa Origins and Historical Anthropology*. University of Utah Press, Salt Lake City.

Reid, J. Jefferson, and Stephanie M. Whittlesey. 2007. Migration, Population Movement, and Process at Grasshopper Pueblo, Arizona. In *Anthropological Archaeology: Perspectives on Method and Theory*, edited by James M. Skibo, Michael W. Graves, and Miriam T. Stark, pp. 218–235. University of Arizona Press, Tucson.

Schachner, Gregson. 2001. Ritual Control and Transformation in Middle-Range Societies: An Example from the American Southwest. *Journal of Anthropological Archaeology* 20:168–194.

———. 2008. Imagining Communities in the Cibola Past. In *The Social Construction of Communities: Agency, Structure, and Identity in the Prehispanic Southwest*, edited by Mark D. Varien and James M. Potter, pp. 171–190. AltaMira Press, Lanham, Maryland.

———. 2011. Ritual Places and Landscapes: Connecting Southwest Peoples Across Time and Space. In *Movement, Connectivity, and Landscape Change in the Ancient Southwest*, edited by Margaret C. Nelson and Colleen Strawhacker, pp. 423–441. University Press of Colorado, Boulder.

———. 2012. *Population Circulation and the Transformation of Ancient Zuni Communities*. University of Arizona Press, Tucson.

Smith, Watson, Richard B. Woodbury, and Nathalie F. S. Woodbury. 1966. *The Excavation of Hawikuh by Frederick Webb Hodge: Report of the Hendricks-Hodge Expedition*. Contributions from the Museum of the American Indian, No. 20. Heye Foundation, New York.

Snead, James E. 2008. *Ancestral Landscapes of the Pueblo World*. University of Arizona Press, Tucson.

Van Dyke, Ruth M. 2007. *The Chaco Experience: Landscape and Ideology at the Center Place.* School for Advanced Research Press, Santa Fe, New Mexico.

Watkins, Joe E. 2003. Beyond the Margin: American Indians, First Nations, and Archaeology in North America. *American Antiquity* 68:273–285.

Whiteley, Peter M. 2002. Archaeology and Oral Tradition: The Scientific Importance of Dialogue. *American Antiquity* 67:405–415.

Wilcox, Michael. 2009. *The Pueblo Revolt and the Mythology of Conquest: An Indigenous Archaeology of Contact.* University of California Press, Berkeley.

Wolverton, Steve, Robert Melchior Figueroa, and Porter Swentzell. 2016. Archaeology, Heritage, and Moral Terrains: Two Cases from the Mesa Verde Region. *Ethnobiology Letters* 7(2):23–31.

14

THE NATIVE SHAPING OF ANTHROPOLOGICAL INQUIRY

PETER M. WHITELEY

THIS CHAPTER WILL examine the influence of Native thought on the development of anthropological explanation. The main focus is my own ethnographic fieldwork and writing, both of which have been profoundly influenced by Leigh Kuwanwisiwma especially, among other Hopi intellectuals. My inquiry here is therefore necessarily somewhat autobiographical and autoanalytical. The intent is not reflexivist per se, but rather to use scholastic self-scrutiny as a means to the furtherance of anthropological knowledge in the tradition of Clifford Geertz's (1974) classic essay "'From the Native's Point of View': On the Nature of Anthropological Understanding."

Let me begin with an anecdote, originally told by Leigh Kuwanwisiwma near the beginning of my fieldwork at the Hopi village of Paaqavi in 1980–1981:

In the 1970s, the Indian Health Service was installing a water and sewer system at Paaqavi, when Leigh's father, Marshall Jenkins, was governor. A lagoon was built in the valley, a quarter mile below. The main sewage pipe ran from the mesa edge to the lagoon, dropping down about 220 feet over its course. A high-tech Japanese pump was put in to assist passage through the pipe to the lagoon. But the pump quickly broke down. At considerable expense, another was installed. But that broke down too, and so another was brought in—which broke down. Was someone profiting from these failures perhaps? Governor Jenkins, a World War II veteran who knew his way around quite a few machines (and a few bureaucracies too), was concerned about both the mechanical failure and the expense. He politely pointed out that, at least according to the Hopi theory of gravity, liquids—yes, even those liquids—tend to flow downhill, so why have such a fancy pump anyway? Caught with his pants down, the Indian Health Service manager furiously retorted: "I'm the engineer: you're just an Indian!"

Uncomfortable though it is, this anecdote echoes all too closely the practices of anthropologists working with native peoples over the last century. Notwithstanding welcome moves toward more explicitly collaborative work in recent decades, anthropologists continue to claim authority as the professional experts, whose opinions are always superior. Indeed, the latest manifestation of this is the ironic byproduct of the move toward collaboration. While indigenous knowledge is suggested to be valuable, it somehow cannot be accommodated within the explanatory frameworks of orthodox scientific anthropology (cf. Wilcox 2010). The two perspectives are each valid, but they are incommensurable, and it is implied, there is no point in trying to bring them into actual dialogue. This seems to me a dodge, defensible neither on logical nor ultimately on ethical grounds.

LOCATING ANTHROPOLOGICAL KNOWLEDGE

In a paper first published in 1987 (Whiteley 1987:711, 1998:18), I quoted a Fredrik Barth passage that resonated then but now seems surpassingly important in the history of anthropology:

> We [anthropologists] should capitalize on our unique advantage [in comparison to other human sciences]: that our "object of study" can help us actively to transcend our categories by teaching us their *own*. This means recognizing that the actors' categories provide a way to understand reality, *as well as* being part of that reality. In practice, probably most of the productivity of the anthropologist derives from this source. Even though his arrogance as a professional academic, and his defensiveness when his own reality is being threatened by the enchanted world of another culture, both militate against such learning. (Barth 1981:9–10; italics original)

Barth points up one of anthropology's dirty little secrets: that notwithstanding their claims to distinctive professional expertise, anthropologists depend greatly on the intellectual positions of their interlocutors in order to generate meaningful cultural explanations. It really could be no other way, of course. Usually inexpert in the cultures of their investigation at the outset of fieldwork and typically spending limited amounts of time within them, anthropologists seek out those who provide expert local knowledge.

Since Barth wrote, debates over perspectival interests have grown apace (e.g., Hastrup 1996; Kempny 2012; Ranco 2006; Smith 1999; Tengan and Fonoti 2010). Is there a "native point of view" constitutively distinct from or antithetical to "the anthropologist's view?" Is the latter "scientific" under some description, and is science justified in claiming to have cornered the market on objective explanation? Can there genuinely be a "native anthropology" or is this a "contradiction in terms" (Hastrup 1996)? Is "native anthropology" an essentialized project attached to the personhood of the practitioner? Some have argued that a different form of anthropological inquiry can emerge from direct engagement by native anthropologists (Ranco 2006). This may be true in certain respects, but we should remember that the history of anthropology includes some prominent Native American practitioners like Francis La Flesche, J. N. B. Hewitt, Arthur C. Parker, Ella Deloria, D'Arcy McNickle, Edward Dozier, Bea Medicine, and Alfonso Ortiz. And, as I shall argue, ethnography is ipso facto a hybrid scheme of knowledge whose discursive space is grounded in mediatory encounter across difference (cf. Whiteley 2004b).

The key question of this volume, it seems to me, pivots on the epistemological conditions and possibilities of anthropological practice and knowledge. I do believe scientific description and explanation are the hallmarks of a serious comparative anthropology. Philosophically, I am uncomfortable with the idea that some cultural perspectives are irremediably incommensurable with others (cf. Keane 2013). This is as much as to say that utterances in one language can under no circumstances be translated into another, that neurological operations manifest differently according to cultural context, or that laws of nature (like gravity or physiology) operate selectively in different parts of the world. Clearly, beyond a certain postmodern point, such arguments are patently absurd. We are all members of the same species, hard-wired in the same ways: cultural perspectives are subsidiary and responsive to the objective biological conditions and forms of human life. To deny that is to question our common humanity, and if anthropology is at base about explaining human behavior, this is an unacceptable proposition ethically as well as logically.

NATIVE EXPLANATION IN THE ANTHROPOLOGICAL DIALOGUE

While not ignoring the connections between knowledge and power (Whiteley 1993) and the academic construction of privileged perspectives, my premise here is that there needs to be a resituating of epistemological perspectives. Natives have often been depicted just as *informants*, who, while they may reliably report experiences and recollections, are not imagined as engaging in critical analysis, evaluation of competing views, or negotiating interpretations both within and beyond a particular cultural framework. We might summarize these prejudices as anthropologists think etically, Natives only emically.

In the past, Native explanations were frequently just dismissed, as in Robert Lowie's (1917) infamous denunciation of oral history. Nowadays, when Native knowledge is recognized in research, it often gets compartmentalized as the "cultural perspective," as distinct from scientific explanation and thus—like some epistemological orphan—permitted a presence at the table, but not one to be taken too seriously. The effect is that Native and scientific perspectives appear to exist in parallel universes, and while pronounced as equally valid, with no attempt to reconcile or address any of their epistemological differences, this is a false sense of equality.

I do not believe this divide is insurmountable, and if the dialogue is to move forward, we should not permit it to be, for the sake of both explanation and intercultural understanding. With the examples that follow from my own work, I will try to demonstrate how local knowledge directly informs anthropological explanation and often guides research in practice. Let me here state an article of faith: Native knowledge is intrinsic to anthropological thought. The debates over "native anthropology" (referenced above) are in my view somewhat misconceived in this regard. Hastrup's denial that there could be such a thing as Native anthropology—i.e., arguing that Native knowledge occupies one epistemological space forever separated from anthropological knowledge—probably represents the views of most professional anthropologists. But this misconceives anthropological knowledge as a disciplinary monologue rather than as an inherent and implicit reflection of the conjunctural thought of subjects party to both investigation and analysis. To be sure, anthropology has developed multiple conceptual schemes for organizing its ethnographically constituted knowledge base. But the very constitution of that knowledge base depends on the translation of systematic ways of thinking cross-culturally. Could there be a theory of "The Gift" (i.e., Mauss 1925) without the Kula Ring or the Kwakwaka'wakw potlatch? Insofar as those ethnographically specific customs rest on indigenously conceptualized practices and organized actions, they reflect a detailed ontology of gift exchange. Similarly, structuralist analysis of mythological, totemic, and other symbolic operations depends on the detailed expression and its implicit analytical registers of such ideas in indigenous modes of thought. While Lévi-Strauss (1970:12) argued that myths think themselves through human minds without the thinkers being conscious of the fact, this seems to me myopic. It suggests that native thought is captive to a mindless stream of collective consciousness without allowing for the possibility of conscious analytical evaluation resting on collective critical standards. Surely, for example, there are poor, as well as good, myth tellers in indigenous societies who may be corrected when they get things wrong, including things that do not conform to "mythologic" principles, in

Lévi-Strauss's sense. In my view, structuralist thought in anthropology could not exist without indigenous thinkers who preserved, transmitted, and extended organized conceptual schemes (bricolage or no) encoded in structured narratives and ritual discourse.

Practically speaking, it is a truism that, ever since Lewis Henry Morgan and Ely Parker, ethnographic research has been dialogical. Indeed, it could be no other way. Consider Franz Boas and George Hunt, Francis La Flesche and Alice Fletcher (and colleagues), Elsie Clews Parsons and several named Pueblo interlocutors, Ruth Benedict and Santiago Quintana, Mischa Titiev and Don Talayesva, Alfonso Ortiz and Tony Garcia, and so on. Even a Native ethnographer depends on particular mentors, who often shape the direction and contours of both learning and explanation. Most ethnographers emphasize in prefaces that their research would not have succeeded without "key informants" in the host community taking a direct interest in their project. This message is frequently effaced in finished ethnographic texts, especially problem-oriented journal articles, leaving the impression that research conclusions derive simply from the ethnographer's own insights. That is the case with my own work too, in part because at Hopi and other Pueblo communities, consultants have typically not wished to be named in ethnographic texts. But whether "professional arrogance" (per Barth), local mores prescribing anonymity, or a mixture of both, the effect is the same, and what are in fact conjuncturally developed ideas appear as the products of the ethnographer's thought alone. By way of setting the record straight, let me address some processes of learning and explanation in my own practice.

A HISTORICAL ANTHROPOLOGY OF PAAQAVI

My first ethnographic research at Paaqavi in 1980–1981 focused on history and social change. How this came to be typifies the conjuncture I am trying to describe. As a graduate student I was certainly interested in ethnohistory and had chosen it as one of three fields of concentration for doctoral examinations at the University of New Mexico. Ethnohistory emerged in the 1950s, a byproduct of research for Indian Claims Commission cases and the attendant establishment of a dedicated journal (*Ethnohistory*). As a field, however, it was largely untheorized, and while my doctoral committee did not object, they were unenthusiastic about it as a legitimately analytical focus. "Historical anthropology," a more explicitly theorized approach, had not yet entered the anthropological mainstream. (Geertz's *Negara* [1980] and Sahlins's *Historical Metaphors and Mythical Realities* [1981] are plausibly the founding monographs of this field.)

From my perspective, the main interest in reading ethnohistory was methodological and ancillary to my prime theoretical focus on symbolic anthropology, especially as mediated in classes with Alfonso Ortiz and as an undergraduate with Edmund Leach. Symbolic anthropology was where most of the intellectual action seemed to lie in those days (the 1970s), especially with the work of Clifford Geertz, Mary Douglas, and Victor Turner (as well as Leach and Ortiz). Given the Pueblos' antipathy to research on ritual and religion, it was unclear how my interest could be channeled into a field problem that would satisfy my committee and at the same time be acceptable to a Hopi community. Fred Eggan also pointed out that Hopi was not the place to launch such an ethnographic interest, as Hopi symbology was just too complex (wise advice!). Fred directed me to some initial contacts nonetheless (cf. Whiteley 1998:22).

So, like not a few graduate students, I was flummoxed: standing on the edge of proposing a plan for doctoral fieldwork without knowing how to frame it or to go about the practical arrangement of whatever I might conceive as a proposal. In addition, I was also skeptical of the logic of creating a problem to be investigated before having experience in the field. Perhaps this came from my experience in the British system, more open in this regard, with doctoral dissertations typically titled "A Contribution to the Ethnography of the [named society]." There was no programmatic requirement that field research should be organized by the identification a priori of an analytical research "problem." This contrasts of course with American graduate schools, where the problem-oriented approach remains the sine qua non of proposals for doctoral research. The wisdom of that still seems to me dubious when compared, say, to a field like evolutionary biology, where there is a body of unitary theory and standard methodologies (contested to be sure) to guide the (often collective) development of research projects.

In anthropology, ever since Malinowksi, ethnographic research has mostly been stipulated as an individual project—indeed this is the necessary rite of passage for incorporation into the discipline. Moreover, unlike biology, where the object of investigation is readily designated in the natural world, ethnographic research is from day one inherently dialogical and negotiated on an ongoing basis: the problem itself undergoes transformation as unanticipated information often of a radical kind enters into the picture. The first premise of ethnography requires engagement with interlocutors in a specific time and place. I contend that most genuine anthropological problems emerge only in and through such dialogue. There would be no field of kinship in anthropology (at least in the way it developed) had Morgan not been adopted into the Seneca Hawk Clan and been instructed to classify his new relatives according to Iroquois rules. Unless there is extensive real-time knowledge of the field situation (that some native anthropologists do have beforehand) it is unlikely that an outsider could know what a meaningful problem for field investigation might be, even if directed by an academic mentor with experience of a neighboring society. Neophyte

anthropologists who insist on sticking to the terms of initial fieldwork proposals usually do not produce work of much interest. Ethnography is fundamentally about listening and attending to what one hears and sees: listening ipso facto requires openness
to evolving dialogue that may transform the initial terms of inquiry.

In the Hopi case, there was also the practical matter of obtaining permission to
do fieldwork, which would require demonstrating a commitment not to trespass
against community norms (by asking detailed questions about religious practices, for
example). Shortly after my first visit to Powamuya (the Bean Dance) in spring 1980,
I was invited to a gathering and fortuitously learned there was interest at Paaqavi in
recording its history: the older attendees lamented that historical knowledge was no
longer routinely passed on to younger village members. This sparked my interest, a
serendipitous conjunction with my ancillary focus on ethnohistory. Some weeks later
I crafted a proposal for Paaqavi's governing body to record oral history and combine
this with a search for documentary records. I half persuaded my doctoral committee
to allow me to proceed while they deferred presentation of a research colloquium
out of concern that I did not clearly have a problem-oriented project. After surveying
the community, the village board agreed to my proposal and to allow me to use this
research for my doctoral dissertation.

Within a few months of residing in the village, a genuine analytical problem
became manifest. Paaqavi had been founded from the split of its mother village,
Orayvi, in 1906. My beginning assumption (embryonically problem oriented), building on some statements in Titiev's *Old Oraibi* (1944), was that the villages resulting
from the split would have sought to reconstitute their social and cultural systems on
the model of Orayvi. I quickly learned that this view was not shared by Paaqavi elders,
who regarded the split as a radical, world-changing event—a genuine cultural revo-
lution. This suggested a new sort of problem and a real one in the collective thought
of the host community, concerning social structural dynamics in the Orayvi split and
the reformation of sociocultural order. Happily, over time, I was able to persuade my
committee and the University of New Mexico Anthropology faculty as a whole that
this was a genuine analytical problem for field investigation (one virtue of choosing a
field site within a five-hour drive of one's graduate school). But my point here is that,
from the outset, this project was not crafted in a vacuum of self-referential theoretical
imagination; rather it was direct Hopi interests and perspectives that guided not only
the practical possibilities for research but also the emergence of a genuine anthropological problem. Those interests and perspectives played out in particular ways, leading
to a series of new anthropological understandings about Hopi social and political
structures. In short, in order to understand the perspectives on historical origins and
subsequent sociocultural processes over time at Paaqavi, I was required by my hosts to
engage with their analyses of how Hopi society operates structurally, politically, and

diachronically. Thus, from the very outset, my research—whether or not I wanted it that way—was governed directly by the community's own intellectual discourse.

Ethnographic fieldwork proceeds in fits and starts. Weeks pass without any major insights; then suddenly, often unpredictably, a conversation begins and sheds completely new light on a subject. After some initial contacts with elders and daily discussions with Herschel Talashoma of the Badger Clan, then in his forties, I had begun to establish some limited rapport, but something was still missing. One day Leigh Kuwanwisiwma came to visit. I had been advised to seek him out, as someone of my own generation with a passionate intellectual curiosity and interest in Hopi culture and history, but had not yet had the opportunity to do so. He took the initiative and thus began a rich conversation that continues to this day. In retrospect, I have often wondered whether this was just curiosity on his part or perhaps concern too. As a neophyte fieldworker, I was rather a pathetic sight. A foreigner on a student visa, I had very few resources: no major grant, just two small local awards via the intercession of my doctoral committee. Occasionally, as the snow began to fall, I could be spotted walking out from the village and returning with a meager bundle of gleaned firewood. Then shortly after that first meeting, and much to my relief, Leigh again appeared out of nowhere, this time with a truckload of coal. So, while his initial motivation may have been simple curiosity, there is always the possibility that it was also alarm that a British student was going to die on the village's doorstep!

Over time, Leigh took on an active role in the project. While I had spoken with several elders individually, he realized the most effective setting would be a group meeting of knowledgeable older men. Including only men was culturally constructed: Hopi males are charged with responsibility for sociopolitical history, and they felt more comfortable meeting to discuss such matters as they would in a kiva setting. While over time I spoke with most older women in the village too, my anthropological perspective carries a certain gender bias (probably all do), both as a result of gendered Hopi constructions of formal discourse as well as my standing as a male outsider in the community (cf. Ardener [1975] on women as an anthropologically "muted group"). In February 1981, Leigh arranged a meeting at the village's community building of several older men who had been present as children at the founding of the village in 1909 or who had been born shortly thereafter. It was an extraordinary meeting that lasted several hours; each man spoke in succession, beginning with the oldest, with the others listening attentively and never interrupting. Hopi discourse is typically conducted in that way: you listen until someone has had their say before contributing your own view. (In 1985, after a two-month period of resident field research at Paaqavi, I moved to New York, where the norm of interrupted conversations and voices agonistically competing to speak came as a profound culture shock.) The same emphasis on age-graded ordering of speakers, indicating privileged expertise, is reflected in the arrangement of performers in a sodality ceremony: the oldest men, as chief-priests, take the lead, followed in age order by their juniors and finally by the new initiates at the end of the line. This was graphically demonstrated at the first ceremony I witnessed in 1978, Hotvela's Snake Dance; that experience left a powerful impression and still serves as a mnemonic image of the successive continuation of tradition from deep in the ancestral past.

Some of the men attending this group meeting spoke at greater length than others, but all represented their stories of the village's founding and early years. There are obviously other advantages to one-on-one interviews in ethnographic fieldwork, but group dialogue can be especially productive. In the first place, these men had all known each other intimately since birth; none of them was going to say anything the others found implausible without being called out for it. You might tell the Pahaana (white person) something privately that could be invented or embellished, but you would not do that publicly in front of your oldest peers. Secondly, the dialog filled out a multifaceted past; an incident recalled by one would jog the memory of another. Historical and philosophical knowledge of this sort—or even traditional ecological knowledge—is collective in key respects. If the research object is to learn about a system of knowledge, it is clearly advantageous to engage those who understand it systemically. Individual members of a culture have, within limits, separate understandings of its premises and practices, and in all cultures certain individuals are more interested in and expert about certain topics. In a community like that of the Hopi, people of the same gender are all expected to engage in a broad variety of tasks—including farming, weaving, hunting, and ritual performances for males and child-rearing, agricultural distribution, basketry, and different ritual performances for females. But talents vary and individual specialty, as a more focused angle on systemic knowledge, gives more comprehensive understanding of the area of interest, especially when it is described for an audience consisting primarily of participants experienced in that system.

Individual ability is also emphasized in the Hopi community, and some individuals are selected for certain roles early in life, based on a combination of inherited privileges and particular aptitude. But although specialists, no one is a solo practitioner; rather some are more expert than others. Speaking to an outsider requires much more explanation—as Keith Basso (e.g., 1996) memorably demonstrated with Apache discourse using place-names—than speaking publicly to others of the same social cohort. Information transacted, while condensed in sometimes unexplicated ways, tends to be much richer and more layered. In the face of such expert discourse, the ethnographer's task is to unpack the saliences after the fact (or, in this instance, the recording). Leigh Kuwanwisiwma was a critical voice in that dimension of the research also.

This group discussion (and that of a follow-up meeting convened some months later) was all in Hopi, and my understanding was very limited. Over days and weeks afterward Leigh translated and I typed up the recordings. I had heard some of the accounts in one-on-one conversations with individuals, but none so richly as in this dialogue. For Leigh too there were new insights—indeed, this was partly his interest in arranging the colloquy—although he was certainly familiar with the main themes. Most striking was the view, pervasive among all participants, that the Orayvi split was the intentional product of decision making by village leaders, with specific intended after-effects (a view I would later come to index as "deliberate acts"). This explanation was reported as having been only inside knowledge at the time of the split. However, all participants in this Paaqavi elders' meeting reported that as youths (i.e., in the decades following the split) they had individually heard older relatives reveal this explanation. Moreover, these older relatives included both the factional leaders themselves and other men who were socially prominent at the time of the split. For the meeting participants, naming these sources vouchsafed the validity of their accounts. Proximate causes of this critical historical transformation were thus brought to light by invoking the knowledge of individuals with direct experience of them who were leading protagonists in the events described. As discussed in the following paragraph, this orientation toward verisimilitude of reported knowledge and quotative speech is a part of Hopi grammar as well. A few of the key individuals invoked by the group as sources of knowledge and reports were Lomahongiwma (Spider Clan), Tawakwaptiwa (Bear Clan), Kuwannömtiwa (Sand Clan), Nakwave'yma (Eagle Clan), Nasikwaptiwa (Badger Clan), Polingyawma (Parrot Clan), Pongyaletstiwa (Coyote Clan), and Qötsakwahu (Sand Clan). Naming these men for their specific roles in events at the time of the split and/or as direct sources of orally transmitted information guaranteed the validity of the information reported. Thus, Hopi discourse among knowledgeable older people has its own system of checks and balances: an account attributed to one of these men (for example, by a youngster lying on a pallet pretending to be asleep) was in effect checked and confirmed by auditors of the same cohort, each of whom had heard part or all of the account independently.

As a general matter, and as I have reported in court testimony for the Hopi Tribe on the validity of oral history (in opposition to the legal profession's stipulated skepticism of hearsay evidence), I have found older Hopis to be very truthful about their recollections of important events in the past—when measured, for example, against contemporary documentary sources describing the same events. There are strong culturally reinforced sanctions to ensure accuracy and faithfulness to experienced events. When, for example, a man returns from a distant ceremonial pilgrimage to collect spruce boughs, he is often asked to give a full accounting in the kiva of the details he can recall at each phase of the journey. Because some details may be treated as omens or signs of the outcome of the upcoming ceremony, it is important to report fully and precisely. The doctrine of *maqastutatvo*, literally "fear teaching," compels truthfulness in important discourse at the risk of supernatural consequences. Schooled since childhood to respect and act within this belief system, Hopis are strongly encouraged to remember accurately and to value (even magically, perhaps) accurately reported knowledge. Valuing the reports of experienced events is framed grammatically in Hopi utterances: distinct verbal aspects and other features like quotative particles (e.g., *yaw*, "it is said") mark reports of events by a third party as opposed to those directly experienced by the speaker. This correlates with the cultural emphasis on evaluative epistemological distinctions among observation statements and statements about events not personally witnessed but described as witnessed by identified sources.

This sort of background is an essential part of Hopi understandings of historical narrative and of the value of oral history of certain kinds. Academic appraisal of oral tradition and history frequently neglects or is unaware of such culturally embedded codes to ensure the accuracy of reported knowledge. Oral presentation of Hopi historical narratives is not the same as explicit statements of testable hypotheses in science, but it contains a parallel form of rigor based on recognized standards of sourced authoritative knowledge and measured against inherited and formally transmitted sets of accounts within community discourse. It is not the same as bald assertions of claims from untestable authority in individualistic Western discourse because the truth claims of historical statements in formal Hopi explanations are subjected to the appraisal of cohorts who collectively share—again, quite intimately and over a lifetime—the terms for this cultural knowledge. Specific valued knowledge is *navoti*, sometimes referred to as Hopinavoti, to mark its distinctive cultural status, as opposed to other ways of knowing.

REFIGURING HOPI SOCIAL STRUCTURE

As noted, the anthropological side of my research on Paaqavi's history was emerging as a problem of a social order's reconstitution following major societal fission (i.e., the Orayvi split of 1906). Orayvi society—its clans, sodalities, and calendrical cycle—had been well described by Titiev (1944), informed especially by the perspectives of Tawakwaptiwa, the *kikmongwi* (village chief), and interpreted by Don Talayesva (Sun Chief). My initial line of inquiry to individual Paaqavi interlocutors considered Titiev's description of Orayvi social structure as the ideal-typical baseline that I expected Paaqavi would have sought to reestablish so far as possible. Thus, the assemblage of Orayvi's clans, lineages, households, sodalities, and kiva groups, ritual and economic entitlements, arrangement of landholdings by corporate matriclans with joint estates, and so on was conceptualized as a received model—a model both *of* and *for* in Geertz's (1966) terms—in Third Mesa's collective consciousness of its social structure.

Consequently, I asked elders repeatedly about the reestablishment of ceremonies and sodalities and how long these were maintained. Who were the ceremonial leaders? Was there ever a Snake Dance or Flute ceremony? Where were Paaqavi's clan lands and how had these been distributed—by a *kikmongwi* or by some other instituted system of authority? In 1980, Paaqavi had none of the higher order religious societies, practicing only the *katsina* religion, and periodic women's society ceremonies (O'waqölö), as well as social dances (Butterfly, Buffalo, etc.) that did not require initiation.

I asked whether Paaqavi ever had Wuwtsim, the manhood society rituals—regarded as so crucial within the old order that Harry Kewanimptewa, one of the elders, referred to them as "the Hopis' government." The answer was that, although the individual members of the four societies (Wuwtsim, Aa'alt [Two-Horns], Kwaakwant [One-Horns], and Taatawkyam [Singers]) did conduct annual public and private obligations throughout their lives, no young man had ever been initiated at the new village. This was a mystery (especially when I was told that some of the priests at Paaqavi had played an important role in the reestablishment of Wuwtsim at Hotvela when relations between the two villages were somewhat antagonistic) and certainly counter to expectations deriving from Titiev's account. Elders both in this first and in subsequent group meetings, as well as in private conversations, were consistently clear that the failure to initiate at Paaqavi was a deliberate decision by the founding leaders. Some noted that they too had been perplexed and frustrated about this in their youth; they had wanted to be initiated, but had been refused. One said, "We used to ask my father and our uncles, 'why don't you initiate us into the religious sodalities, like Wuwtsim?' All they would say was, 'this was what was decided at the Orayvi split.'" This was the case, even though some leading priests from Orayvi's sodalities had been principal founders of the village, as emphasized elsewhere (Whiteley 1988a, 1988b; see Whiteley 2008 for the specific composition of post-split communities and ritual positions held in each).

HOPI STRUCTURE AND AGENCY

Although I did not have the theoretical vocabulary to present this perspective at that time, this Hopi discourse highlighted the importance of agency in social process—from a Hopi point of view. In 1981, prevailing models of sociocultural and social structural change were lingeringly structural-functionalist, evolutionist, ecologically oriented, acculturationist, Marxist, or various combinations. All attributed change to abstract social or environmental forces rather than to the intentional decisions and actions of social leaders, who collectively imagined and predicted future outcomes on the basis of preexisting structures of knowledge and practice. In 1981, "structure and agency" was hardly more than a reflected gleam from the eye of sociologist Anthony Giddens (1979). As a theoretical perspective, it had certainly not penetrated my anthropological consciousness.

Here then is a major theoretical conjuncture of Hopi analytical knowledge with anthropological explanation. Hopi historical discourse foregrounds agency in relation to structural change; indeed, I subsequently became a structure-and-agency type of anthropologist (viz. *Deliberate Acts* [1988b]), directly owing to my learning from Hopi discourse. Elders delved into some of the specific decisions and their modes of execution, both private and public, by the factional leaders at Orayvi that resulted in the split (e.g., Whiteley 1988a, 1988b). It remains a remarkable fact that, despite the intense animosities and conflicts resulting in the deprivation of more than half of Orayvi's population of their property and their (formal, ritualized) expulsion from the village, not a single person was killed. (This is confirmed in detailed accounts by non-Hopi witnesses in the documentary record—see Whiteley 2008, volume 2.) In itself this partially corroborates the Paaqavi elders' reports of deliberate planning. In short, the elders' accounts and interpretations of these historical events—the way they unfolded and how specific actions were prosecuted—have some objectively testable or falsifiable features in the same manner as scientific propositions.

As I have been suggesting, if we see this Hopi historical discourse through the lens of now established anthropological categories, we can describe it as a Hopi dialectic of structure and agency—just as I earlier (Whiteley 1988b) described Hopinavoti as a sort of Hopi hermeneutics. Further evidence of its status as a systematic principle of social explanation—a model both *of* and *for*—was encapsulated in an axiom stated by Marshall Jenkins (Musangnuvi/Paaqavi Bear Clan): "*Tunatya, pasiwni, okiw antani*— this is the cornerstone of the Hopi way." If there was a single moment in my first fieldwork that was truly epiphanous, this was it (cf. Whiteley 1988b).

Marshall, a lifelong traditional Hopi farmer, went on to explain via the metaphor of planting seeds and bringing corn to bear from them. *Tunatya* is an intention, the germ of an idea, so to speak—the "seed of thought." *Pasiwni* (planning) refers to bringing all the necessary elements together to allow the seed to germinate and grow. This includes the whole intricate array of Hopi technical and ritual measures applied in floodwater and dune agriculture: evaluating soil temperature, planting in sufficiently deep and moist ground, building windbreaks, and protecting against myriad crop pests. While low-tech and characteristically conservative, Hopi agricultural technology was and is immensely varied, thought out, and somewhat open to experimentation for proven enhancement. This illustrates the depth of the metaphor for Hopi analytical thought in general. And lastly, *okiw antani*—literally, "now, let it be this way"— expresses a prayerful attitude and committed purposiveness. Finally, this careful deliberative approach to cultivation allows for *natwani* (the reflection of one's character, will, and practical efforts) to be realized in a successful harvest. In the metaphorical context, it adumbrates the social mechanics of planning the events of the Orayvi split for what the leaders jointly identified as a desired social outcome. And as my ethnographic writing has attempted to show, this was what indeed occurred—at a sophisticated political and ritual level—at Orayvi.

LESSONS FOR THE ENHANCEMENT OF ANTHROPOLOGICAL EXPLANATION

Elsewhere (especially, Whiteley 1988b, 1998, 2008) I have suggested how predictions of social structural transformation deriving from the received anthropological model (notably Titiev 1944 and Eggan 1950) founder in the face of the quite different explanations of social forms and political processes articulated by Hopi elders. First, according to Hopi elders, clans were not jurally corporate groups with joint estates in material property; neither were they composed by discrete, nested unilineal lineages (Whiteley 1985, 1986). Second, in contrast to the then prevailing anthropological wisdom, Orayvi society was not egalitarian, but contained an instituted and ritually legitimated hierarchy managed by politico-religious leaders (*pavansinom* or "powerful people") who engaged in deliberative social decision making (Whiteley 1987, 1988b; cf. Levy 1992). Third, there were no clan lands as represented in the ethnographic literature for Orayvi. Attempts by other scholars (Bradfield 1971, 1995, Levy 1992) to interpret the split as a direct result of field resources diminished by erosion of the Oraibi Wash and/or unequal access to (hypothesized) clan lands depend utterly on the received structural-functionalist model to the exclusion of Hopi explanations. That model provides a fictitious lens through which Orayvi landholding was constructed anthropologically (see Whiteley 2008:59–193). Fourth, on the historical side of this same argument, Bradfield's explanation of the split—which rejected his informants' accounts that down-cutting of the Oraibi Wash followed the split rather than preceding it—provides perhaps the starkest object lesson for my main point. Bradfield needlessly perpetuated a misconception of Orayvi's material environment, together with an erroneous representation of the social organization of production. Subsequently, both aspects of Bradfield's argument guided Levy's influential explanation of the split. Hopi perspectives that falsify both aspects and that manifestly correspond to the contemporary documentary record of hydrogeological events (Whiteley 2008:90–181) were actively ignored in favor of an externally projected model lacking corroboration.

CONCLUSION

The Hopi analytical and historical perspectives regarding social, political, economic, and adaptive forms are indispensable if we are interested in the furtherance of anthropological explanation. In countless ways, it has become clearer to me that most of my interventions have been shaped and guided by Hopi thinkers and Hopi analytical statements. From the poetics and social import of personal names (Whiteley 1992), to the collective assault on Awat'ovi in 1700 (Whiteley 2002b), the meaning of a diplomatic message to President Fillmore (Whiteley 2004a), and the nature of environmental cognition (Whiteley 2011), the great majority of my analyses have been motivated or directed by Hopi thought. As discovered by several other scholars engaged in collaborative research at Hopi (e.g., Bernardini 2005; Ferguson and Colwell-Chanthaphonh 2006; Kuwanwisiwma and Ferguson 2009), the enhancement of anthropological explanation by explicit attendance to Hopi explanation is palpable.

Purported incommensurability of knowledge systems should not be accepted (cf. Whiteley 2002a). This is not a philosophically sustainable position in any rigorous sense. To be sure, translation—the key anthropological act—is prerequisite to effectively situating epistemological conjuncture. That should be the challenge for explanation, however, not its obstacle. In short, anthropology, to adapt Frederick Maitland's famous dictum, is either Native or it is nothing. This, it seems to me, is the most valuable anthropological lesson of all, especially for all those who would claim to be engineers rather than just Indians.

REFERENCES CITED

Ardener, Edwin. 1975. Belief and the Problem of Women. In *Perceiving Women*, edited by Shirley Ardener, pp. 1–17. Malaby Press, London.

Barth, Fredrik. 1981. *Process and Form in Social Life*. Routledge, London.

Basso, Keith H. 1996. *Wisdom Sits in Places: Landscape and Language Among the Western Apache*. University of New Mexico Press, Albuquerque.

Bernardini, Wesley. 2005. *Hopi Oral Tradition and the Archaeology of Identity*. University of Arizona Press, Tucson.

Bradfield, R. Maitland. 1971. *The Changing Pattern of Hopi Agriculture*. Occasional Paper 30. Royal Anthropological Institute, London.

———. 1995. *An Interpretation of Hopi Culture*. Privately printed, Derby, England.

Eggan, Frederick R. 1950. *Social Organization of the Western Pueblos*. University of Chicago Press, Chicago.

Ferguson, T. J., and Chip Colwell-Chanthaphonh. 2006. *History Is in the Land: Multivocal Tribal Traditions in Arizona's San Pedro Valley*. University of Arizona Press, Tucson.

Geertz, Clifford. 1966. Religion as a Cultural System. In *Anthropological Approaches to the Study of Religion*, edited by Michael Banton, pp. 1–46. Tavistock, London.

———. 1974. "From the Native's Point of View": On the Nature of Anthropological Understanding. *Bulletin of the American Academy of Arts and Sciences* 28(1):26–45.

———. 1980. *Negara: The Theatre State in Nineteenth Century Bali*. Princeton University Press, Princeton, New Jersey.

Giddens, Anthony. 1979. *Central Problems in Social Theory: Action, Structure, and Contradiction in Social Analysis*. University of California Press, Berkeley.

Hastrup, Kirsten. 1996. Anthropological Theory as Practice. *Social Anthropology* 4(1):75–81.

Keane, Webb. 2013. Ontologies, Anthropologists, and Ethical Life. *HAU: Journal of Ethnographic Theory* 3(1):186–191.

Kempny, Marta. 2012. Rethinking Native Anthropology: Migration and Auto-ethnography in the Post-Accession Europe. *International Review of Social Research* 2(2):39–52.

Kuwanwisiwma, Leigh J., and T. J. Ferguson. 2009. *Hopitutskwa* and *Ang Kuktota*: The Role of Archaeological Sites in Defining Hopi Cultural Landscapes. In *The Archaeology of Meaningful Places*, edited by Brenda J. Bowser and Maria Nieves Zedeño, pp. 90–106. University of Utah Press, Salt Lake City.

Lévi-Strauss, Claude. 1970. *The Raw and the Cooked*. Jonathan Cape, London.

Levy, Jerrold. 1992. *Orayvi Revisited: Social Stratification in an "Egalitarian" Society*. School of American Research Press, Santa Fe.

Lowie, Robert H. 1917. Oral Tradition and History. *Journal of American Folklore* 30(116):161–167.

Mauss, Marcel. 1925. Essai sur le Don [Essay on the Gift]. *L'Année Sociologique* (new series) 1: 30–186.

Ranco, Darren J. 2006. Toward a Native Anthropology: Hermeneutics, Hunting Stories, and Theorizing from Within. *Wicazo Sa Review* 21(2):61–78.

Sahlins, Marshall D. 1981. *Historical Metaphors and Mythical Realities: Structure in the Early History of the Sandwich Islands Kingdom*. University of Michigan Press, Ann Arbor.

Smith, Linda Tuhiwa. 1999. *Decolonizing Methodologies: Research and Indigenous Peoples*. Zed, New York.

Tengan, T., T. Ka'ili, and R. Fonoti (editors). 2010. Genealogies: Articulating Indigenous Anthropology in/of Oceania (special issue). *Pacific Studies* 33(2/3).

Titiev, Mischa. 1944. *Old Oraibi: A Study of the Hopi Indians of Third Mesa*. Papers of the Peabody Museum of American Archaeology and Ethnology XXII(1). Harvard University, Cambridge, Massachusetts.

Whiteley, Peter M. 1985. Unpacking Hopi "Clans": Another Vintage Model Out of Africa? *Journal of Anthropological Research* 41:359–374.

————. 1986. Unpacking Hopi "Clans," II: Further Questions about Hopi Descent Groups. *Journal of Anthropological Research* 42:69–79.

————. 1987. The Interpretation of Politics: A Hopi Conundrum. *Man* (new series) 22:696–714.

————. 1988a. *Bacavi: Journey to Reed Springs*. Northland Press, Flagstaff, Arizona.

————. 1988b. *Deliberate Acts: Changing Hopi Culture through the Oraibi Split*. University of Arizona Press, Tucson.

————. 1992. *Hopitutungwni*: 'Hopi Names' as Literature. In *On the Translation of Native American Literatures*, edited by Brian Swann, pp. 208–227. Smithsonian Institution Press, Washington, D.C.

————. 1993. The End of Anthropology (at Hopi)? *Journal of the Southwest* 35(2):125–157.

————. 1998. *Rethinking Hopi Ethnography*. Smithsonian Institution Press, Washington, D.C.

————. 2002a. Archaeology and Oral Tradition: the Scientific Importance of Dialogue. *American Antiquity* 67(3):405–415.

————. 2002b. Re-imagining Awat'ovi. In *Archaeologies of the Pueblo Revolt: Identity, Meaning, and Renewal in the Pueblo World*, edited by Robert Preucel, pp. 147–65. University of New Mexico Press, Albuquerque.

————. 2004a. Bartering Pahos with the President. *Ethnohistory* 51(2):359–414.

————. 2004b. Ethnography. In *A Companion to the Anthropology of American Indians*, edited by Thomas Biolsi, pp. 435–471. Blackwell, Malden, Massachusetts.

————. 2008. *The Orayvi Split: A Hopi Transformation*. Anthropological Papers of the American Museum of Natural History no. 87. 2 vols.

————. 2011. Hopi Place Value: Translating a Landscape. In *Born in the Blood: On Native American Translation*, edited by Brian Swann, pp. 84–108. University of Nebraska Press, Lincoln.

Wilcox, Michael. 2010. Saving Indigenous Peoples from Ourselves: Separate But Equal Archaeology Is Not Scientific Archaeology. *American Antiquity* 75(2):221–227.

APPENDIX

*Primary Research Reports and Publications from Projects
Sponsored by the Hopi Cultural Preservation Office*

COMPILED BY STEWART B. KOYIYUMPTEWA, CHIP
COLWELL, MICHAEL YEATTS, AND T. J. FERGUSON

REPORTS AND PUBLICATIONS

Albert, Steve and Chip Colwell-Chanthaphonh. 2007. *Hopi Cultural and Natural Resources
Report for the Navajo Transmission Project*. Prepared by Parametrix and Anthropological
Research, LLC, in collaboration with the Hopi Cultural Preservation Office. Hopi Cultural
Preservation Office, Kiqötsmovi, Arizona.

Anyon, Roger. 1999. *Migrations in the North: Hopi Reconnaissance for the Rocky Mountain
Expansion Loop Pipeline*. Prepared by Anthropological Research, LLC, in collaboration
with the Hopi Cultural Preservation Office. Hopi Cultural Preservation Office, Kiqötsmovi, Arizona.

———. 1999. *Migrations in the South: Hopi Reconnaissance in the Barry M. Goldwater Range*.
Prepared by Anthropological Research, LLC, in collaboration with the Hopi Cultural Preservation Office. Hopi Cultural Preservation Office, Kiqötsmovi, Arizona.

Bernardini, Wesley. 2005. *Hopi Ethnographic Overview for the Grand Staircase-Escalante
National Monument*. Report on file at the Hopi Cultural Preservation Office, Kiqötsmovi,
Arizona.

———. 2005. *Hopi Oral Tradition and the Archaeology of Identity*. University of Arizona Press,
Tucson.

———. 2005. Reconsidering Spatial and Temporal Aspects of Prehistoric Cultural Identity: A
Case Study from the American Southwest. *American Antiquity* 70(1):31–54.

———. 2005. *The Tutuveni Petroglyph Site*: Report of field work conducted by the University
of Redlands in collaboration with the Hopi Cultural Preservation Office. Report on file at
the Hopi Cultural Preservation Office, Kiqötsmovi, Arizona.

———. 2006. Jeddito Yellow Ware and Hopi Ethnogenesis. *Kiva* 72(3):295–328.

———.2007. *Ancestral Hopi Villages Mapping Project*. Report on file at the Hopi Cultural Preservation Office, Kiqötsmovi, Arizona

———. 2007. Understanding Ancestral Hopi Migration and Identity, A.D. 1275–1400. *Archaeology Southwest* 21(2):9.

———. 2008. Identity as History: Hopi Clans and the Curation of Oral Tradition. *Journal of Anthropological Research* 64:483–509

———. 2009. *Hopi History in Stone: The Tutuveni Petroglyph Site*. Arizona State Museum Archaeological Series 200. Arizona State Museum, University of Arizona, Tucson.

———. 2011. Migration in Fluid Social Landscapes: Units and Processes. In *Current Developments in the Anthropological Study of Past Human Migration*, edited by Graciela Cabana and Jeffery Clark, pp. 31–44. University of Florida Press, Gainesville.

———. 2012. Hopi Clan Traditions and the Pedigree of Ceremonial Objects. In *Enduring Motives: Religious Traditions of the Americas*, edited by Warren DeBoer and Linea Sundstrom, pp. 172–184. University of Alabama Press, Tuscaloosa.

———. 2012. North, South, and Center: An Outline of Hopi Ethnogenesis. In *Religious Transformation in the Late Prehispanic Pueblo World*, edited by Donna M. Glowacki and Scott Van Keuren, pp. 196–220. University of Arizona Press, Tucson.

———. 2014. Ceramic Connections: Investigating Ties Between Hopi and Perry Mesa. In *Alliance and Landscape on Perry Mesa in the Fourteenth Century*, edited by David R. Abbott and Katherine A. Spielmann, pp. 145–160. University of Utah Press, Salt Lake City.

Bernardini, Wesley, and Severin Fowles. 2011. Becoming Hopi, Becoming Tewa: Two Pueblo Histories of Movement. In *Movement, Connectivity, and Landscape Change in the Ancient Southwest*, edited by Margaret Nelson and Colleen Strawhacker, pp. 253–274. University Press of Colorado, Boulder.

Bernardini, Wesley, and Leigh J. Kuwanwisiwma. 2010. Hopi Perspectives on the Archaeology of the Grand Staircase-Escalante National Monument. In *Learning from the Land: Grand Staircase-Escalante National Monument Science Symposium Proceedings*, edited by Marietta Eaton, pp. 336–354. Bureau of Land Management, Cedar City, Utah.

Bernardini, Wesley, and Lee Wayne Lomayestewa. 2016. Hopi Perspectives on Cultural Resources at Chimney Rock National Monument. Manuscript on file at the Hopi Cultural Preservation Office, Kiqötsmovi, Arizona.

Bungart, Peter W., and Anne Raney. 2005. *An Archaeological Survey of Components of the Black Mesa Project Crossing Hopi Tribal Lands in Northeastern Arizona*, with contributions by Michael Yeatts and Lanell Poseyesva. Circa Cultural Report No. 05-23. Hopi Cultural Preservation Office and Circa Cultural Consulting, Flagstaff, Arizona.

Carver, Larrynn Occhiello. 1996. *A Cultural Resources Inventory of State Route 87 from the Hopi Reservation Boundary to the State Route 264 Junction, Navajo County, Arizona*. Hopi Cultural Preservation Office project 96-029. Hopi Cultural Preservation Office, Kiqötsmovi, Arizona.

———. 1997. *A Cultural Resources Inventory of State Route 264 from Polacca Wash to the State Route 87 Junction, Navajo County, Arizona.* Hopi Cultural Preservation Office project 96–064. Hopi Cultural Preservation Office, Kiqötsmovi, Arizona.

Colwell, Chip, and T. J. Ferguson. 2017. Tree-Ring Dates and Navajo Settlement Patterns in Arizona. *American Antiquity* 82(1):25–49.

Colwell-Chanthaphonh, Chip. 2003. Signs in Place: Native American Perspectives of the Past in the San Pedro Valley of Southeastern Arizona. *Kiva* 69(1):5–29.

———. 2004. Remembrance of Things and Things Past: Museums as Memorials and Encounters with Native American History. *Museum Anthropology* 27(1):37–48.

———. 2005. Footprints of the Hisatsinom: Hopi Interpretations of Ancient Images in the San Pedro Valley of Southern Arizona. In *Making Marks: Graduate Studies in Rock Art Research in the New Millennium,* edited by Jennifer K. K. Huang and Elisabeth V. Culley, pp. 221–228. Occasional Paper No. 5. American Rock Art Research Association, Tucson.

———. 2011. Sketching Knowledge: Quandaries in the Mimetic Reproduction of Pueblo Ritual. *American Ethnologist* 38(3):451–467.

Colwell-Chanthaphonh, Chip, and Stewart B. Koyiyumptewa. 2006. *Investigation of Hopi Traditional Cultural Properties and Cultural Landscape for the Desert Rock Energy Project.* Report on file at the Hopi Cultural Preservation Office, Kiqötsmovi, Arizona.

———. 2011. Translating Time: A Dialogue on Hopi Experiences of the Past. In *Born in the Blood, On Native American Translation,* edited by Brain Swann, pp. 61–83. University of Nebraska Press, Lincoln.

Colwell-Chanthaphonh, Chip, and T. J. Ferguson. 2004. Virtue Ethics and the Practice of History: Native Americans and Archaeologists Along the San Pedro Valley of Arizona. *Journal of Social Archaeology* 4(1):5–27.

———. 2006. Memory Pieces and Footprints: Multivocality and the Meanings of Ancient Times and Ancestral Places Among the Zuni and Hopi. *American Anthropologist* 108(1):148–162.

———. 2010. Intersecting Magisteria, Bridging Archaeological Science and Traditional Knowledge. *Journal of Social Archaeology* 10(3):425–456.

Colwell-Chanthaphonh, Chip, T. J. Ferguson, and Douglas W. Gann. 2011. Multivocality in Multimedia: Collaborative Archaeology and the Potential of Cyberspace. In *New Perspectives in Global Public Archaeology,* edited by Katsuyuki Okamura and Akira Matsuda, pp. 239–249. Springer, New York.

Colwell-Chanthaphonh, Chip, T. J. Ferguson, and Roger Anyon. 2008. Always Multivocal and Multivalent: Conceptualizing Archaeological Landscapes in Arizona's San Pedro Valley. In *Archaeologies of Placemaking: Monuments, Memories, and Engagements in Native North America,* edited by Patricia E. Rubertone, pp. 59–80. Left Coast Press, Walnut Creek, California.

Davis, Hester A. 2008. *Remembering Awatovi: The Story of an Archaeological Expedition in Northern Arizona.* Peabody Museum Press, Harvard University, Cambridge, Massachusetts.

Dongoske, Cindy. 1998. *A Cultural Resources Survey and Inventory Report of State Route 264 from the Hopi-Navajo Reservations Boundary Line to the Coconino-Navajo County Line, Hopi Indian Reservation, Coconino County, Arizona.* Hopi Cultural Preservation Office project 98–001. Hopi Cultural Preservation Office, Kiqötsmovi, Arizona.

———. *Antelope Mesa Archaeological Survey 1995–1998.* Hopi Cultural Preservation Office project 96–001. Hopi Cultural Preservation Office, Kiqötsmovi, Arizona.

———. 2000. *Antelope Mesa Rock Art Documentation Project, Hopi Indian Reservation, Navajo County, Arizona.* Hopi Cultural Preservation Office Project 99–001, National Park Service Grant 04–97-NA-0412. Report on file at the Hopi Cultural Preservation Office, Kiqötsmovi, Arizona.

———. 2002. *A Cultural Resources Survey and Inventory Report of Two Hundred Navajo Properties Within the Hopi Partitioned Lands, Hopi Indian Reservation, Coconino and Navajo Counties, Arizona.* Hopi Cultural Preservation Office project 2001–046. Hopi Cultural Preservation Office, Kiqötsmovi, Arizona.

Dongoske, Kurt E., T. J. Ferguson, and Michael Yeatts. 1994. Ethics of Field Research for the Hopi Tribe. *Anthropology News* 35(1):56.

Dongoske, Kurt E., Leigh Jenkins, and T. J. Ferguson. 1993. Understanding the Past Through Hopi Oral History. *Native Peoples* 6(2):24–31.

———. 1994. Issues Relating to the Use and Preservation of Hopi Sacred Sites. *Historic Preservation Forum* 8(2):12–14

———. 1996. Managing Hopi Sacred Sites to Protect Religious Freedom. *Cultural Survival Quarterly* 19(4):36–39.

Dongoske, Kurt E., Michael Yeatts, Roger Anyon, and T. J. Ferguson. 1997. Archaeological Cultures and Cultural Affiliation: Hopi and Zuni Perspectives in the American Southwest. *American Antiquity* 62(4):600–608.

Dongoske, Kurt, Michael Yeatts, T. J. Ferguson, and Leigh Jenkins. 1995. Historic Preservation and Native American Sites. *SAA Bulletin* 13(4):13, 39.

Driscoll, Daniel E. 2006. Golden Eagle Nest Non-development Zones Established by Exhibit C of the 1934 Reservation Mediation Compact. Manuscript on file at Hopi Cultural Preservation Office, Kiqötsmovi, Arizona.

Duff, Andrew I., T. J. Ferguson, Susan Bruning, and Peter Whiteley. 2008. Collaborative Research in a Living Landscape: Pueblo Land, Culture, and History in West-Central New Mexico. *Archaeology Southwest* 22(1):1–24.

Ferguson, T. J. 1993. *Assessment of Hopi and Zuni Traditional Cultural Properties in the Vicinity of the Dead Wash Housing Cluster, the Interstate Housing Cluster, and the N-2013 Access Road on ONHIR Lands, Apache County, Arizona.* Zuni Archaeology Program Report No. 433. Pueblo of Zuni, New Mexico.

———. 1997. *Hopi Reconnaissance of the Carlota Copper Project: Ethnohistoric Overview and Cultural Concerns.* Prepared for SWCA, Inc., Flagstaff, Arizona. Report on file at the Hopi Cultural Preservation Office, Kiqötsmovi, Arizona.

———. 1997. *Hopi Traditional Cultural Properties in the US 89 Highway Right-of-Way from Fernwood to Wupatki*. Prepared for the Arizona Department of Transportation, Phoenix. Report on file at the Hopi Cultural Preservation Office, Kiqötsmovi, Arizona.

———. 1998. Hopi Footprints in the Jeddito Valley: Interpretation of Ethnohistory and Archaeology. In *Ethnohistorical Interpretation and Archaeological Data Recovery along Navajo Route 9101, Jeddito Road, Navajo County, Arizona*, edited by David C. Eck, pp. 639–680. Zuni Cultural Resource Enterprise Report No. 562. Pueblo of Zuni, New Mexico

———. 1998. *Öngtupqa Niqw Pisisvayu (Salt Canyon and the Colorado River): The Hopi People and the Grand Canyon*. Manuscript on file at the Hopi Cultural Preservation Office, Kiqötsmovi, Arizona.

———. 2000. Western Pueblos and the Petroglyph National Monument: A Preliminary Assessment of the Cultural Landscapes of Acoma, Laguna, Zuni, and Hopi. In *"That Place People Talk About": Ethnographic Landscapes Literature Essays, Petroglyph National Monument*, edited by Kurt Anschuetz, pp. 4.1–4.29. Community and Cultural Landscape Contribution V. Rio Grande Foundation for Communities and Cultural Landscapes, Santa Fe, New Mexico

———. 2004. *Hopi Agriculture and Water Use*. Prepared for the Hopi Tribe for Use in General Adjudication of all Rights to Use Water in the Little Colorado River System and Source, Superior Court of Arizona, Case No. CV-6417. Manuscript on file at the Hopi Cultural Preservation Office, Kiqötsmovi, Arizona.

Ferguson, T. J. (compiler). 2003. *Yep Hisat Hoopoq'yaqam Yeesiwa (Hopi Ancestors Were Once Here): Hopi-Hohokam Cultural Affiliation Study*, with contributions by Patrick D. Lyons, Micah Loma'omvaya, Gregson Schachner, and Laurie D. Webster. Hopi Cultural Preservation Office, Kiqötsmovi, Arizona.

Ferguson, T. J., and Roger Anyon. 2001. Hopi and Zuni Cultural Landscapes: Implications of History and Scale for Cultural Resources Management. In *Native Peoples of the Southwest: Negotiating Land, Water, and Ethnicities*, edited by Laurie Weinstein, pp. 99–122. Bergin and Garvey, Westport, Connecticut.

———. 2001. *Hopi Traditional Cultural Properties along the Questar Southern Trails Pipeline*. Prepared by Heritage Management Research Consultants in collaboration with the Hopi Cultural Preservation Office. Report on file at the Hopi Cultural Preservation Office, Kiqötsmovi, Arizona.

Ferguson, T. J., G. Lennis Berlin, and Leigh J. Kuwanwisiwma. 2009. Kukhepya: Searching for Hopi Trails. In *Landscapes of Movement: The Anthropology of Paths, Trails, and Roads*, edited by James E. Snead, Clark L. Erickson, and J. Andrew Darling, pp. 20–41. University of Pennsylvania Press, Philadelphia.

Ferguson, T. J., and Chip Colwell-Chanthaphonh. 2006. *History is in the Land: Multivocal Tribal Traditions in Arizona's San Pedro Valley*. University of Arizona Press, Tucson.

Ferguson, T. J., Chip Colwell-Chanthaphonh, and Roger Anyon. 2004. One Valley, Many Histories: Tohono O'odham, Hopi, Zuni, and Western Apache History in the San Pedro Valley. *Archaeology Southwest* 18(1):1–16.

Ferguson, T. J., and Kurt E. Dongoske. 1994. *Navajo Transmission Project EIS Hopi Ethnographic Overview*. Report on file at the Hopi Cultural Preservation Office, Kiqötsmovi, Arizona.

Ferguson, T. J., Kurt E. Dongoske, Leigh Jenkins, Mike Yeatts, and Eric Polingyouma. 1993. Working Together: The Roles of Archaeology and Ethnohistory in Hopi Cultural Preservation. *CRM* 16 (special issue):27–37.

Ferguson, T. J., Kurt E. Dongoske, Mike Yeatts, and Leigh J. Kuwanwisiwma. 2000. Hopi Oral History and Archaeology. In *Working Together: Native Americans & Archaeologists*, edited by Kurt E. Dongoske, Mark Aldenderfer, and Karen Doehner, pp. 45–60. Society for American Archaeology, Washington, D.C.

Ferguson, T. J., Kurt Dongoske, Mike Yeatts, and Leigh Jenkins. 1995. Hopi Oral History and Archaeology, Part 1: The Consultation Process. *SAA Bulletin* 13(2):12–15.

———. 1995. Hopi Oral History and Archaeology, Part 2: Implementation. *SAA Bulletin* 13(3):10–13.

———. 2001. Hopi Perspectives on Southwestern Mortuary Studies. In *Ancient Burial Practices in the American Southwest: Archaeology, Physical Anthropology, and Native American Perspectives*, edited by Judy Brunson Hadley and Douglas Mitchell, pp. 9–26. University of New Mexico Press, Albuquerque.

Ferguson, T. J., E. Richard Hart, and G. Lennis Berlin. 1995. *Hopi and Zuni Trails and Traditional Cultural Properties in and Near the Interstate, Dead Wash, and Kelsey Housing Clusters on Chambers-Sanders Trust Lands, Apache County, Arizona*. Prepared by Institute of the North American West in association with the Zuni Heritage and Historic Preservation Office. ZHHPO Report No. 484. Pueblo of Zuni, New Mexico.

Ferguson, T. J., and Stewart B. Koyiyumptewa. 2006. *Hopi Traditional Cultural Properties Investigation for the Black Mesa Project*. Prepared by Anthropological Research, LLC, in association with the Hopi Cultural Preservation Office. Report on file at the Hopi Cultural Preservation Office, Kiqötsmovi, Arizona.

———. 2009. *Footprints and Clouds in a Living Landscape: Notes on Hopi Culture and History Relating to Chaco Canyon, Aztec Ruin, and Mount Taylor*. Report on file at the Hopi Cultural Preservation Office. Kiqötsmovi, Arizona.

Ferguson, T. J., Stewart B. Koyiyumptewa, and Chip Colwell-Chanthaphonh. 2007. *Hopi Traditional Cultural Properties along the US 160 Highway Corridor*. Prepared by the Hopi Cultural Preservation Office and Anthropological Research, LLC. Hopi Cultural Preservation Office, Kiqötsmovi, Arizona.

Ferguson, T. J., Stewart B. Koyiyumptewa, and Maren P. Hopkins. 2015. Co-creation of Knowledge by the Hopi Tribe and Archaeologists. *Advances in Archaeological Practice* 3(3):249–262.

Ferguson, T. J., and Leigh J. Kuwanwisiwma. 2017. Traditional Cultural Properties. In *Handbook of Southwestern Archaeology*, edited by Barbara J. Mills and Severin Fowles, pp. 177–191. Cambridge University Press.

Ferguson, T. J., Leigh J. Kuwanwisiwma, Micah Loma'omvaya, Patrick Lyons, Gregson Schachner, and Laurie Webster. 2013. *Yep Hisat Hoopaq'yaqam Yeesiwa* (Hopi Ancestors Were Once Here): Repatriation Research Documenting Hopi Cultural Affiliation with the Ancient Hohokam of Southern Arizona. In *Global Ancestors, Understanding the Shared Humanity of our Ancestors*, edited by Margaret Glegg, Rebecca Redfern, Jelena Bekvalac, and Heather Bonney, pp. 104–133. Oxbow Books, Oxford, England.

Ferguson, T. J., and Micah Lomaomvaya. 1999. *Hoopoq'uaqam niqw Wukoskyavi (Those Who Went to the Northeast and Tonto Basin): Hopi-Salado Cultural Affiliation Study*. Report on file at the Hopi Cultural Preservation Office, Kiqötsmovi, Arizona.

———. 2011. Nuvatukya'ovi, Palatsmo Niqw Wupatki: Hopi History, Culture, and Landscape. In *Sunset Crater Archaeology: The History of a Volcanic Landscape*, edited by Mark D. Elson, pp. 144186. Anthropological Papers 37. Center for Desert Archaeology, Tucson, Arizona.

Ferguson, T. J., and Lee Wayne Lomayestewa. 2007. *Kwaatu: Collection and Use of Golden Eagles on the Hopi Indian Reservation*. Report on file at the Hopi Cultural Preservation Office, Kiqötsmovi, Arizona.

Ferguson, T. J., and Eric Polingyouma. 1991. Statement on Hopi Concerns about Traditional Cultural Properties Affected by the Salt River Project's Fence Lake Mine and Transportation Corridor. Report on file at the Hopi Cultural Preservation Office, Kiqötsmovi, Arizona

———. 1993. *Sio Önga*, An Ethnohistory of Hopi Use of Zuni Salt Lake. In *Traditional Cultural Properties of Four Tribes: The Fence Lake Mine Project*, edited by E. Richard Hart and T. J. Ferguson. Institute of the North American West, Seattle, Washington.

Gilpin, Dennis. 2014. Building Awatovi: The Architecture of Awatovi Pueblo, Northeastern Arizona, A.D. 1200–1700. Draft report submitted to the Peabody Museum of American Archaeology and Ethnology, Harvard University, Cambridge, Massachusetts.

Gumerman, George, Joëlle Clark, Elmer J. Satala, and Ruby Chimerica. 2012. Footprints of the Ancestors: Reengaging Hopi Youth with Their Culture. *Museums & Social Issues* 7(2):149–166.

Hays, Kelley A., and Richard V. N. Ahlstrom. 1991. *Hopi Cultural Resources Inventory: Phase I*. SWCA Archaeological Report No. 91–21. Report on file at the Hopi Cultural Preservation Office, Kiqötsmovi, Arizona.

Hedquist, Saul L. 2013. *Hopi Traditional Cultural Properties Investigation for the Proposed Payson Ranger District Administration Site Sale Parcel*. Report prepared by Anthropological Research, LLC, and the Hopi Cultural Preservation Office for Tonto National Forest, U.S. Forest Service, Phoenix. Hopi Cultural Preservation Office, Kiqötsmovi, Arizona.

Hedquist, Saul L., Stewart B. Koyiyumptewa, Wesley Bernardini, T. J. Ferguson, Peter M. Whiteley, and Leigh J. Kuwanwisiwma. 2015. Mapping the Hopi Landscape for Cultural Preservation. *International Journal of Applied Geospatial Research* 6(1):40–59.

Hedquist, Saul L., Stewart B. Koyiyumptewa, Peter Whiteley, Leigh J. Kuwanwisiwma, Kenneth C. Hill, and T. J. Ferguson. 2014. Recording Toponyms to Document the Endangered Hopi Language. *American Anthropologist* 116(2):324–331.

Hopi Cultural Preservation Office. 2005. *Awatovi Ruins National Historic Landmark Boundary Definition Project.* National Park Service Grant No. 04–00-NA-0419 and Hopi Cultural Preservation Office Report 2005–048. Report on file at the Hopi Cultural Preservation Office, Kiqötsmovi, Arizona.

Hopi Language Assessment Project. 1997. *Presentation of Hopi Language Survey Results.* Hopi Cultural Preservation Office and Bureau of Applied Research in Anthropology, University of Arizona, Tucson.

Hopkins, Maren P., and T. J. Ferguson. 2013. *Hopi, Zuni, and Western Apache Interpretations of Sites Along State Route 77.* Prepared for Desert Archaeology, Inc., Tucson, Arizona. Report on file at the Hopi Cultural Preservation Office, Kiqötsmovi, Arizona.

Hopkins, Maren P., Saul L. Hedquist, T. J. Ferguson, and Stewart B. Koyiyumptewa. 2014. *Talwi'pikit Tuuwuhiyat Ang Hopit Navoti'at: Hopi Traditional Knowledge on the Arizona Public Service 500kV El Dorado Transmission Line Corridor on the Hopi Reservation.* Prepared for Arizona Public Service Company. Report on file at the Hopi Cultural Preservation Office, Kiqötsmovi, Arizona.

Hopkins, Maren P., T. J. Ferguson, and Stewart B. Koyiyumptewa. 2013. *Hopisinmuy Wu'ya'mat Hisat Yang Tupqa'va Yeesiwngwu (Hopi Ancestors Lived in These Canyons): Hopi History and Traditions at Glen Canyon National Recreation Area and Rainbow Bridge National Monument.* University of Arizona, School of Anthropology. Colorado Plateau CESU Cooperative Agreement H1200-09-0005. Report on file at the Hopi Cultural Preservation Office, Kiqötsmovi, Arizona.

Hopkins, Maren P., Stewart B. Koyiyumptewa, Leigh J. Kuwanwisiwma, and T. J. Ferguson. 2016. Comprehending Hopi Footprints: Hopi History and Traditions at Glen Canyon National Recreation Area and Rainbow Bridge National Monument. *Journal of Arizona Archaeology* 4(1):50–59.

Hopkins, Maren P., and Barry Price Steinbrecher. 2016. *Mootisinmuy Piisisvayu ang Yesqamuy Kukveniam (Artifacts of the First People to Live on the Colorado River): Summary of Museum Research with Hopi Cultural Advisors.* Prepared by Anthropological Research, LLC, in collaboration with the Hopi Cultural Preservation Office for Glen Canyon National Recreation Area, National Park Service. Report on file at the Hopi Cultural Preservation Office, Kiqötsmovi, Arizona.

Hopkins, Maren P., Barry Price Steinbrecher, Chip Colwell, T. J. Ferguson, Saul Hedquist, Stewart B. Koyiyumptewa, and Leigh J. Kuwanwisiwma. 2017. *Hopi Ethnographic Study of the Navajo Generating Station and Kayenta Mine Complex.* Prepared by Anthropological Research, LLC, in collaboration with the Hopi Cultural Preservation Office for Salt River Project and Bureau of Reclamation, Kiqötsmovi, Arizona. Report on file at the Hopi Cultural Preservation Office, Kiqötsmovi, Arizona.

Huisinga, Kristin, and Michael Yeatts. 2003. *Sooysoy Himu Naanamiwiwyungwa: An Analysis of the Grand Canyon Monitoring and Research Center's Terrestrial Ecosystem Monitoring*

Program and the Development of a Hopi Long-term Plan. Report on file at the Grand Canyon Monitoring and Research Center, Flagstaff, Arizona.

———. 2014. *Öngtupqa pas Qatsi: Hopi Life in Salt Canyon. A Hopi Handbook to the Grand Canyon*. Report on file at the Hopi Cultural Preservation Office, Kiqötsmovi, Arizona.

Koyiyumptewa, Stewart B., and Chip Colwell-Chanthaphonh. 2011. The Past Is Now: Hopi Connections to Ancient Times and Places. In *Movement, Connectivity, and Landscape Change in the Ancient Southwest*, edited by Margaret C. Nelson and Colleen Strawhacker, pp. 443–455. University Press of Colorado, Boulder.

Koyiyumptewa, Stewart B., and T. J. Ferguson. 2009. *Hopi Cultural Resources Inventory for the N309 Bridge Project in the Vicinity of Sand Springs, Coconino County, Hopi Indian Reservation, Arizona*. Submitted to Western Regional Office Bureau of Indian Affairs Phoenix, Arizona. Report on file at the Hopi Cultural Preservation Office, Kiqötsmovi, Arizona.

Koyiyumptewa, Stewart B., and Leigh J. Kuwanwisiwma. 2009. *Hopi Stories and Connections to the Flagstaff Area National Monuments: Wupatki, Sunset Crater, and Walnut Canyon*, with contributions by Marie Schaefer, Shannon Caplan, and Chelsea Susan Kuiper. Report on file at the Hopi Cultural Preservation Office. Kiqötsmovi, Arizona.

Krall, Angie and T.J. Ferguson. 2003. *Hopi Traditional Cultural Properties in the US 89 Highway Right-of-Way from Antelope Hills to US 160 Junction*. Prepared by Heritage Resources Management Consultants in association with the Hopi Cultural Preservation Office. Report on file at the Hopi Cultural Preservation Office, Kiqötsmovi, Arizona.

Kuwanwisiwma, Leigh J. 2002. *Hopi Navotiat*, Hopi Knowledge of History: Hopi Presence on Black Mesa. In *Prehistoric Culture Change on the Colorado Plateau: Ten Thousand Years on Black Mesa*, edited by Shirley Powell and Francis E. Smiley, pp. 161–163. University of Arizona, Tucson.

———. 2002. Hopi Understanding of the Past: A Collaborative Approach. In *Public Benefits of Archaeology*, edited by Barbara J. Little, pp 46–50. University Press of Florida, Gainesville.

———. 2004. *Yupkövi*: The Hopi Story of Chaco Canyon. In *In Search of Chaco: New Approaches to an Archaeological Enigma*, edited by David Grant Noble, pp. 41–47. SAR Press, Santa Fe.

———. 2008. Collaboration Means Equality, Respect, and Reciprocity: A Conversation About Archaeology and the Hopi Tribe. In *Collaboration in Archaeological Practice: Engaging Descendant Communities*, edited by Chip Colwell-Chanthaphonh and T. J. Ferguson, pp. 151–169. AltaMira Press, Lanham, Maryland.

Kuwanwisiwma, Leigh J., and T. J. Ferguson. 2004. Ang Kuktota: Hopi Ancestral Sites and Cultural Landscapes. *Expedition* 46(2):25–29.

———. 2009. *Hopitutskwa* and *Ang Kuktota*: The Role of Archaeological Sites in Defining Hopi Cultural Landscapes. In *The Archaeology of Meaningful Places*, edited by Brenda J. Bowser and Marìa Nieves Zedeño, pp. 90–106. University of Utah Press, Salt Lake City.

———. 2014. Hopitutskwa: The Meaning and Power of Maps. In *Mapping Native America: Cartographic Interactions Between Indigenous Peoples, Government, and Academia*, Vol. III, edited by Daniel G. Cole and Imre Sutton, pp. 132–147. Printed by CreateSpace Independent Publishing Platform (Amazon).

Kuwanwisiwma, Leigh J., T. J. Ferguson, and Michael Yeatts. 2008. Öngtupqa: The Enduring Association of the Hopi People and the Grand Canyon. In *Reflections of Grand Canyon Historians; Ideas, Arguments, and First-Person Accounts*, edited by Todd R. Berger, pp. 89–95. Grand Canyon Association, Grand Canyon, Arizona.

Kuwanwisima, Leigh J., Stewart B. Koyiyumptewa, and Anita Poleaha. 2015. Pasiwvi: Place of Deliberations. In *Hisat'sinom: Ancient Peoples in a Land Without Water*, edited by Christian E. Downum, pp. 7–10. School for Advanced Research Press, Santa Fe, New Mexico.

Kuwanwisiwma, Leigh J., Michael Yeatts, Kurt E. Dongoske, and T. J. Ferguson. 1997. The Hopi People, the Operation of Glen Canyon Dam, and Management of Cultural Resources in the Grand Canyon. In *Making Protection Work: Proceedings of the 9th Conference on Research and Resource Management in Parks and on Public Lands*, edited by David Harmon, pp. 79–84. George Wright Society, Hancock, Michigan.

Laurila, Erick M., David A. Bild, and Erin Davis. 2011. *A Cultural Resources Survey of 34 Miles (927 Acres) of Hopi Tribal Lands for the Arizona Public Service Company 500-1 (Four Corners-Moencopi-El Dorado) 500-kK Transmission Line, Coconino and Navajo Counties, Arizona*. Logan Simpson Design Inc. Technical Report 075107 (500–1e). Report on file at the Hopi Tribe and Arizona Public Service Company.

Leap, Lisa M., and Michael Yeatts. 1998. *Proposed Data Recovery and Site Management at C:13:010, Grand Canyon National Park*. River Corridor Monitoring Project and the Hopi Tribe. RCMP Report No. 54. Report on file at Grand Canyon National Park, Arizona.

———. 1999. *Proposed Data Recovery at AZ C:13:099 and AZ C:13:100, Palisades Delta, Grand Canyon, Arizona*. Report on file at Grand Canyon National Park, Arizona.

Leap, Lisa M., Michael Yeatts, and Jennifer L. Kunde. 1999. *Data Recovery at Four Sites Along the River Corridor, Grand Canyon National Park, AZ*. River Corridor Monitoring Project Report No. 61. Report on file at Grand Canyon National Park, Arizona.

———. 1999. *Data Recovery Proposed for C:13:010, Feature 24*. River Corridor Monitoring Project Report No. 62. Report on file at Grand Canyon National Park, Arizona.

Lomaomvaya, Micah, and T. J. Ferguson. 2003. *Hisatqasit Aw Maamatslalwa*—Comprehending Our Past Lifeways: Thoughts About a Hopi Archaeology. In *Indigenous People and Archaeology* (Proceedings of the Chacmool Conference), edited by G. Oetelaar, T. Peck, and E. Siegfried, pp. 43–51. University of Calgary, Canada.

Lomaomvaya, Micah, T. J. Ferguson, and Michael Yeatts. 2001. *Öngtuvqava Sakwtala, Hopi Ethnobotany in the Grand Canyon*. Report on file at the Hopi Cultural Preservation Office, Kiqötsmovi, Arizona

Lyons, Patrick D. 2003. *Ancestral Hopi Migrations*. Anthropological Papers of the University of Arizona 68. University of Arizona Press, Tucson.

Maxson, Rachel, Chip Colwell-Chanthaphonh, and Lee Wayne Lomayestewa. 2011. Lost in Translation: Rethinking Hopi Katsina Tithu and Museum Language Systems. *Denver Museum of Nature & Science Annals* 2:1–137.

Sheridan, Thomas E., Stewart B. Koyiyumptewa, Anton Daughters, Dale S. Brenneman, T. J. Ferguson, Leigh Kuwanwisiwma, and Lee Wayne Lomayestewa (editors). 2015. *The Moquis and Kastiilam: Hopis, Spaniards, and the Trauma of History*, Vol. 1: 1540–1679. University of Arizona Press, Tucson.

Sheridan, Thomas E., Stewart B. Koyiyumptewa, Anton T. Daughters, T. J. Ferguson, Leigh Kuwanwisiwma, Dale S. Brenneman, and LeeWayne Lomayestewa. 2014. Moquis and Kastiilam: Coronado and the Hopis. *Journal of the Southwest* 55(4):377–434.

Swidler, Nina, David Eck, T. J. Ferguson, Leigh Kuwanwisiwma, Roger Anyon, Loren Panteah, Klara Kelley, and Harris Francis. 2000. Multiple Views of the Past, Integrating Archaeology and Ethnography in the Jeddito Valley. *CRM* 23(9):49–53.

Varien, Mark D., Scott G. Ortman, Paul Ermigiotti, Timothy A. Kohler, and Leigh Kuwanwisiwma. 2011. Modeling Agricultural Potential in the Mesa Verde Region: Combining Computer Simulation with Experimental Gardening. Paper presented at the Annual Meeting of the Society for American Archaeology, Sacramento, California.

Webster, Laurie D., and Micah Loma'omvaya. 2004. Textiles, Baskets, and Hopi Cultural Identity. In *Identity, Feasting, and the Archaeology of the Greater Southwest: Proceedings of the 2002 Southwest Symposium*, edited by Barbara J. Mills, pp. 74–92. University Press of Colorado, Boulder.

Welch, John R., and T. J. Ferguson. 2007. Putting *Patria* Back into Repatriation: Cultural Affiliation Assessment of White Mountain Apache Tribal Lands. *Journal of Social Archaeology* 7(2):171–198.

———. 2013. Apache, Hopi, and Zuni Perspectives on Kinishba History and Stewardship. In *Kinishba Lost and Found: Mid-Century Excavations and Contemporary Perspectives*, edited by John R. Welch, pp. 261–287. Arizona State Museum Archaeological Series 206. Arizona State Museum, University of Arizona, Tucson.

———. 2016. Preservation Spotlight: Apache, Hopi, and Zuni Perspectives on Kinishba History and Stewardship. *Archaeology Southwest* 30(1):26–27.

Whiteley, Peter M. 1989. *Hopitutskwa: An Historical and Cultural Interpretation of the Hopi Traditional Land Claim. Expert Witness Report for the Hopi Tribe in Masayesva vs. Zah vs. James ('1934 Reservation case')*. U.S. District Court, Phoenix, Arizona.

Yeatts, Michael. 1991. *A Cultural Resources Inventory of the Lower Little Colorado River, Coconino County, Arizona*. Hopi Cultural Preservation Office, Kiqötsmovi, Arizona.

———. 1996. *High Elevation Sand Deposition and Retention from the 1996 Spike Flow: An Assessment for Cultural Resources Stabilization*. Final report submitted to the Grand Canyon Monitoring and Research Center, Bureau of Reclamation, Flagstaff, Arizona.

———. 1997. *An Archaeological Inventory of State Route 264 from Polacca Wash to Keams Canyon, Navajo County, Arizona.* Hopi Cultural Preservation Office project 96–047. Report on file at the Hopi Cultural Preservation Office, Kiqötsmovi, Arizona.

———. 1997. *High Elevation Sand Retention Following the 1996 Spike Flow.* Final report submitted to the Grand Canyon Monitoring and Research Center, Bureau of Reclamation, Flagstaff, Arizona.

———. 1998. *1997 Data Recovery at Five Sites in the Grand Canyon, Final Report.* River Corridor Monitoring Project and the Hopi Tribe, RCMP Report No. 60. Report on file at Grand Canyon National Park, Arizona.

———. 2000. *Testing at Site AZ:C:09:051 (GRCA), Grand Canyon National Park.* Report on file at the Bureau of Reclamation, Upper Colorado River Office, Salt Lake City, Utah.

———. 2004. *A Cultural Resources Inventory of the Lower Moencopi Village Residential and Commercial Development Site.* Hopi Cultural Preservation Office project 2003–019. Hopi Cultural Preservation Office, Kiqötsmovi, Arizona.

———. 2011. *A Cultural Resources Inventory of the Tawa'ovi Community Development, Hopi Indian Reservation, Navajo County, Arizona.* Hopi Cultural Preservation Office project 2010–017. Hopi Cultural Preservation Office, Kiqötsmovi, Arizona.

———. 2013. *A Cultural Resources Inventory of the Hopi Arsenic Mitigation Project (HAMP), Hopi Indian Reservation, Navajo County, Arizona.* Hopi Cultural Preservation Office project 2011–024. Hopi Cultural Preservation Office, Kiqötsmovi, Arizona.

———. 2015. *A Class III Cultural Resources Inventory of the Hopi Twin Arrows Property, Twin Arrows, Arizona for the Hopi Land Team.* Hopi Cultural Preservation Office project 2015–011. Report on file at the Hopi Cultural Preservation Office, Kiqötsmovi, Arizona.

Yeatts, Michael, and Cindy Dongoske. 1993. *An Archaeological Inventory of State Route 264 from the County Line to State Route 87, Navajo County, Arizona.* Hopi Cultural Preservation Office project 91–003. Report on file at the Hopi Cultural Preservation Office, Kiqötsmovi, Arizona.

Yeatts, Michael, and Kristin Huisinga. 2006. *A Hopi Long-Term Monitoring Program for Öntupqa (the Grand Canyon).* Report on file at the Bureau of Reclamation, Upper Colorado River Office, Salt Lake City, Utah.

———. 2010. *2009 Report of the Hopi Long-Term Monitoring Program for Öngtupqa (the Grand Canyon).* Hopi Cultural Preservation Office, Kiqötsmovi, Arizona.

———. 2011. *2010 Report of the Hopi Long-Term Monitoring Program for Öngtupqa (the Grand Canyon).* Hopi Cultural Preservation Office, Kiqötsmovi, Arizona.

———. 2012. *2011 Report of the Hopi Long-Term Monitoring Program for Öngtupqa (the Grand Canyon).* Hopi Cultural Preservation Office, Kiqötsmovi, Arizona.

———. 2012. *2012 Report of the Hopi Long-Term Monitoring Program for Öngtupqa (the Grand Canyon).* Hopi Cultural Preservation Office, Kiqötsmovi, Arizona.

———. 2013. *2013 Report of the Hopi Long-Term Monitoring Program for Öngtupqa (the Grand Canyon)*. Hopi Cultural Preservation Office, Hopi Tribe, Kiqötsmovi, Arizona.

———. 2014. *2014 Report of the Hopi Long-Term Monitoring Program for Öngtupqa (the Grand Canyon)*. Hopi Cultural Preservation Office, Kiqötsmovi, Arizona.

———. 2014. *Öngtupqa pas Qatsi: Hopi Life in Salt Canyon. A Hopi Handbook to the Grand Canyon*. Hopi Cultural Preservation Office, Kiqötsmovi, Arizona.

———. 2015. *2015 Report of the Hopi Long-Term Monitoring Program for Öngtupqa (the Grand Canyon)*. Hopi Cultural Preservation Office, Hopi Tribe, Kiqötsmovi, Arizona.

———. 2016. *2016 Report of the Hopi Long-Term Monitoring Program for Öngtupqa (the Grand Canyon)*. Hopi Cultural Preservation Office, Hopi Tribe, Kiqötsmovi, Arizona.

Yeatts, Michael, and Lisa M Leap. 1996. *Proposal for Data Recovery at Six Sites in the Grand Canyon During FY 1997*. The Hopi Tribe and the River Corridor Monitoring Project Report No. 45. Report on file at Grand Canyon National Park, Arizona.

———. 1997. *Proposed Testing at AZ:C:09:051 (GRCA)*. The Hopi Tribe and the River Corridor Monitoring Project Report No. 49. Report on file at Grand Canyon National Park, Arizona.

MASTER'S THESES AND DOCTORAL DISSERTATIONS

Brenton, Barrett P. 1994. *Hopi Foodways: Biocultural Perspectives on Change and Contradiction*. PhD dissertation, Department of Anthropology, University of Massachusetts Amherst.

Chip Colwell-Chanthaphonh. 2004. *The Place of History: Social Meanings of the Archaeological Landscape in the San Pedro Valley of Arizona*, PhD dissertation, Indiana University, Bloomington.

Higgins, Daniel B. 2001. *Language Decline and Stabilization: A Narrative of the Revitalization of the Hopi Language*. Master's thesis, Liberal Studies, Northern Arizona University, Flagstaff.

Hedquist, Saul L. 2017. *A Colorful Past: Turquoise and Social Identity in the Late Prehispanic Western Pueblo Region, A.D. 1275–1400*. PhD dissertation, School of Anthropology, University of Arizona, Tucson.

Hopkins, Maren P. 2012. *A Storied Land: Tiyo and the Epic Journey Down the Colorado River*. Master's thesis, School of Anthropology, University of Arizona, Tucson.

Johnson, Tai E. 2007. *Surviving the Transformation: Hopi Farming, Food, and Labor, 1936–2007*. Master's thesis, Department of History. Northern Arizona University, Flagstaff.

Lyons, Patrick D. 2001. *Winslow Orange Ware and the Ancestral Hopi Migration Horizon*. PhD dissertation, Department of Anthropology, University of Arizona, Tucson.

Reed, Trevor. 2010. *Returning Hopi Voices: Toward a Model for Community-Partnered Repatriation of Archived Traditional Music*. Master's thesis, Teachers College, Columbia University, New York,

Secakuku, Ferrell H. 2006. *Hopi and Quetzalcoatl—Is There a Connection?* Master's thesis, Department of Anthropology, Northern Arizona University, Flagstaff.

Steinbecher, Barry Ellen Price. 2015. *The Geography of Heritage: Comparing Archaeological Culture Areas and Contemporary Cultural Landscapes.* Master's thesis, School of Anthropology, University of Arizona, Tucson.

FILMS

Holzman, Allan. 2007. *Beyond the Mesas: Indian Boarding Schools, Keeping the Culture Alive.* Produced by Culture of Children, LLC, Allan Holzman, Stewart Koyiyumptewa, Gerald Eichner, Matthew Sakiestewa Gilbert, and Eric Jerstad.

McLeod, Christopher and Malinda Maynor. 2001. *In the Light of Reverence.* A Sacred Land Film Project of Earth Island Institute.

WEBSITES

CyArk. 2010. Hopi Petroglyph Sites. CyArk in partnership with the Hopi Cultural Preservation Office, the Navajo Nation Historic Preservation Department, and the University of Redlands. Electronic document, http://www.cyark.org/projects/hopi-petroglyph-sites, accessed February 5, 2017.

Northern Arizona University Department of Anthropology. 1998. Hopi Cultural Preservation Office Website. Electronic document, http://www8.nau.edu/hcpo-p, accessed February 5, 2017.

CONTRIBUTORS

E. Charles Adams is curator of archaeology at the Arizona State Museum and professor of anthropology in the School of Anthropology at the University of Arizona. He is the director of the Homolovi Research Program and director of the Rock Art Ranch Field School. He is the author of *The Origin and Development of the Pueblo Katsina Cult*, as well as numerous books and articles about Southwestern archaeology.

Wesley Bernardini is associate professor in society and anthropology at the University of Redlands in California. His research combines archaeological data with Native American oral tradition, ethnography, historical records, and geographic information systems to trace the development of social groups through time. He is the author of *Hopi Oral Tradition and the Archaeology of Identity* and *Hopi History in Stone: The Tutuveni Petroglyph Site*.

Joëlle Clark, MA, MAST, is associate director for Professional Development Programs at the Center for Science Teaching & Learning, Northern Arizona University. She is a science educator and applied anthropologist/archaeologist who has designed, written, and implemented science and cultural curricula and professional development programs for K-12 educators, informal educators, and Indigenous communities. She is active in science education reform efforts and has led numerous grant-funded science, technology, engineering, and math (STEM) projects. She co-created and managed the Hopi Footprints of the Ancestors program for Hopi youth as a collaboration among the Hopi Cultural Preservation Office, Hopi elders, educators, archaeologists, and technology specialists.

Chip Colwell is senior curator of anthropology at the Denver Museum of Nature & Science. He has published more than fifty academic articles and book chapters and ten books, most recently *Plundered Skulls and Stolen Spirits: Inside the Fight to Reclaim Native America's Treasures.*

T. J. Ferguson is professor of anthropology at the University of Arizona in Tucson, where he also a principal investigator at Anthropological Research, LLC, a company specializing in research with and for American Indian tribes. He has worked on numerous projects for the Hopi Tribe since 1991, including research related to traditional cultural properties, repatriation, and land and water rights.

Dennis Gilpin is an archaeologist, ethnographer, and historian at PaleoWest Archaeology. His research interests include Pueblo architecture, prehistoric agriculture, and historical archaeology, and he is best known for his discoveries of early maize in the Chinle Valley and his research on the Chacoan system and the transition to modern Puebloan settlement. Since 2011 he has been assistant principal investigator and principal ethnographer for the Navajo-Gallup Water Supply Project, a 272-mile pipeline that will supply water from the San Juan River to Gallup and Navajo communities in northwestern New Mexico.

Kelley Hays-Gilpin is professor and chair of anthropology at Northern Arizona University and Edward Bridge Danson chair of anthropology at the Museum of Northern Arizona. Her current research, undertaken in collaboration with the Hopi Cultural Preservation Office, explores Hopi history and culture from prehistory to present through cross-media comparison of style and iconography (including pottery, textiles, basketry, mural painting, and rock art), visual and verbal metaphors, traditional ecological knowledge, and gender arrangements.

George Gumerman IV is professor of anthropology and director of the honors program at Northern Arizona University. In addition to his long-term collaboration with the Hopi Cultural Preservation Office to develop a Hopi culture curriculum for Hopi schools, he conducts archaeological research on food and culture on the north coast of Peru.

Saul L. Hedquist is senior archaeologist and ethnographer with Logan Simpson Design. His research interests include Pueblo ethnography, landscape anthropology, and American Southwest archaeology, particularly that of northern Arizona. He has worked with the Hopi Cultural Preservation Office on multiple projects since 2010.

Maren P. Hopkins is director of research for Anthropological Research, LLC, a research company in Tucson, Arizona, that works with Indian tribes to identify traditional cultural places and evaluate their eligibility for the National Register of Historic Places. She has fifteen years of experience in conducting historic preservation research in Arizona and New Mexico, including many projects with the Hopi Cultural Preservation Office.

Stewart B. Koyiyumptewa is a member of the Badger Clan from Hotvela on Third Mesa. Since 2000 he has been employed as the archivist for the Hopi Cultural Preservation Office. He is a co-author of *Hopi People* and *Moquis and Kastiilam: Hopis, Spaniards, and the Trauma of History*. He is currently finishing an MA in cultural anthropology at Northern Arizona University in Flagstaff.

Leigh J. Kuwanwsiwma is a member of the Greasewood Clan from Paaqavi on Third Mesa. He has directed the Hopi Cultural Preservation Office since 1989. He has published numerous articles and technical reports and is a co-author of *Moquis and Kastiilam: Hopis, Spaniards, and the Trauma of History*.

Lee Wayne Lomayestewa is a member of the Bear Clan from Songòopavi on Second Mesa. He has worked as research assistant at the Hopi Cultural Preservation Office since 1993. He is a co-author of *Moquis and Kastiilam: Hopis, Spaniards, and the Trauma of History*.

Patrick D. Lyons is director of the Arizona State Museum, associate professor in the School of Anthropology at the University of Arizona, and research associate at Archaeology Southwest. His research focuses on ancient migrations in the U.S. Southwest, the use of ceramics in understanding the lives of ancient peoples, the use of tribal oral traditions in archaeological studies, and the archaeology, history, ethnography, and ethnohistory of the Hopi people. He has primarily conducted fieldwork in the ancestral Hopi settlements of the Homol'ovi area, near present-day Winslow, Arizona, and in the San Pedro Valley of southeastern Arizona. He is the author of *Ancestral Hopi Migrations* and co-editor of *Migrants and Mounds: Classic Period Archaeology of the Lower San Pedro Valley*.

Shirley Powell is vice president of programs at Crow Canyon Archaeological Center, where she has worked since 2007. She directed and was co-principal investigator of the Black Mesa Archaeological Project in northeastern Arizona between 1978 and 1987. She has published numerous journal articles and is senior author of *Pueblo of the Mesa,* *the Archaeology of Black Mesa Arizona*, and senior editor of *Prehistoric Culture Change on the Colorado Plateau: Ten Thousand Years on Black Mesa.*

Gregson Schachner is associate professor in the Department of Anthropology and Cotsen Institute of Archaeology at the University of California, Los Angeles. His research interests include mobility, the origins of villages and leadership in early agricultural societies, and the analysis of settlement systems. In addition to publishing numerous journal articles, he is the author of *Population Circulation and the Transformation of Ancient Zuni Communities* and co-editor of *Crucible of Pueblos: The Early Pueblo Period in the Northern Southwest* (with Richard Wilshusen and James Allison). His current fieldwork is aimed at understanding agriculture, demography, landscape use, and mobility practices on the Hopi Mesas, in the Petrified Forest of Arizona, and in the El Malpais region of New Mexico.

Thomas E. Sheridan is a Distinguished Outreach Professor at the University of Arizona, where he is research anthropologist at the Southwest Center and professor in the School of Anthropology. He has written or co-edited fourteen books and monographs including *Arizona: A History; Landscapes of Fraud: Mission Tumacácori, the Baca Float, and the Betrayal of the O'odham; Stitching the West Back Together: Conservation of Working Landscapes* (with Susan Charnley and Gary Nabhan); and *Moquis and Kastiilam: Hopis, Spaniards and the Trauma of History*, vol. I (with Stewart Koyiyumptewa, Anton Daughters, Dale Brenneman, T. J. Ferguson, Leigh J. Kuwanwisiwma, and Lee Wayne Lomayestewa).

Mark D. Varien is executive vice president of the Crow Canyon Archaeological Center Research Institute in Cortez, Colorado. In this position he seeks to further Crow Canyon's three-part mission: to increase knowledge of the human experience through archaeological research, to conduct that research in the context of public education programs, and to partner with American Indians on the design and delivery of those research and education programs. He has authored numerous journal articles and five books, most recently *Emergence and Collapse of Early Villages: Models of Central Mesa Verde Region Archaeology.*

Laurie D. Webster is an anthropologist and independent scholar who specializes in the perishable material culture of the American Southwest. Her research interests include textile craft production and innovation, technological change, cultural affiliation, and the documentation and interpretation of older museum collections. She is adjunct faculty in the Department of Anthropology at Northern Arizona University and research associate at the American Museum of Natural History and the Crow

Canyon Archaeological Center. In addition to numerous articles about pre-Hispanic perishable technologies, she edited *Beyond Cloth and Cordage: Archaeological Textile Research in the Americas* and *Collecting the Weaver's Art: The William Claflin Collection of Southwestern Textiles*.

Peter M. Whiteley is curator of North American ethnology at the American Museum of Natural History. His ethnographic and ethnohistorical research has focused on Hopi, with long-term fieldwork since 1980. Major publications include *Deliberate Acts: Changing Hopi Culture through the Oraibi Split* (1988), *Bacavi: Journey to Reed Springs* (1988), *Rethinking Hopi Ethnography* (1998), and *The Orayvi Split: A Hopi Transformation* (2008). His research also addresses several New Mexico Pueblos (especially Isleta, Kewa, Laguna, and Tesuque) and Native American cultures in the Northeast (Cayuga, Oneida, Akwesasne Mohawk, and Shinnecock), California (Hupa, Yurok, and Karuk), Southeast (Choctaw and Chickasaw), and Pacific Northwest (especially Skagit).

Michael Yeatts obtained his master's degree in archaeology from Arizona State University in 1990. He has been employed as an archaeologist in the Southwest since the 1980s. In 1991, he was hired by the Hopi Tribe's Cultural Preservation Office to coordinate its participation in environmental studies in the Grand Canyon, a role that continues today. He is currently the Hopi Tribe's senior archaeologist.

INDEX

Hopi Buttes. *See* Tùutukwi
Hopi Cultural Preservation Office
(HCPO), 3–4, 16, 159, 216; archaeology
and, 73–74, 157–58; burial agreements
of, 94–95; collaborative research and,
12–14, 100, 124; cultural preservation at,
32–34; development and roles of, 5–8;
corn research, 163, 173–74; educational
programs, 179–81, 183–92; Grand Canyon and, 40, 46–48; language program,
182–83; NTP consultation, 17, 22–23;
repatriation issues, 9–12
Hopi Footprints program, 179–81; curriculum development, 183–92; goals of,
181–82
Hopi History Project, 204, 207, 208
Hopi Iconography Project, 124
Hopilavayi Project, 5, 182–83
Hopi Long-Term Monitoring Program,
48, 49
Hopi Place Names Project, 61
Hopi Reservation, 54(fig.), 59, 60(fig.)
Hopitutskwa, 52, 180; concepts of, 53–60;
place-names in, 61–63; Tiyo's journey
and, 65–67
Horn Clan, 142
Hotvela, 4, 29, 208, 241
houses: as living beings, 135, 136
human remains, 96; HCPO-ASM agree-
ments, 94–95; repatriation and burial
of, 9–11

Ibarra, Francisco de, 208
identity: farming and, 221–22; Hopi, 191–92;
and oral memories, 209
Indian Claims Commission, 60(fig.), 218,
234; Hopitutskwa and, 53, 59
informants, 232–33
intangible heritage, 178–79
intellectual genealogies: of archaeology,
214–16
intellectual property rights, 9, 163

James, Harry, 207, 208
Jenkins, Marshall, 230–31, 242

Kabotie, Fred: Hopitutskwa map, 53, 55(fig.);
Tiyo's journey, 64(fig.)
katsinam, 84, 28–29, 135–36, 153, 172–73
Kawàyka'a, 123, 126(fig.), 128–30, 134, 149, 208
Kawestima (Tsegi Canyon), 26, 28, 56,
62(fig.), 63, 185; and NTP viewshed,
29–30
Kayenta, 128, 130, 147; migrants from, 104,
105, 109, 110–11, 115–16, 117–18
Keresan speakers, 128, 133, 134
Kewanimptewa, Harry, 241
kiikiqö, 21–22, 53, 62(fig.), 63, 91; Davis
Ranch Site as, 105, 116–17
kilts: embroidered, 150, 152(fig.), 153
kivas, 130, 133, 147; Davis Ranch, 107–8, 110,
111–12, 113–14; Homol'ovi, 95–96, 98;
storytelling in, 204–5
knowledge, knowledge systems, 100, 184,
233–34, 239, 244; anthropological,
230–31; of clan migrations, 77–78, 116–
17; cultural, 8, 67–68; in ethnographic
research, 235–36; local, 231–32; oral histories and, 204–5, 205, 208; traditional,
24–25, 64–65
Kokop (Firewood) clan, 125, 128
Kòoninhahàwpi (Havasupai Descent Trail), 56
Kooyahoema, Wilton, 10, 28, 29
Kuwannömtiwa (Sand Clan), 14, 239
kyaptsi, 8, 25, 135, 189, 242–43
Kyeekeltuy Kiiöam (Fledgling House), 30

Laguna Pueblo, 128, 134
Lalkont society, 154
land, 5, 52, 243; knowledge of, 67–68. *See
also* Hopitutskwa
landscapes, landforms, 8, 73, 80, 219; perspectives on, 74–75; Pueblo perspectives
on, 75–76; of salt pilgrimage trail, 31–32;
storytelling and, 63–67; visual, 76–77